MARTIN LUTHER
AND THE
MODERN MIND

FREEDOM, CONSCIENCE, TOLERATION, RIGHTS

Edited
by

Manfred Hoffmann

Toronto Studies in Theology
Volume 22

The Edwin Mellen Press
New York and Toronto

Library of Congress Cataloging In Publication Data

Main entry under title:

Martin Luther and the modern mind.

(Toronto studies in theology ; v.22)
"Originally presented at a symposium held in
November 1983 at Emory University, sponsored by the
Candler School of Theology, co-sponsored by the
Goethe Institute, Atlanta."
Includes bibliographies.
1. Luther, Martin, 1483-1546--Congresses.
2. Reformation--Congresses. I. Hoffman, Manfred.
II. Lindbeck, George A. III. Candler School of
Theology. IV. Goethe Institute (Atlanta, Ga.) V. Series.
BR323.7.M33 1985   230'.41'0924   85-3054
ISBN 0-88946-766-8

Toronto Studies in Theology
Series ISBN 0-88946-975-X

Printed in the United States of America

In memoriam

James Franklin Hopewell

1929 - 1984

theologian of the church

caring priest

unfailing friend

gifted teacher

faithful servant

Professor of Religion and the Church

Candler School of Theology

Emory University

1972 - 1984

CONTENTS

INTRODUCTION

Major anniversaries provide special opportunities for assessing how, why, and to what extent significant historical events have informed present thought and life. But such occasions of retrospect also serve, conversely, to shed light on those features in the present profile of consciousness which are distinctly different from past forms. So the identification of both the common contours of the present ethos with, and the dissimilarities of current traits from former situations, ideas, and persons help in understanding the contemporary identity.

This impulse to historical comparison seems particularly strong in the case of the Protestant Reformation and Luther. Their position at the beginning of the 16th century has continued to evoke reflection on the differences between the Middle Ages and the Modern Period - a reflection necessary to clarify many of the peculiar characteristics of modernity. The commemoration of Luther's birth in 1483 or of his 1517 theses on indulgences, to mention but the most obvious dates, have produced besides the stream of regular literature periodic floods of special publications (but so far none as abundant as that of the 1983 quincentennial celebration). Each *dies festus* was taken to call for an extraordinary engagement with the historic subject, eulogistic or critical to varying degrees as the case may be depending on disposition and orientation. For confessionally committed Lutherans or

otherwise attracted admirers the festive mood would
elevate the interpretation of the Reformation to the
level of its 'world-historical effects,' escalate the
status of its founder to that of a religious hero, and
even exalt his memory to a downright Lutherolatry. Of
course, zealous proponents on the other side of the
denominational demarcation line would not need a
special occasion for a criticism, in measure of defamation not unequal to that of their opponents' exalta-
tion. Non-committed observers, on the other hand, saw
in Luther either a progenitor of their own views or the
representative of a bygone age. Yet times have changed
meanwhile; extreme praise or blame by and large have
given way to a more balanced and differentiated view on
all sides.[1]

Such positive or negative evaluations notwith-
standing, coming to terms with the historic subject
means to interpret from the perspective of contemporary
experience with the sometimes unacknowledged intention
of finding in history at least an orientation for the
present time, if not securing for the present a place
in history, by using the past identity as some kind of
Rorschach test for individual and social identification. The history of special Luther-interpretations
shows that the figure of the Reformer, the shape of his
thought, and his impact on his environment have again
and again been fit for bringing to light one's own
sense of individuality and sociality, of self, community, culture, society, church, and world, be it by
contrast or similarity, or any combination of both.
Luther could be seized upon as a source for modern
enlightenment, and we are, for better or worse, heirs
to such an interpretative tradition, conditioned by it
as if by osmosis. Therefore, a re-assessment of Luther

for current understanding has to take this tradition of interpretation into critical consideration.

While the Luther celebrations in Germany over the centuries reveal fascinating shifts in the appropriation of the reformer's image according to the characteristic hermeneutic prevailing at a particular time, the Luther reception in America began slowly but then developed distinct features, in part inspired by continental precedent but mostly resembling the traits of the American experience.[2] The fledgling republic, its political independence just internationally recognized, found neither time nor taste for a tricentennial anniversary of Luther's birth in 1783. Its founders looked elsewhere for models of liberty. Their rare and marginal references to the German Reformer, who by then had in Europe already long become a herald of enlightened freedom,[3] totally lacked the inspiration Roger Williams more than a century earlier had drawn from him for his concept of religious toleration.[4] Yet, 100 years later, in 1883, the situation had changed 100 percent from a virtual Luther oblivion to a full-blown Luther enthusiasm. The tributes to his 400th birthday hailed him as a veritable source of the American freedoms, even as George Washington's forerunner. What had happened in the meantime amounted to a remarkably fast Luther appropriation, beginning at the turn of the century, first by Unitarians who saw in him the advocate of the Enlightenment human rights to moral, religious, and political liberty. But also evangelical Protestants from various denominations discovered Luther around the time of the Second Great Awakening, except that they found in him the Bible-bound pious person, God's unique prophet fighting for the truth against all falsehood - an image that could

be easily turned by many of them and by others, as
well, into the bigotted rationale for the upsurge of
anti-Catholicism and American nativism in reaction to
the waves of immigrants in the early 1830's. Just
about the same time another group got hold of Luther,
the Transcendentalists. They unearthed Luther the
genius, the unique personality endowed with an extraordinary imagination and poetic power, the autonomous
individual who demonstrated the superiority of mind
over matter.

The period following the 1883 apex of interest in
Luther was overshadowed by the relativizing effects of
the problems attending the phenomenon of religious
pluralism in an industrialized society. Furthermore,
the sobering World War I experiences created a critical
climate toward Germany in general and Luther in particular. As it turned out, the high tide of Luther
reception at the end of the 19th century was but a
short-lived episode. In fact, it was Calvin who,
though never as ardently embraced as Luther, actually
fared much better in the long run.[5] No wonder, then,
that Luther's fate in 20th century America is something
of a mixed bag. A unified, generally adopted Luther
image failed to emerge among the experts here as well
as across the ocean. Rather, research concentrated on
the study of manageable topics and, perhaps because of
the American preoccupation with pragmatic and psychological problems, increasingly engaged in social and
psycho-history more so than in essaying interpretative
overviews within the history of ideas. But American
scholarship has come into its own and its relation to
its European counterpart moved from an associate status
to that of partnership.[6]

The question of how the deluge of publications commemorating on both continents the 500th anniversary of Luther's birth will eventually figure in the overall history of interpretation must be left to those in the future who can take the longer view from the vantage point of historical distance. This goes also for the present collection of essays. Written by an ecumenical group of Americans and Germans (Lutheran, Calvinist, Methodist, Roman Catholic) and from varied academic fields of interest (church history, social history, historical theology, systematic theology), the papers address the problem of Luther's relation to modernity in view of some key concepts that characterize modern mentality: freedom, conscience, toleration, and rights. **Luther and the Modern Mind:** extremely complex as this issue is, it hardly can be expected to result in a consensus in every respect. Yet common denominators have emerged. Luther is seen as neither the hero of Enlightenment, nor the true Christian of Pietism, nor the genius of Romanticism. Rather, the assessment of his contribution to modern times produces a more differentiated picture. While his influence is estimated as more limited than generally assumed, criticism also turns to modernity itself for having created a Luther in its own image and thereby having inverted, lost, or failed to receive significant but less comfortable emphases in the Reformer's legacy.

These papers were originally presented at a symposium held in November 1983 at Emory University, sponsored by the Candler School of Theology, co-sponsored by the Goethe Institute, Atlanta, and financially assisted by a grant from the National Endowment for the Humanities through the Georgia Endowment for the Humanities. D. Michael Bennethum assisted in

preparing the manuscript for publication; Jane Statham
and David Leonard committed it to the word processor;
Larry Williams formatted the document.

Emory University, Atlanta, Georgia   M. H.

NOTES

1. Convenient surveys and bibliographies can be found
    in: J. Wicks, S. J., *Luther and His Spiritual
    Legacy* (Wilmington, 1983), 11-34; B. Lohse, *Martin
    Luther, Eine Einführung in sein Leben und sein
    Werk*, 2nd ed., (München, 1982), 210-248; and E. W.
    Gritsch, *Martin - God's Court Jester, Luther in
    Retrospect* (Philadelphia, 1983), 203-213.

2. For the following compare H. Lehmann, "Die Ent-
    deckung Luthers im Amerika des frühen 19. Jahr-
    hunderts," in: *Luther in der Neuzeit*, ed. B.
    Moeller, Schriften des Vereins für Reformations-
    geschichte 192 (Gütersloh, 1983), 151-159.

3. Cf. H. Bornkamm, *Luther im Spiegel der deutschen
    Geistesgeschichte*, 2nd ed., (Göttingen, 1970).

4. See for instance R. H. Bainton, *The Travail of
    Religious Liberty* (New York, 1958), 208-228.

5. So U. M. Kremer, *Die Reformation als Problem der
    amerikanischen Historiographie*, Veröffentlichungen
    des Instituts für europäische Geschichte Mainz 92
    (Wiesbaden, 1978).

6. See L. W. Spitz, "Luther in America," in: *Luther
    in der Neuzeit*, 160-177.

MARTIN LUTHER
AND THE
MODERN MIND

George Lindbeck

MODERNITY AND LUTHER'S UNDERSTANDING OF
THE FREEDOM OF THE CHRISTIAN

It is the task of this essay to explore the relation between Luther's understanding of Christian freedom and modern culture - a task which by definition crosses the lines, not only of historical periods, but also of scholarly disciplines. The 16th and 20th centuries are both pertinent, as well as the intervening periods, and sociological, political, cultural, and intellectual developments of many kinds all need to be taken into consideration. It is perhaps a disadvantage to be too much of a Luther scholar. Anyone who knows the Reformer well is likely to eschew the crude and sweeping generalizations which the theme demands.

From this point of view, my own qualifications are excellent. I am not a Luther scholar: much more of my life has been spent reading medieval and modern texts than burrowing in the hundred volumes of the Weimar edition of Luther's works. Yet, as it often happens to those of Lutheran upbringing, the Reformer keeps constantly tugging at my attention. I think of him frequently as I read other authors, and cannot help but develop ideas as to how his thought relates to theirs. The temptation to try out some of these ideas on genuine experts has proved irresistible, and that is really my only excuse for essaying this topic. I would like to say that I am following Luther's advice by "sinning boldly," except my courage, I fear, does not come from the faith which he recommends, but rather from ignorance. That, however, is something for others to judge.

As befits my lack of expertise, I shall start by reviewing resemblances others have seen between Luther's understanding of Christian freedom and certain modern notions. After sketching these resemblances, I shall make some remarks on the treacherous question of historical causation; and then, in the third place, discuss the inversion of meaning which takes place when an originally religious view of freedom is secularized.

I

The most obvious similarity between Reformation and modern views of freedom is in the attitude towards law. For both, laws and obedience to them are not the way to conquer whatever powers hold human beings in thrall. Luther's way of putting this goes back to the Apostle Paul's insistence that men and women "are justified by faith apart from the works of the law" (Rom. 3:28), but he intensified and generalized this principle beyond any previous thinker in the mainstream Christian tradition. Paul was thinking primarily of the specifically Jewish law, the Torah, and his concern was to include the Gentiles in the church without requiring them first to become Jews; but Luther, developing what he thought were the implications of the Apostle's thought, argued against the liberating efficacy of moral and ethical systems of any kind. Most educated people in our society seem to agree. We naturally think as did the Reformers - and, for that matter, Freud[1] - that socially enforced behavioral rules are necessary for the sake of civilization, but we often talk as if the effort to obey these rules, to become virtuous, to acquire moral merit, was deeply repressive and hypocritical and likely to damage psychic health or personal authenticity. Our culture is perhaps uniquely suspicious of those who are ethically or religiously strenuous. We suspect them of being self-righteous, of being holier-than-thou; and such characteristics are, in our lexicon of vices, among the very worst. The Reformation case against the law, to be sure, is not the same as the contemporary one, and more successfully avoided permissive or antinomian consequences; but whatever the differences, most of us have no difficulty understanding and accepting the proposition that liberated human beings are free from the endeavor to justify themselves by the works of the law.

We are also open, in the second place, to the suggestion that at least on the personal level it is faith which liberates. Faith for the Reformers, we remember, does not mean intellectual assent to the truth of unprovable propositions, but is, rather, a trust or confidence of the whole being which persists no matter how unhappy the circumstances, great the failures, or grave the doubts. Most of our contemporaries, it seems, take more or less for granted this emphasis on the importance of faith in the sense of basic confidence as formulated, for example, by Erik Erikson[2] (who, it is not irrelevant to note, thinks of himself quite self-consciously as at this point agreeing with Luther). Without some measure of this underlying confidence, we human beings go disastrously astray. Perhaps this insight is now more prevalent outside than inside the church. There is, then, a

sense in which even secularists agree with Paul and the
Reformers that the disciplines of the law are not the
way to personal freedom, but that faith is.

A third agreement then becomes inescapable, this
time specifically with the Reformation. If freedom
comes through trust or faith, then the basic bondage
must be lack of faith or lack of trust. The essence of
original sin for Luther has a distinct family resemblance to what modern existentialists call "anxiety."[3]
For him, in contrast to St. Augustine and much of the
tradition, rebellious pride and consequent concupis-
cence were not the fundamental flaw, but rather what
Kierkegaard was later to characterize as the "fear of
freedom," the insecurity induced, when basic confidence
is lacking, by multiplicity of choices. This theme has
become a familiar one in the twentieth century through
such writers as Sartre, Camus, and Heidegger; but even
if we do not happen to have read these authors, most of
us find it easy to picture the self, as they did, as an
isolated center of finite freedom, thrown into a
hostile universe, threatened by the three fundamental
fears, as Paul Tillich puts it, of morality, meaninglessness, and guilt. It is these anxieties which are
the source of our attempts to free ourselves from
insecurity, to justify ourselves, either by conformity
to social expectations (that is, to law), or by becoming individually or collectively masters of our fate
and captains of our soul. We are, as Luther put it,
incurvatus in se, turned in on ourselves. We depend
upon ourselves to make a case for the worthwhileness of
our existence, to free ourselves from fear of failure.
We seek to bolster our fragile self-esteem by becoming
good or virtuous, or by success or popularity, or by
gaining power over ourselves and others. When striving

becomes unbearable, some of us lapse compulsively into distractions of which the most common in our technologically advanced civilization is television, and the most effective, drugs. Others of us turn inwards in search of peace of mind by means of, for example, transcendental meditation; but nothing, whether striving, distractions, or the inward turn, delivers us, in St. Paul's words, from "the body of this death." Something like this analysis of human bondage is involved both in the Reformation understanding of sin and in widespread contemporary ways of thinking.

There is in the fourth place, oddly enough, a curious affinity between some modern modes of thought and the Reformation insistence that basic confidence or liberating faith is wholly a gift, wholly a grace. It seems in our day intuitively self-evident that the crucial period for the origins of basic confidence is the first months of life when nothing depends on the infant and everything on the parental bond.[4] It is a truism for most of us that unless a child has some experience of unconditional love, or unconditional acceptance, by the seemingly omnipotent significant others of its early life, that its chances for uninhibited development are minimal. Prolonged psychoanalysis in later years can perhaps to some extent repair the damage, but, once again, this happens by transference, that is, by the analyst becoming a kind of surrogate parent who liberates by being non-judgmental. Thus, freeing confidence is communicated precisely through the experience of being accepted despite unacceptability, of being loved despite unloveableness, by God-like parents or therapists. This freedom, to repeat, is a gift, not an achievement. The parallel to the Reformation insistence that saving or justifying faith is *sola gratia*, by grace alone, is unmistakable even if incomplete.

A fifth and final point of resemblance has to do with the consequences of justification, or what was traditionally called "sanctification." Justifying faith, like the basic confidence which is its contemporary analogue, has as its first and fundamental effect the freedom to accept oneself as one is rather than some more dramatic transformation of the self. Luther's way of putting this was to say that the justified are simultaneously sinners, *simul justus et peccator*. Liberating faith does not eliminate unfaith, but rather enables those who have it to acknowledge its destructive presence in their lives without being overwhelmed by despair. Selfishness, idolatry, sensuality, and rebellious pride remain, but not as unrecognized tyrants reigning over the self, as Luther puts it,[5] but as known enemies which can be struggled against without self-righteousness or the delusion of being holier than others. Perhaps here more than at any other point the Reformation seems emphatically modern. It freed its adherents from struggling for an earth-transcending saintliness, and was reluctant to identify anyone as exceptionally holy (that is, to canonize and venerate saints). Even Luther's favorite Biblical heroes, such as Abraham and David in the Old Testament and Paul in the New, were not, as he describes them, notable for what we ordinarily think of as saintliness. Faith freed them to accept their earthiness, rather than from earthiness.

In summary, then, we have noted five resemblances between Reformation teaching and a widespread contemporary outlook: (1) freedom is freedom from the law; (2) faith or basic confidence is the liberating force; (3)

unfaith or anxiety is the fundamental source of bondage; (4) there is a radical need for unconditional love, unconditional acceptance; and (5) to be a free human being is to accept oneself, warts and all, rather than to repress awareness of mortality, meaninglessness, and guilt. These five resemblances in their modern forms have both existentialist and psychoanalytic roots, and contribute greatly to what Philip Rieff has called the "therapeutic culture of modernity."[6] Taken in conjunction, they look like a secular version of liberation through justifying faith; and this raises the question of whether the similarities are simply accidental or whether they are historically dependent on Luther's teaching. It is to this question that we now turn.

II

Causal connections in matters historical are notoriously speculative, and this is particularly true in the present instance. Those who emphasize the secular form of freedom through faith which we have reviewed, are for the most part not conscious of dependence on Luther. They draw on existentialists and psychoanalysts who, as in the case of Sartre and Freud, were often anti-religious and not Protestant in background. To be sure, there are also more distant progenitors such as Schelling, Hegel, Kierkegaard, Schopenhauer and Nietzsche who, according to some historians, were documentably influenced negatively or positively by the strongly Lutheran environments in which they were reared.[7] Yet even here the literary and ideational connections are debatable.

Yet, on the other hand, there is *prima facie* plausibility in the supposition that assiduously inculcated religions shape the deep cognitive and emotive dispositions of the populations in which they are established.[8] Even those who reject or rebel against them do not escape their influence. Thus, classical paganism influenced early Christians: the church fathers became partly platonist despite themselves. Similarly, as one self-professed atheist has remarked, there is no such thing as atheism in general,[9] but only Calvinist, Catholic or Jewish varieties. Religiously implanted patterns of thought and feeling are likely to persist long after the religion itself has changed or lost its dominance.

When one pursues this line of thought, the resemblances we have spoken of begin to look like consequences. For hundreds of years, Luther's understanding of liberating faith had a powerful impact on Protestant preaching, worship, and, above all, Bible reading. The effects on Biblical interpretation must especially be emphasized, because Scripture constituted the imaginative and conceptual world in which the whole of Christendom, and particularly Reformation Christendom, lived. The establishment of schools and the spread of literacy had already become a religious duty for many in the Middle Ages, but the Reformation doctrines of the primacy of Scripture and the spiritual equality of all Christians, emerging, as they did, at the same time as printing and vernacular literatures, led to an explosion of literacy even in remote and poverty-stricken lands such as Scotland, Sweden, and New England.[10] Protestants followed Luther's insistence that girls as well as boys should be taught to read the Bible and the catechism for sake of their souls' salvation, and they often agreed with him that, given the indifference of illiterate parents, school attendance should be made compulsory. From that point on, whatever Luther may have said or thought about women, modern feminism became inevitable in the long run. Well into the nineteenth century, furthermore, elementary schooling consisted largely in drilling in the Bible. Most people never became personally devout, and large portions of the better educated classes were increasingly skeptical from the eighteenth century on, but no one escaped the Scriptural imprint.

When evolutionary theory began to develop, for example, even rationalist scientists found it difficult to shake themselves loose from their Biblically derived notion that the earth is, as we would now put it, recently formed.[11] They were, in that respect, quite different from medieval theologians who followed Aristotle in thinking that, apart from revelation and faith, there is no reason to suppose that the world is not everlasting.[12] This influence of the Bible, to be sure, was not a uniquely Protestant phenomenon. The parameters of what a Rabelais or a Voltaire could conceive as possible were also in large part set by the Christian tradition and thus indirectly by Scripture.[13] Yet it is in Reformation lands that the power of Holy Writ is most closely manifest. It constituted the *lingua franca* of the culture, and as William Blake and Jacob Boehme illustrate, provided the conceptual and imaginative vocabulary in which even heretical thoughts were expressed.

It is in this context that the liberating role of justification by faith can be best appreciated. Especially (though not only) in Lutheran lands, the chief function of this doctrine was a guide to the interpretation and assimilation of Scripture. The basic pattern in terms of which everyone learned to construe the sacred text was provided by Luther's *Small Catechism*. All children were expected to memorize it from beginning to end. The word "justification" does not, as it happens, appear in it, but it nevertheless impelled its readers to find everywhere in Holy Writ the five themes we earlier considered. Justification by faith, one might say, reshaped the Biblical world in which the society lived, and it is by this reshaping rather than directly that it exerted its major cultural influence. Generation after generation was taught to read the Bible as the story of, among other things, the liberation of anxious and guilt-ridden human beings from bondage to accursed law by a gift of inward confidence which frees them to be themselves. Everything else in the Bible was interpreted in a fashion compatible with this central cluster of convictions about the human problem and its solution.

It is scarcely surprising, therefore, that there were many anti-Christians such as Nietzsche (himself the product of a Lutheran parsonage) who retained this set of convictions after jettisoning everything else which the Bible teaches. His supermen have an uncanny formal resemblance to those who are justified as described by Luther.[14] In both cases, to be authentically human is to be freed from anxious and guilt-ridden bondage to accursed law by an inward confidence which liberates human beings for spontaneous action. Nor is it surprising that these convictions should be popular in a variety of secularized forms among Catholics and Jews as well as Protestants. Modern culture everywhere in the traditionally Christian West, but perhaps especially in the United States, is in large part secularized Protestantism, and everyone who participates in this culture becomes in some measure an heir of the Reformation.

This view of the Reformation's influence in shaping modern secular notions of what it means to be free cannot, it is true, be demonstrated. The most which can be claimed is that it has the kind of plausibility possessed by the similar and more familiar claim that Marxist utopianism, for example, is a secularized form of Messianic hope which would be unthinkable apart from the Biblical sources of Western culture.[15] In any case, I shall in the remainder of this essay assume (whether plausibly or implausibly) that the modern therapeutic version of liberation by inward confidence is a secularized form of the Reformation doctrine and ask about the difference made by its secularization.

III

One basic difference between the Reformation and modern versions of justification by faith is that saving confidence liberates in the first case for service to others, while in the second, it liberates for self-realization. Luther speaks, in what is perhaps his best known writing,[16] of the Christian as the free lord of all, who is yet the free servant or slave of all. The freedom from self-concern which comes from trust in God's love is freedom to be concerned about others. In the modern doctrine, in contrast, love-bestowed deliverance from self-preoccupation frees human beings to actualize their potentialities whatever these may be. Self-love or self-esteem of the right kind is considered indispensable in the

modern outlook while the Reformers, in contrast both to
their contemporary successors and their medieval
predecessors, avoided the concept.

Clearly, two different notions of the self are
involved. To be liberated is to acquire a new identity
quite discontinuous with the old, according to Reformation teaching, while true selfhood is generally primor-
dial or innate in secularized versions of the doctrine.
Instead of thinking of saving confidence as enabling
human beings to become what they really are deep down,
the Reformers spoke of it as producing new selves, free
selves. For Luther, as Wilfried Joest has put it,
Christian selfhood is exocentric:[17] Christians live
outside themselves in Christ or, alternatively, Christ
lives within. To be free is to receive a new being
founded on the almighty promises of God in Christ. It
is not a matter of developing what one already is.

Liberating confidence is communicated in very
different ways in these two outlooks. The Reformers
emphasized what they called the external or outer word
(which ultimately is Jesus Christ)[18] as imparted
through Scripture, preaching, and celebratory rites,
that is, sacraments. It is by internalizing this
external word of God that the new and trustful self is
created. Contemporary social psychologists might say
that selfhood for the Reformers is a product of successful socialization into the appropriate world view -
that is, the world of the Bible. The Reformers in
effect agree with this description though they, of
course, understand the relevant socializing processes
as the means of grace God uses to create new selves.
Conversely, the therapeutic model pictures true selfhood as hidden deep in every person. The role of basic
confidence is to remove the anxieties and inhibitions

which prevent its exfoliation. Thus, the basic conceptual contrast is between two models of the self and
only secondarily between more or less optimistic views
of human nature or of human goodness and sinfulness.
Looked at non-theologically, the Reformers have a more
empirically psycho-social, and their therapeutic
successors a more idealistically transcendental view of
what constitutes the self or ego.[19]

Given these formal contrasts, the concrete meaning
of self-acceptance and of freedom is also very different in the two outlooks. Here we need to recall that
for the Reformers the new identity never simply re-
places the old, at least not before death. Until the
end of life, the old Adam and Eve struggle against the
new and trust-filled self which is the free lord and
servant of all. The heteronomous demands of the law
remain in force against the old though not the new
self. Furthermore, believers cannot be neatly separated into their old and new selves because they are
simultaneously and completely both new and old, free
and bound, trustfully loving and anxiously selfish.
Their freedom is freedom to fight.[20] Their existence
is one of conflict both within and without, against
what Luther liked to call "the world, the flesh, and
the devil."[21] The self-acceptance which faith makes
possible is acceptance and persistence in this warfare.
Trust in the unrestricted love of the God who is
unrestrictedly powerful was not supposed to bring what
we ordinarily think of as peace and quiet, but rather
to confer the capacity to bear stress and strain. From
this perspective, therapeutic self-acceptance is
incomplete because it stops short with accepting and
integrating the old Adam and Eve, but not the battle
against them. It makes the mistake of supposing that

liberating confidence confers harmony within and
adjustment to the world without. This mistake is
perhaps inevitable whenever self-realization is the
ideal, and confidence is derived from partial and
faltering acceptance by other human beings (whether
parents, friends, therapists, or society) rather than
from God's almighty affirmation. Thus, whatever the
formal similarities, the practical meaning and cultural
significance of the two outlooks are contradictory.
The therapeutic version of liberation by faith aims at
the free unfolding of the self (including, to be sure,
the capacity to love others) while the Reformation
version seeks to undergird the non-self-righteous
service of neighbors, and through neighbors, of God.

The story of how this Reformation emphasis on
freedom to serve worked itself out in later Protestantism is a familiar one, but it should at least be
mentioned. Protestants redirected the dutifulness and
devotion once lavished on monastic disciplines to
secular vocations for, so the Reformers argued, it is
by faithfulness in the mundane tasks God calls us to
that we are most helpful to others in the place where
they actually live, that is, the world. Those devoted
to Christ are as free to serve in the familial, economic, and political domains as in overtly religious
activities. As Ernst Troeltsch in particular has
phrased it, the other-worldly asceticism of medieval
Catholicism was channeled into the inner-worldly
asceticism of post-Reformation Protestantism;[22] and if
Max Weber and others are to be believed, this displace-
ment of transcendentally sanctioned energies from the
sacred to the profane contributed much to the rise of
capitalism, nation states, Puritan revolutions, New
England and modern democracy.[23] Perhaps the Protestant

emphasis on the secular which has replaced pre-Reformation sacralism is now as oppressively dysfunctional as were medieval patterns in the sixteenth century, but at least the long transition from old to new was experienced by multitudes as immensely liberating, and the Reformation stress on freedom to work for human welfare in the world played no little part in the change.

The Reformation freedom to serve the neighbor had its limits, however. It did not in the 16th century situation include the freedom to engage in revolutionary action on behalf of the oppressed. Modern notions of progress had not yet developed, and the world of human affairs was conceived as fundamentally static. Radical improvements in economic, social, and political patterns were assumed to be impossible this side of the eschaton. Thus for those like Luther who rejected apocalyptic efforts to help bring in the Kingdom by force, the only way genuinely to help the disadvantaged was within the prevailing structures rather than by overturning them. One, even if not the most important, of his reasons for opposing the Peasants' Revolt was his conviction that its success would lead at best to a different rather than better government.[24] Calvin's views were not dissimilar,[25] although in his case the attempt to reorder the church along New Testament lines resulted in new models of social organization which in the long run, some historians maintain,[26] were of crucial importance in the development of democratic institutions especially in the United States of America. The training grounds for democracy of the American type were presbyterian and congregational ways of running the church. This kind of democratic social liberation, however, was an unintended consequence of Reformation teaching, not a deliberate goal.

Much the same can be said of modern notions of
tolerance, individual autonomy, and freedom of conscience, speech, and religion. These can be understood
as spinoffs of developments occasioned by the Reformation, but they were not part of its understanding of
Christian liberty. That liberty consisted quite simply
of deliverance from egotistic entrapment into free
service of others in whatever social world one finds
oneself. If the world in which God places one happens
to be ruled by the Turks, so Luther says, then Christian captives will pray and work for the earthly
welfare of the city of their sojourn just as the Jews
did in Babylon or Persia; and they will be as good
subjects of the Muslim sultan as of a Christian
prince.[27] He would presumably give much the same
advice regarding the Christian role in contemporary
communist countries, for these are no more antagonistic
to Christianity than were the Turks. Thus, Christian
freedom from self-concern and for the neighbor includes
the liberty to be good citizens of any kind of polity
except when the government commands the believer to do
that which is against Christ.

It would be wrong to conclude from this, however,
that the political implications of Luther's position in
our present situation are what we now ordinarily think
of as conservative. For him, it will be recalled, the
proper ordering of the earthly kingdom cannot be
deduced from Scripture. We must draw on reason and
experience, not on the Bible, in attempting to discover
the polities and policies most likely to promote our
neighbors' welfare in a given set of circumstances.
Our world, however, is so vastly different from that of
the 16th century that it becomes idle to speculate
regarding what he might now favor. His traditionalist

conservatism is neither capitalist nor socialist in the modern senses of those terms. Both the major ideologies of the contemporary world are in a sense secularized forms of the messianic radicalism which Luther fought in the Left-Wing Reformation. They share a common commitment to human improvement through endless and ever-accelerating scientific, technological, and economic advances of a kind which constantly revolutionizes the patterns of everyday life, fosters alienated individualism together with its counterpart, impersonal bureaucratic collectivism, undermines elemental social structures, weakens the transmission of traditions, dissolves the moral standards of the past, and threatens to destroy the environment and exterminate humanity. From this point of view, the traditionalist conservatism Luther thought most reasonable in his day is not an option, and it is idle to ask what policies he might now consider the most likely to avoid present perils. Perhaps he would be a rightist, perhaps a leftist, but in any case he would insist that Christians are free to differ in politics. They are delivered by faith from the need to absolutize the policies or polities for which they fight.

It is not our business to debate whether this is a tenable interpretation of the doctrine of the two kingdoms (for that is what the above paragraph is about), but it is part of our purpose to emphasize that if Luther is right, then reformers and revolutionaries stand in need of Christian freedom just as much as do defenders of the *status quo*. The bane of all social and political action on both the left and right is ego-tripping. Liberal politics and welfare states are as susceptible to the corruptions of self-interest as are the conservative varieties. Liberation movements

are regularly subverted by the lust for power, and
victorious radicals often end by being more oppressive
than the elites they displaced. It is thus not idle to
speculate that the efficacy of both reforming and
conserving action in Protestant cultures has at times
been enhanced by the influence of justification by
faith, by the conviction that human beings are not
justified by the presence, absence, success, or failure
of good works, and that both radicals and defenders of
establishments are sinners in need of grace and forgiveness. Christian freedom in this specifically
Reformation sense, so it can be plausibly argued, once
did much to spur and at the same time temper that
astonishing Protestant activism which inspired both
conservative and progressive movements and did much to
shape the modern world. In both Reformed and Lutheran
lands - in Switzerland, Holland, Britain, and the
United States as well as Scandinavia and Germany - that
activism was often characterized by an ethically
strenuous, self-critical, and non-utopian concern for
the welfare of the neighbor which can be viewed as a
legitimate offspring of Brother Martin's understanding
of the liberty of the justified.

From Luther's perspective, however, a similar
legitimacy cannot be ascribed to the therapeutic
understanding of liberating faith. This may well be
the currently most influential part of Luther's cultural legacy, but he would repudiate it every whit as
strenuously as he did the anabaptist and antinomian
versions of his teaching on justification. The corruption of the best is the worst, and perversions of
the gospel are in their way more diabolical than
outright denials of it. If the argument of this paper
is correct, the high culture of our day is pervaded by

a surprisingly Lutheran understanding of what it means, on the personal level, to be an authentically free human being, but in the absence of reference to the full range of Biblical teaching, this understanding, from Luther's perspective, is a recipe for disaster, not only religiously and theologically, but also ethically, socially, and politically. In the absence of the *coram deo* and the *simul justus et peccator*, the Reformation insight that authentic liberty is faith-given freedom from the law is a truth too explosively dangerous for human beings to bear. It contributes to a chaotically permissive individualism incompatible with any viable social order, and proves once again, as did the 16th century misappropriations of Biblical insights, that nothing is more destructive than the Biblical message when taken piecemeal.

The discussion of whether this polemic is justified lies beyond the scope of this essay. My main purpose has simply been to suggest that an understanding of human freedom which dominates one major strand of contemporary culture inside as well as outside the churches[28] is descended from Luther's insights. I have tried to describe what happens to Luther's anthropology when this is abstracted from his theology, but whether the change is good or bad must be left to the reader to judge.

NOTES

1. S. Freud, *Civilization and its Discontents* (New York: Norton, 1961), 42.

2. For a discussion of Erikson's interpretation of Luther, see G. Lindbeck, "Erik Erikson's *Young Man Luther*: A Historical and Theological Reappraisal," *Soundings* 16 (1973), 210-227, reprinted in D. Capps et. al., eds., *Encounter with Erikson* (Missoula, 1977), 7-28.

3. P. Tillich notes this resemblance in his *Systematic Theology*, Vol. 2 (Chicago, 1957), 47. For a remainder of the discussion in this paragraph, see G. Lindbeck, "An Assessment Reassessed: Paul Tillich on the Reformation," *The Journal of Religion* 63 (1983), 376-393.

4. This again is Erikson's view. See n. 2.

5. WA 8, 91-96; LW 32, 206-208, 210-213.

6. P. Rieff, *The Triumph of the Therapeutic: Uses of Faith after Freud* (New York, 1966).

7. The connections between Luther and some of these thinkers, especially Nietzsche, became the subject of much controversy during and after the Nazi period, but earlier they were taken for granted. See, e.g., K. Holl, "Der Neubau der Sittlichkeit" (1919) and "Die Kulturbedeutung der Reformation" (1911). Both essays are reprinted in his *Gesammelte Aufsätze zur Kirchengeschichte* Vol. I (Tübingen, 1948). See esp. 222 and 532-533. See also E. Hirsch, "Luther und Nietzsche," *Jahrbuch der Luthergesellschaft* 2 (1921), 61 ff.

8. The works of cultural anthropologists such as C. Geertz are particularly persuasive on this point. See his *The Religion of Java* (Glencoe, Ill., 1960), *Islam Observed* (Chicago, 1968), and various essays in his *The Interpretation of Cultures* (New York, 1973).

9. A. MacIntyre (with P. Ricoeur), *The Religious Significance of Atheism* (New York, 1966), 14. MacIntyre's comment concerns the difference between Russell's and Sartre's atheisms because these are denials of two different Gods.

10. Luther's influence on education is dealt with in other essays in this volume.

11. C. Gillispie, *Genesis and Geology* (New York, 1959).

12. See, e.g., Th. Aquinas, *Summa Theologiae* I, 46.

13. In regard to Rabelais, this thesis has been argued at length by Lucien Febvre in a classic study first published in 1942 and now available in English translation: *The Problem of Unbelief in the Sixteenth Century: The Religion of Rabelais* (Cambridge, 1983).

14. See n. 7.

15. The Marxist way of putting this thesis, to be sure, is that Christianity is implicitly atheistic. See E. Bloch, *Atheism in Christianity* (New York, 1972).

16. *The Freedom of a Christian*, WA 7, 42-73; LW 31,333-377.

17. W. Joest, *Ontologie der Person bei Luther* (Göttingen, 1967), 233 ff.

18. Joest also provides a good discussion of the relation of Christ and the word. See pp. 355-391.

19. The non-theological contrast I here have in mind is developed in terms of the differences between "cultural-linguistic" and "experiential-expressive" views of religion in G. Lindbeck, *The Nature of Doctrine* (Philadelphia, 1984), esp. chapters 1 & 2, and with specific reference to the Reformation, 34, 43, 118-119.

20. The passages from *Contra Latomus* referred to in n. 5, esp. WA 8, 95f; LW 32, 212, exemplify this emphasis.

21. E.g., in the explanation of the Third Petition of the Lord's Prayer in Luther's *Small Catechism*.

22. E. Troeltsch, *The Social Teachings of the Christian Churches*, Vol. 2 (New York, 1931), 602-612. Troeltsch differentiates between Calvinist and Lutheran attitudes on pages 605-606. For his

summary of the later developments of "ascetic Protestantism," see 807-820.

23. For a bibliographical essay surveying the discussions for and against Weber's thesis see D. Little, *Religion, Order, and Law* (New York, 1969), 226-237.

24. WA 19, 635-636, 639-640; LW 46, 106-107, 112.

25. B. Gerrish, "Strasbourg Revisited: A Reformed Perspective," in: *The Augsburg Confession in Ecumenical Perspective*, ed. H. Meyer (Geneva, 1980), esp. 146-147, 156-158. These pages contain a review of recent literature comparing Calvin's and Luther's views of the two kingdoms and of church-state relations.

26. E.g., A. D. Lindsay in his classic, *The Modern Democratic State* (New York, 1962), 117 ff.

27. E. Grislis, "Luther and the Turks," *The Muslim World* 64 (1974), esp. 278.

28. For evidence of the penetration of the therapeutic version of Luther's understanding of Christian freedom into the churches, see E. B. Holifield, *A History of Pastoral Care in America: From Salvation to Self-Realization* (Nashville, 1983).

Otto Hermann Pesch

FREE BY FAITH

Luther's Contribution to a Theological Anthropology

The question of "freedom by faith" is of special
significance because it introduces us, on the one hand,
into the center, the core of Luther's theology, while
it presents us, at the same time, with a Luther who is
a stranger in today's world. Of course, contemporary
Christians believe they know Luther as a hero of
freedom: didn't he successfully fight to set the
Christians free from the "tyranny" of ecclesiastical
hierarchy? Didn't he struggle for the freedom of
conscience from the tutelage by the priests? Hasn't he
dissolved the illegitimate marriage of church and
state, church and worldly power, church and society?
Hasn't he liberated the Christian theology from philosophical alienation and precisely thereby, vice versa,
freed philosophical reason from the illicit control of
theological guidance, particularly in the area of
social and political life, the field of professions,
economy, and law? Isn't Luther, in the final analysis,
the father of the Enlightenment, of the secular state,
of human rights? Isn't he, after all, the spiritual
and theological grandfather of the United States with
their guarantee of religious toleration both by the
government and even by church leaders?

This is no doubt the image of Luther in the eyes of countless Christians and non-Christians, not only in our century but also in the past. Yet, for Luther scholars and those who know Luther more intimately, this image appears almost entirely false, not simply and primarily because Luther was not that hero of liberty he is reputed to be, but above all because his idea of "freedom by faith" deals with quite other dimensions than those of ecclesiastical, political, and academic freedom; it points to quite different essentials of human being. And it is precisely due to these essentials that Luther is a stranger to us: we have to understand that "freedom by faith" belongs to Luther's concept of human being *coram deo*, in the eyes of God. "Free by faith:" that is the summary of Luther's theological anthropology. However, can it make a contribution to a contemporary theological anthropology?

I. A "PESSIMISTIC" PICTURE OF THE HUMAN BEING?

Now, even benevolent Luther scholars, particularly among Catholics but also among Protestants, regard Luther's anthropology as "pessimistic." He teaches, one thinks, that human beings are living so much under the power of sin that God's good creation seems entirely destroyed. Even the justified sinner is, according to Luther's famous formula *simul iustus et peccator*, "righteous and a sinner at the same time." And that means according to countless explications by Luther himself: the sin of the human being remains in its reality so that the sinner is righteous only through God's act of "non-imputation," i.e., by the fact that God does not reckon human sin as condemning.[1]

The well-known Catholic reply (which is so much more plausible to all human sciences) reads as follows: no fall into sin can be so deep that God's good work of creation is annihilated. Even the sinner who lives separated from God, retains elements of the "image of God": the ability to know the good (otherwise he/she could not know that he/she lives in sin) and the freedom to resist the sin (although the inclination to sin, in fact, could become a compulsion). God's grace redeeming the sinner can use those elements as points of contact. Thus, in the area of theological anthropology, one contrasts a "moderate optimism" with the Lutheran "pessimism" - and this contrast seems to be the ultimate obstacle to regarding the Lutheran-Catholic controversy as obsolete. But the Lutheran theology counters: the Catholic view of humankind does not take its own tradition seriously! It promotes the self-achievement of the human being - of the sinner! - over against God instead of degrading the human being in favor of the "new creation" which God builds up by God's own power and love. Catholic theology is said to fall back into that humanistic optimism of the Renaissance which was one of the reasons the Reformation happened in the first place. The intimate relationship between Catholic anthropology and human sciences, which regard humankind as good in principle, and social ideologies and programs, which hope to create a new humanity by means of political liberation and social changes - this relationship confirms the Lutheran objections to, or at least the Lutheran suspicion of, the Catholic anthropology. For Luther, in the name of Augustine and the great tradition of the church fathers, always contradicted that kind of anthropological humanism, and that from the very beginning of his

career, even before the conflict with Rome. Moreover,
one can say, his conflict with Rome only came into
being because he, following Paul and Augustine, maintained an anthropological "pessimism."

From the Reformation time on to our days this
basic conflict between two theological images of human
being comes to a head in the question of human freedom.
Already the young Luther declared freedom to be an
illusion. "The free will is a matter of mere title,
even a title without matter" (*res de solo titulo, immo
titulus sine re*).[2] Catholic theologians consider this
thesis of Luther's a monstrosity with disastrous
consequences for Christian ethics. Therefore, already
Pope Leo X, and respectively his counsellors, included
this thesis in the list of the *Errors of Martin
Luther*,[3] on the basis of which Luther was first asked
to recant and finally excommunicated. We shall come
back to this thesis later on.

To conclude our preliminary remarks, an illustra-
tion of the old and yet acute controversy by a characteristic example is appropriate: there is an old
thesis pervading the history of theology which became a
kind of focus for both a "pessimistic" and an "optimistic" anthropology. It is found in a work which for a
long time had been attributed to Augustine even in
Luther's time, which, however, as we know today, has
been written by an unknown scholar in Augustine's
school: the so-called *Hypognosticum*.[4] The thesis
goes: the sinner has lost the freedom to do the good;
he/she is only able "to build houses and to plant
vineyards."[5] This sentence was quoted wherever theologians raised the question of the sinner's ethical
faculties. Also Thomas Aquinas referred to it when he
wanted to show what, or better how little, good the

sinner is able to do.[6] We find it with a similar
meaning also in the *Augsburg Confession*, at the point
where Melanchthon described the abilities of the
sinner.[7] It is evident from the use of this thesis
that the abilities of the sinner are considered to be
extremely limited. Only such neutral and irrelevant
achievements as building houses and planting vineyards
are in the sinner's power to produce. Any good deed
which could make the sinner righteous, or even more
righteous before God is an impossibility.

After the Reformation, however, Catholic theologians used this text **against** Luther: **in any case**, as
Thomas says, the sinner is **able** to build houses and to
plant vineyards! But why didn't Thomas illustrate his
thesis by examples directly from the ethical field, if
he wanted to demonstrate the positive capability of the
sinner? The commentator's answer: "Because the
Augustinian text came into his mind!"[8] Thus on account
of an anti-Reformation prejudice, Catholic theologians
turned the clearly "pessimistic" thesis of the Augustinian tradition into a traditional argument for a "moderate optimism" which they felt obliged to maintain over
against Luther's "pessimism." In view of such a
distortion one has to agree with those Protestant
scholars who at this point defend Thomas against the
Thomists.[9]

I think this much is clear now: the topic "Free
by Faith" casts Luther's understanding of human being
into sharp relief. Only faith makes free - by their
own power sinners are no longer free at all. And
because this topic includes virtually the entire
Lutheran-Catholic controversy, the question Luther
raised is **the** central question for both the Catholic
church and present-day human self-understanding.

II. UNFREE BY UNBELIEF - SIN

It must be clear from the very beginning: we cannot discuss Luther's understanding of "freedom by faith" as the focus of his anthropology unless we talk first of all about the most unpopular theme in our time - sin. Certainly, Luther represented to some extent the "dawn of the modern era,"[10] for he was the first theologian trying to answer modern existential questions. Nevertheless, taking Luther to be the first theologian of the modern era can only be justified if we do not avoid the gloomy, touchy topic of sin. Otherwise, as Gerhard Ebeling justly said, we would not only give away Luther but also betray the modern era.[11]

1. The Basic Sin

Let us begin with that point which usually is for Catholics (and already for the fathers of the *Council of Trent*) the most inconceivable one: **the** sin, i.e., the basic sin, indeed the "natural" sin is **unbelief.** Therefore, it is essentially identical with original sin. Of course, such a notion of sin is total nonsense if we define "belief" and "faith" the way the medieval tradition and, following it, the Catholic catechisms still in our century understand them, namely, as the consent of reason to the revealed word of God, or in the language of the catechisms: "to take as true."[12] Here unbelief is one sin among others, such as uncharitableness, despair, pride, and, of course, all sins against the "second table" of the Ten Commandments. Yet if we see sin this way, Luther is completely misunderstood.

This is so first of all because Luther, supported by the Bible, conceived of faith as an event between

God and the whole of human being, between the person's complete devotion and God's merciful love. Consequently, unbelief cannot be one sin among others. In this connection Protestant Luther scholars underline the fact (and Catholics accept it, in the meantime, at least as a fact of theological history)[13] that Luther's emphasis on the notion of sin does not concern the **sins**, that is to say, **each and every** actual single sin, but **the** sin, the basic sin, the fountain of all other actual single sins. Here we encounter Luther's "radicalism" in interpreting sin: he traces the single sin back to its origin, to the person as a sinner. In the Catholic tradition this question was indirectly raised in the context of the problem: what is the "greatest" sin (particularly when pride and hatred against God were discussed).[14] In Luther's theology, however, this question became a direct topic: the concentration of all single sins in their substance as fundamental aversion from God.

> This is **the real capital sin.** If there were
> not this sin, there would not be any real sin
> at all. This sin is not committed just like
> all the other sins, not even as the most
> important one among others. It is not
> committed just for a time and in a place, but
> it lasts as long as the human being lives.
> It is only this natural sin that God takes
> into account.[15]

Once one understands Luther's notion of faith, it is no longer difficult to comprehend his conception of sin. According to his immortal definition in the *Large Catechism*

> "to believe means to trust God with our whole
> heart, ... to look for all good from God and

> to find refuge in God in every time of need,
> ... to set one's heart on God" or, as God
> would express it: "Whatever good thing you
> lack, look to me for it and seek it from me,
> and whenever you suffer misfortune and
> distress, come and cling to me. I am the one
> who will satisfy you and help you out of
> every need. Only let your heart cling to no
> one else."[16]

In other words, "to believe" means to **receive** oneself
from God and to be **willing** to receive oneself, i.e., to
renounce any attempt to obtain life, deliverance from
misery, and salvation by one's own efforts. Unbelief
signifies the opposite: to be someone through one's
own power and effort, to extract oneself from misery by
one's own endeavors, to do good by one's own abilities;
in short, literally to be in the attitude of self-glorification and, therefore, of selfishness. It is
clear, then, if unbelief (concretely expressed by
ingratitude, selfishness, and pride)[17] is dominating
the whole existence of a person, then single deeds will
represent nothing else than that which expresses and
satisfies precisely this fundamental unbelief. This
same selfishness and eagerness for power will necessarily also control the relationship to the neighbor.
It is not by chance that Luther, in the passage of the
Large Catechism just quoted, ties the notion of faith
to the first of the Ten Commandments. Belief or unbelief decides on which side we are standing, whether it
is the true God to whom we can pray "in every time of
need"[18] or whether it is the "idol" of self-glorification which, although flattering us, will finally betray
us. In theological terminology that is to say: unbelief is **the** basic sin for the very reason that it

is the transgression of the First Commandment, the focus of which is the demand or rather the permission to believe.[19]

2. The Slavery of Sin

The gloomy word of slavery under sin (yet a word coined by the Apostle Paul[20] and explained in the Christian tradition particularly by Augustine[21] - a fact which should prevent us from hasty judgments of Luther) is now no longer inconceivable. Already the classical Catholic tradition had argued that human beings cannot act without a final goal which determines everything one does.[22] If this goal is the person him/herself, then action amounts to a real slavery for, on the one hand, the person must refer everything to him/herself, i.e., the person cannot act in a way that is **not** selfish, and, on the other hand, such acting can result only in a radical disillusion because the finite person cannot satisfy the infinite desire for freedom and self-fulfillment. Luther, too, was guided by the same fundamental idea. However, he did not interpret it in the framework of a metaphysics of finite freedom but in simple terms of daily experience.

Selfishness "takes from God what is God's and from people what is theirs, and out of all it is and all it has and all it can do gives nothing either to God or (humanity)."[23] In all people do or leave undone, they rather seek their own advantage and their own way. They seek their own honor rather than God's and that of the neighbor. Therefore, all their works, all their words, all their thoughts, all their lives are evil and not Godly.[24]

Human beings are slaves of sin because they set their
hearts on false gods to which one cannot "look for any
good thing and in which one cannot find refuge in every
time of need."[25] In his *Large Catechism*, Luther names
those false gods quite concretely, such as money,
property, erudition, cleverness, power, sympathy,
friendship, honors.[26] Any human being is lost who is
forced to rely on them. And every human being is
forced to do so who cannot rely on the true God who
does not demand any works but only our readiness to
receive.

The culmination of this reversal of all real
relations between God and human beings, and thus the
climax of radical sin, emerges from the fact that human
beings misuse even their **good** works for their own
glory. With the best they can do by themselves they
inevitably will ratify and strengthen their basic,
personal sin. They are forced to do so. Luther did
not hesitate to include even the best ethical efforts,
well-known by pre-Christian history, into that basic
sin, such as the heroic deeds of C.M. Scaevola.[27] This
(by the way already Augustinian[28]) conviction finds its
most severe expression in Luther's following words that
are so confusing for Catholic readers (and not only
Catholics):

> As long as it (free will) does what it is
> able to do (*facit quod in se est*), it commits
> a mortal sin.[29] A good work, even though
> well performed, is a venial sin according to
> God's merciful judgment, and a mortal sin
> according to God's strict judgment.[30]

Luther did not hesitate to say those words in his sermons to the simple faithful, and again and again these
words have caused quite some irritation and disapproval

among good Catholics, at his time and even today. (Of
course, it is not surprising that those words not only
have been misunderstood but also misused, the more so
since even theologians found it difficult to interpret
them correctly.)

3. The Enslaved Will

From all of this it is already quite clear what
Luther intends to point out in his thesis on the
bondage of the human will. He formulated this thesis
already in his early theology, and he continued to
maintain it as long as he lived, although he did not
always press it on to all its extreme consequences as
he did in his treatise against Erasmus' *De servo
arbitrio* (1525).[31] (By the way, Luther considered *On
the Bondage of the Will* one of his best works, and one
among the few he wanted to be preserved from being
forgotten or burned).[32] Let us try to summarize:[33]

(1) Luther's thesis must not be interpreted in
the sense of a philosophical determinism. He never
denied that human beings can decide and act freely in
the area of "nature" i.e., concerning that "which is
below them,"[34] for example, to walk or not to walk, to
eat or not to eat, to build a house or to plant a vine-
yard. Human beings still can decide and choose to do
what is in their power, physically and intellectually.

(2) We have to take into consideration that from
Luther's point of view (Biblical and philosophical
influences merge here) the will is not first a neutral
power, an ability in itself, before it is to be brought
into movement. Rather, the will is a permanent willing, and this willing has a definite direction. Luther
argued against his opponent, Erasmus, that there is no
middle ground between "being able to will the good"

(*posse velle bonum*) and "not being able to will the good" (*non posse velle bonum*). There is no "mere and absolute willing" (*purum et merum velle*). Consequently, the human will is never, like Hercules', placed at a cross-road.[35]

(3) The actual direction of the concrete human will, i.e., of the sinner's will, is selfishness, self-glorification, the intention to do evil, to act against God's will, the search for one's own glory.[36]

(4) This direction of the will has the character of a compulsion. Once it exists and operates, human beings cannot change it any more, not only as to their ability to do any good, but even as to their inability to want to do it. In this regard they cannot escape sin. As soon as Satan rides the "beast of burden," the beast cannot shake off its rider.[37] And human beings do not even realize it. On the contrary, they fall for the illusion that they are free and that they are in charge rather than the beast of burden.[38] Not until they meet God's law can they learn that they are actually perishing in sin.[39]

(5) In Luther's view, this condition is not only a metaphysical necessity (or better: this argument is not so important for Luther) but it is above all God's judgment. God holds sinners in their evil attitude. Since God cannot stop operating in God's almighty way even in the face of the sinful human will, God goes on acting the same way as God is doing in and with everything else. If for human beings the only result is sin, it is not because of God but because of their sinful human will.[40] To illustrate, Luther used a metaphor: even the best rider cannot ride well on a lame horse.[41] Without metaphor: although human beings cannot escape sin, they themselves, not God, are

responsible for their sin. Though human beings are not free to **decide** and to **choose** by themselves, they still are *willing* to do what they do. They are not forced to do so from outside.[42] This clarification shows the one and only focus of his thesis. Luther wants to exclude the blasphemous consequence that God is directly responsible for human sin. Nevertheless, God is never the spectator but the operator of human decisions. By the way, Luther obviated with this thesis a humanistic interpretation of freedom which indeed understood freedom as liberty **over against** God. In contradistinction to this notion of freedom, Luther maintained the position of the classical theological tradition. Reading carefully both Augustine and Thomas Aquinas,[43] we will find that Luther is quite in line with their thought.

In summary, one thing is clear now regarding Luther's concept of sin: the doctrine of the enslaved will is a test of the seriousness and radical strength of his understanding of sin. Luther felt obliged to think in this way for the sake of the glory of God, who by faith alone binds human beings to God's freedom and thus sets them free from Satan's slavery. Luther felt compelled to think in this way for the sake of Christ's glory, because, as he argued against Erasmus, what a poor redeemer Christ would indeed be if we needed him only to get rid of some imperfection at the periphery of our existence rather than being liberated by him from the perversion of the basic attitude of our mind.[44] Therefore, as Hans-Joachim Iwand rightly pointed out, the doctrine of the enslaved will is the "critical point," and at the same time a "law of style" (*Stilgesetz*) of Luther's and Lutheran theology.[45] Given this crucial focus of the bondage of the will,

the next question, "What does it mean for human beings
to be free by faith?" imposes itself all the more
urgently.

III.   FREE BY FAITH ALONE - JUSTIFICATION

1.   Faith

It is almost a tautology to say that faith abolishes sin, for belief abolishes unbelief by being its
opposite. Now everything is going to happen that we
have mentioned above in connection with Luther's notion
of faith.[46] It is going to happen, of course, not by
human efforts but by God's grace, concretely, by the
Holy Spirit who takes hold of human beings when they
are listening to the word of the gospel: faith is the
fulfillment of the First Commandment (but not the
"work" of the First Commandment, as the older Luther
carefully pointed out).[47] Yet what seemed to be so
obvious turns into a matter of reflection as we consider the theoretical and practical implications of faith
- and here, at last, Luther's contribution to a theological anthropology comes fully into focus.

Faith - faith alone, what else? - becomes the
theological definition of human nature. To clarify by
comparison: when defining persons, scholasticism was
especially concerned with the relationship between the
bodily and the spiritual dimension of human being.[48]
This was extremely urgent, for, due to some spiritual-
istic tendencies in pre-Christian Greek philosophy, it
had become an accepted Christian conviction for a long
time that it is the spiritual soul that constitutes
human being while the body is a prison. In the 13th
century, the ancient Greek philosopher Aristotle,
recently discovered and received, became the best

advocate of the Christian belief in creation and of the
Biblical appreciation of the body. With his help, it
was finally possible to advance the following formula
in a **Christian** understanding: the soul is the (unique!)
"form" of the body, therefore, the human being is a
sensitive being, gifted with reason (*animal rationale*).[49] Rather than saying the human being is soul but
has a body, the new statement went: the human being is
bodily spirit and spiritual body. Thus the doctrine of
creation was freed from a dangerous narrowness.

Yet, asked Luther, had one sufficiently taken into
consideration that human beings, concretely, exist as
creatures who **deserted** God, i.e., as sinners, and that
they deserted God **totally**, not only with their body but
also with their soul?[50] Luther did not simply reject
the medieval formula, but he thought that it was
theologically insufficient, if not irrelevant. For him
the central subject matter of theology was nothing else
than the sinful human being and the justifying God.[51]
He defined the human being theologically as *fide
justificandus*, as the one who needs to be justified by
faith.[52] The **whole** human being, without differentiation between body and soul, is in need of justification. In his theses of the *Disputatio de homine* (1536)
Luther sharpened this point into important consequences.[53] If human being is defined by justifying faith,
then faith - or, more precisely, the **call** to faith - is
a constituent part of human nature. Of course, through
unbelief a human being can deny his/her nature, but
then he/she is losing it. Sinners, selfish as they
are, are a caricature of human being. Theologically
speaking (that is to say, from the perspective of the
Christian message) there does not exist a "neutral"
human being who, without any consequences for the

fulfillment of his/her nature, could be asked whether
he/she or his/her will "wants to," or rather "does not
want to," believe. For the sake of the human being's
nature, God calls him/her to receive him/herself, and
if he/she refuses to respond, he/she is not going to be
what he/she is destined to be according to God's will
as creator and redeemer. Therefore, it can no longer
surprise that for Luther faith is the only dimension
where the human being is in the image of God, while
unbelief leads to becoming a distorted picture of what
human beings are called to be.[54]

It is worthwhile mentioning at this point that
Luther's deliberations come surprisingly close to those
of certain tendencies within contemporary theological
anthropology. The human being as "the actor" (*Täter*)[55]
who wants to achieve what he/she is only by own accomplishments in all areas of life, and who chooses to
remain within his/her limits rather than being prepared
to receive him/herself from someone greater than he/she
is - that is indeed today's concept of unbelief, of
atheism. The thesis, "There cannot be and must not be
a God because if God exists, human beings cannot be
free any longer," does not express a Christian suspicion or an unfair reproach against atheism. On the
contrary, it is a philosophical thesis of our present
time which is formulated in plenty of variations.[56] In
this situation the Christian understanding of human
being and Luther's surprising actuality for the field
of theological anthropology becomes completely clear.
By nature the human being is defined as the one who is
called to faith. In other words, at the basis of everything, even at the basis of all activities demanded
from the human being, he/she is the one who **receives**.
The medieval thesis of the human being as a sensual

being, gifted with reason, was very much needed in
order to recover the Christian justification of the
body and of the bodily world. After this thesis had
succeeded, we must say today that Luther's definition
of the human being as the one who is to be justified by
faith, more than ever promises to lead us into the core
of Christian understanding of human nature.

But now a new question must arise: if faith, the
demand of faith and the responsibility of faith,
constitutes human nature, how can faith make free?
Isn't faith a **demand** which exactly has to deny human
self-glorification, or the deep human will to achieve
itself? Does not Luther insist, particularly in the
Large Catechism, that faith is **God's commandment** and
that God's **wrath** will come upon all those who do not
follow it?[57]

2. Freedom by Faith: To Live With Sin

It is time to admit that a closer look at Luther's
understanding of human being and faith makes it appear
more alien to us than it seemed at first sight. There
are simple reasons for this. Luther had no problems
with presupposing that nobody was going to call God's
reality in question. For him, in every respect the
human being is by nature faced with God and therefore
is always responsible to God. Luther's pathos in
speaking about faith did not at all have to deal with
any doubts about God's reality, as is the case today,
but was directed against the works with which the human
being tries to influence, to manage, so to speak, the
relationship to this God and, conversely, God's relationship to him/herself. Furthermore, it was aimed at
the blindness which makes the human being believe that
he/she in fact is able to settle his/her relationship

to God's holy will by his/her own efforts. In other words, Luther's notion of faith struggled against that minimalistic understanding of **sin** that we have described.[58] It is obvious already here that "freedom by faith" in Luther's understanding is something entirely different from "freedom of conscience" in the modern sense, which is a freedom over against state and society, and a human right in the political arena.[59] In Luther's view, however, freedom by faith is freedom to faith which God is demanding of humanity, and which God does not leave at all to human choice. Is this a disappointing answer for a modern reader of Luther? We only have to follow it up within the context of Luther's own thought, then its modern significance becomes obvious.

1. The sinner who is touched by the word of the gospel proclaiming God's forgiving love, the sinner who believes through God's grace and who realizes that he/she is accepted by God's grace - this sinner is free from the condemning power of sin before God. Sin can no longer separate the human being from God because God, so to speak, does not take it into account as an argument against God's love. This is certainly not a "cover-up" of sin, benign but without seriousness - as the traditional Catholic objection against this Lutheran idea of the "non-imputation" of sin has it.[60] On the contrary, in terms of the relationships between persons, "non-imputation" illustrates what it means "to forgive." Among human beings "forgiveness" does not mean that guilt is made undone and thus abolished, but that despite the guilt a new beginning is opened.

2. Freedom by faith signifies that sin (as self-glorification, selfishness, ingratitude, etc.) has been rendered ineffective in its enslaving power.

Every act of faith in God explodes the **vicious circle** within which selfishness always engenders new selfishness, within which persons misuse one another like commodities instead of being a second Christ to their neighbors by acting in their favor like Christ has acted for our sake - according to Luther's well-known words.[61]

3. The deeply rooted will of self-glorification and selfish autonomy, of course, is not automatically killed by faith. At this point Luther is not a "pessimistic" theologian but simply realistic. To receive ourselves is indeed troublesome, and faith has to overcome many obstacles again and again. This process of killing sin will not be completed during a lifetime. In the core of ourselves, the old aversion against God is still active. In Luther's own words: the "old Adam" is alive.[62] And because it is aversion, it is unbelief, and because it is unbelief, it is **the** sin - the basic sin, the ground and reason of all actual sins. Faith does not change this situation with one stroke but it creates a new relationship to it: as God does not take this aversion as an opposition to God's love, so the sinner who believes shall follow suit and do likewise. Therefore, the justified sinner is allowed to take consolation even regarding continuing sin.

In a word: believers are free from sin because **they are allowed to live with their sin,** inspite of the fact that sin, in and by itself, is mortal. In Luther's famous formulation: the faithful one is righteous and sinner at the same time (*simul iustus et peccator*).[63] It is superfluous to underline that this in no way amounts to a slightening of ethics. It rather means, in terms of another version of the reformatory formula by Johann Baptist Metz (which

immediately discloses its actuality): "The Christian
is simultaneously faithful and unbelieving."[64] Consequently, we have always to struggle for our faith, our
devotion to God, our readiness to **receive** ourselves
again and again, and we have to protect it again and
again against our deeply rooted will to **achieve** ourselves, against our will to exist on our own. Do we
really believe that some day we can "manage" faith once
and forever?

3. The Liberated Will - To Live Against Sin
    What about the human **will** concerning which Luther
declared in such a challenging way that it is unfree,
enslaved, indeed an illusion? Now, even in the case of
the truly faithful person, Luther maintained that the
human will is **not** free before **God.** The rider has
changed, not the beast of burden.[65] But, surprisingly,
Luther emphasized that the will, now released from
being "incurved upon itself"[66] is in fact able to
collaborate with God's rule, to "cooperate" with God,
as Luther, following the medieval terminology, formulated without fear of falling into synergism. One
quotation stands for plenty of others: God "does not
work in us without us, because it is for this God has
created and preserved us, that God might work in us and
we might cooperate with God."[67] Luther wrote this
sentence in his most severe treatise against the free
will, *De servo arbitrio.* God will have us as "coopera-
tors."[68] The entire freedom of will toward "natural"
matters, all the willingness of the will (which even
the enslaved will had retained) is now engaged in
establishing the kingdom of God, i.e., in serving
fellow human beings by communicating God's love to
others. To be sure, the will remains **unfree,** for it is

God who operates **through** us, but it is **freed**, released from selfishness and enabled to serve.

How does the will find the power to do so? Scholasticism had answered: because God's grace has touched it and turned it around.[69] Luther answered differently: because the word of the gospel, the word of God's forgiving love has touched the core of human being.[70] Therefore, human beings are freed from the need to establish themselves, to preserve themselves, and to redeem themselves. The essence of freedom is that human beings now have their hands free to serve the world and their neighbors, because they no longer need to care for themselves - in spite of sin. All energies of the former selfishness are, so to speak, to be turned back to true love. And these energies are not reserves to fall back on at a later time. No, if they are not immediately invested in service, they thwart at once that faith which had just crossed out selfishness. This is the way one has to understand Luther's thesis (by which he associated himself with a very old idea of the Christian ethical tradition from Paul to Thomas Aquinas)[71] that faith spontaneously, by its own inner impulse, engenders a new kind of acting.[72] Faith rejects and overcomes unbelief, i.e., selfishness and self-glorification. It can do this only by beginning to kill that selfishness, that is to say, to receive oneself from God and to serve. Otherwise, faith would deny by acting what it affirms by believing.

Therefore, faith by its own substance is a struggle against sin. The liberated will is what it is precisely because it enables the faithful not only to live **with** sin, but also to live **against** sin. Therefore, according to Luther, faith and good works cannot

be separated. As he stated in the famous words of his
Preface to the Epistle to the Romans in his German
Bible:

> Faith, however, is a divine work in us which
> changes us and makes us to be born anew of
> God. It kills the old Adam, makes us alto-
> gether different beings in heart and spirit
> and mind and powers; and it brings with it
> the Holy Spirit. O, it is a living, busy,
> active, mighty thing, this faith. It is
> impossible for it not to be doing good works
> incessantly.[73]

IV.   FREEDOM OF CONSCIENCE - THE CHURCH

Our topic is: Luther's contribution to a theological anthropology. It seems that until now we have
dealt more with Luther's soteriology. But the anthropological significance of what we have considered thus
far will appear more clearly as we connect the freedom
by faith with Luther's notion of conscience.

1.   Freedom of Conscience

As in the case of both the notion of sin and of
faith, Luther's thinking did not replace the traditional significance of the term "conscience"[74] but deepened
and radicalized it. In his treatise *Judgment On
Monastic Vows (De votis monasticis iudicium)* 1521,
Luther gave a clear summary of his understanding of
both the conscience and its freedom.

> Christian or evangelical freedom, then, is a
> freedom of conscience which liberates the
> conscience from works. Not that no works are
> done, but no faith is put in them. For

conscience is not the power to do works, but to judge them.[75]

We realize conscience concerns works, not particular works from the viewpoint of their ethical value, but works in general from the perspective of their significance before God.

Therefore, **freedom** of conscience is not the free choice to do whatever one likes to do, but the permission to do works without being forced to trust in them. In other words, before God human beings are not to be identified with what they do and achieve, but with what they receive. The human dimension in which this freedom is experienced is called by Luther "conscience." He identified this "conscience" explicitly with the "heart" in the Biblical sense, or even with the "intellect" (*intellectus*).[76]

Luther is here original with regard to terminology. He moved beyond certain tendencies in the medieval discussion, particularly on the notion of *synteresis* (the "basic conscience").[77] The end result of his advance is that conscience is identical with the core of human being, or in the words of Gerhard Ebeling: the human being "does not **have** a conscience but **is** conscience."[78] And this is not simply a change of words and their significance, but it is precisely the focus of Luther's contribution to a theological anthropology. For, through the notion of conscience, Luther understood human beings as essentially faced with God (*coram deo*), in whose eyes human beings cannot stand on what they are achieving, but only by faith, i.e., by receiving oneself through God's gift. The result of this fundamental theological description of human beings is Luther's formula in the *Heidelberg Disputation*: "Faith in Christ is a good conscience."[79]

Evidently, the notion of "conscience" epitomizes what we have explained regarding sin and faith.

2. No Freedom of Conscience

This is obviously not the kind of freedom of conscience we normally understand today. Our modern concept of freedom of conscience appears to be an anthropological reality as well: the powerful person- alism of faith which cannot be replaced by delegation to anybody else, neither to the church nor to the representatives of political or social ideologies. However, does not precisely our modern concept of freedom of conscience immediately follow from Luther's statements? Many people certainly think so - but as already indicated in the beginning of this essay, their assumption is erroneous. The disappointing answer is inevitable: Luther is not the **father** of freedom of conscience in the modern sense of the word, nor the father of human rights in general.[80]

In fact, there are some texts which **sound** like supporting our modern understanding, above all Luther's historic answer at the Diet of Worms.[81] Another statement may stand for plenty of others:

> I want to preach it, I want to say it, I want
> to write it, but I do not want to force, to
> coerce anybody by violence. For, faith is to
> be accepted willingly, without compulsion.[82]

Or the famous words in a letter to the Elector: "Let the spirits collide and fight it out."[83] Isn't that what we wish and hope to hear from Luther?

However, we are at a loss fully to understand Luther here. And nobody can help us. For these texts - not accidentally texts from the early Reformation time - refer in fact only to his conflict with Rome and

appeal to the common basis of the Scriptures. Luther
claimed freedom for his own understanding of the
Christian faith, and he supported his contention by the
greatest witnesses of Christian faith, Paul and Augustine, whom his opponents also in general acknowledged
as authorities. To say it briefly (because we cannot
explain here the whole problem of how the theological
conflict between an originally Augustinian theology of
grace and the late medieval practice of piety could
escalate into an institutional conflict, at the end of
which the question of freedom of conscience in the modern sense could arise):[84] the representatives of the
church, involved as they were in a practice of piety
which issued in financial and political practices seriously lacking theological foundation, refused to acknowledge an essential part of their own tradition
which Luther, and his friends, had rediscovered and intensified by solid academic research. That, of course,
is inconceivable to us today, but it is a matter of
fact which even Catholic theologians no longer deny.[85]

Only in this framework, namely by appeal to a
common authority in Scripture, did Luther and his
followers dissent from the "official" church. It is
significant to observe that Luther only in this respect
criticized the ecclesiastical authority, charging that
it had instituted "articles of faith" which can by no
means be proven as being in agreement with the Bible.[86]
Thus, he hoped that the "gospel," freed from human dis-
tortions and misunderstandings, would make its way by
its own power. He also proposed to convince the heretics by the word, not by fire.[87] However, after 1525,
subsequent to the experience of new misunderstandings
of the gospel, as he felt, and in response to new reformatory groups which enlarged his original concern,

Luther turned more or less involuntarily to the conviction that the gospel in fact needed help.[88] The
"idolatry" of the papal faith must be suppressed and
the reformatory newcomers, from the anabaptists to
Zwingli and the antinomians, must be prevented from
advancing their ideas. Who alone could provide help?
The princes and the political authorities, in the case
of emergency even by execution. Once more, it is hard
to understand this attitude today - but Luther felt no
contradiction, for his original concern had neither
changed nor been enlarged. **Other** people tried to en-
large it; he himself was and stayed, as one has justly
formulated, a "conservative reformer."[89]

3. Luther: the Ancestor of Freedom of Conscience

But precisely here not only we but already
Luther's contemporaries began to raise critical questions. Even convinced Lutherans found it hard to understand that the preacher of the "freedom of a Christian"
felt no uncertainty with the assumption that other
theologians interpreted the same Biblical passages in a
different way, and that even he himself changed several
times his own interpretation of important texts of the
Scripture.[90] **Within** the Reformation movement, one came
to realize there was a potential for further freedom of
searching for truth which became effective the longer
and the more the search was pursued.

This development is even more understandable when
we consider the following: Luther's concept of the
freedom of conscience always involved that which the
conscience is faced with, the word of God coming from
outside of the human being. For the sake of this word
he claimed a limited freedom of conscience over against
that social institution which at that time dominated

the whole of society, the church. He could claim this
freedom because the church was subservient to this
word. All conflicts were based on the same foundation,
i.e., Scripture.

But what will happen if the church more and more
ceases to be the only dominating social power? Personal belief is then no longer related to a word which is
publicly taken for granted. Rather, individual belief
itself is the way to discover in the Bible the word of
God. In other words, the act of personal belief includes in itself, in its own self-understanding, the
reality of a divine word which outside of faith is no
longer available. This situation began with the
Enlightenment. Under these novel conditions, the personalism of faith in an ecclesiastical context had to
change to a freedom of conscience **over against** a
post-Christian society and over against a church, or
churches, that no longer represented the unquestioned
basis of social life. Luther was not the **father** of
modern freedom of conscience, because his situation was
still such that he did not yet have to reflect on a
freedom of conscience vis-à-vis the social and ecclesiastical institutions. But he is the **ancestor** of such a
freedom, because he was the first in church history to
underline and focus on a radical personalism, even an
individualism of faith, which can by no means be dele-
gated to any social group, not even to the only one
dominating both political and social life. This, too,
is not the least of Luther's contributions to a theological anthropology.

4. The Church - Model of Freedom of Conscience

The Reformation events had a tragic impact on a
church, the Roman church, which was not prepared to

agree with Luther's theological anthropology according
to which the human being lives before God by faith
alone (not even partly by one's own endeavors and
efforts), and according to which all good things the
human being achieves are **fruits** of God's gift, **answers**
to God's call, **responses** to, rather than initiatives of
salvation. The Reformation was a tragedy precisely
because (and that is the most important result of
present-day Catholic Luther research)[91] the theoretical
presuppositions of the Catholic tradition would have
allowed a basic agreement with Luther. The church had
to pay a high price for this failure - the split of
Western Christendom - in the wake of which the Enlightenment, in order to overcome the perennial denominational controversies, finally claimed, by stressing
Luther's own view, that freedom of conscience which we
enjoy today.

What consequences does the church have to draw
from this tragic history? I think it can only be the
following one: it must become a model of freedom of
conscience - also and especially in its institutional
life. Forced by an anti-ecclesiastical, anti-clerical
development in the Post-Reformation era, the church has
to realize that the gospel is an offer, **the** offer of
real humanization, which can only be accepted by faith.
The church does not have to be afraid of competition by
other views of human life. Atheism in all its various
shapes has not yet proved that its concept of human
beings making themselves over into "new" human beings
has to offer a better chance for real humanization and
better freedom. The church, the churches owe to the
world a model, a demonstration even in their own institutional life, that freedom by faith (in a sense which
includes freedom of conscience as a human right) is

possible and the best, the only way of human self-fulfillment, a freedom which is never without responsibility **because** it is responsibility before the God in
whom faith trusts, and, finally, a responsibility which
reveals its freeing power precisely in that it takes
care of the freedom of all who are unfree under the
various oppressive powers of contemporary life in the
present-day world.[92]

Thus we come to a summary which, in Luther's
words, stresses what the church ought to do today.

V. THE ARTICLE BY WHICH THE CHURCH STANDS AND FALLS

This challenging formula of Luther's[93] would be
entirely nonsensical if Luther's doctrine of justification by faith alone were only **one** topic among others.
For, in this case, Luther would promote arbitrarily and
in a one-sided way one Biblical and theological theme
at the expense of others. Luther would not be, according to the famous critique of Joseph Lortz, a "full
hearer of the Scriptures."[94] Yet, if we recall our
reflection, particularly Luther's understanding of
faith and his corresponding understanding of freedom,
the formula *articulus stantis et cadentis ecclesiae*
is self-evident. Let us summarize as precisely as
possible.

If the church today has to talk about sin - and
without sin it cannot talk about the gospel! - it has
first of all to emphasize that human beings live
against their nature when they refuse to understand
themselves as those who receive. Aren't there thousands and thousands of hints to recognize how urgent
this "message of sin" is - urgent in a world of

pervasive "making" and "producing," in which God's almighty power seems to turn into the might of human beings?[95]

If the church today talks about freedom - and without freedom it cannot talk about the gospel of Christ! - it must make clear that true freedom is the freedom from the compulsion to achieve the meaning of human life by one's own power, and the liberation to a literally free service in favor of the world and for the sake of our fellow human beings, and, finally the release even from all of one's own failures. Aren't there thousands and thousands of hints to acknowledge the importance of such a joyful message in a world of inescapable compulsion and pressure, of manipulations and illusions which offer meaning without being able to keep their promises?

If the church understands itself as the representative of the coming kingdom of God and as the good companion of all those who are on the way towards that kingdom - how could it follow its call in an appropriate way unless it did present a model, an image, an "advertisement" of this kingdom in itself, its structure, its public appearance, its ways of life, its "milieu?" Whether the church really is the church and thus the living contradiction of this world of pressures and selfmade anxieties, that depends on its readiness to announce publicly: freedom does not depend on the church but on the faith which it proclaims. Doing so, the church would be faithful to Luther - even the Catholic church. Thus, late but not too late, it would become clear that Luther does not only belong to the Lutheran church, but to the whole of Christendom.

NOTES

1. Cf. for instance WA 56, 272; 513; WA 2, 469; LW 27, 230; WA 39 I, 492 and 563. For interpretation and literature see O. H. Pesch, *Hinführung zu Luther* (2nd ed., Mainz, 1983), 189-202.

2. This formula (WA 7, 146), a repeated and sharpened version of Thesis 13 of the *Heidelberg Theses* (WA 1, 354; LW 31, 40), was condemned by the pope (DS 1486); see also WA 18, 756.

3. See n. 2.

4. Also called *Hypomnesticon contra Pelagianos et Coelestinos*: PL 45, 1611-1664.

5. PL 45, 1623.

6. *Summa Theologiae*, I-II 109, 2 in corp. art.

7. BSLK 73 f.; BC 39.

8. Cf. Th.-A. Deman, *Der neue Bund und die Gnade. Kommentar zu Thomas von Aquin: Summa Theologiae, I-II 106-114, Die Deutsche Thomas-Ausgabe*, vol. 14 (Heidelberg - Graz, 1955), 253f; 333.

9. See H. Vorster, *Das Freiheitsverständnis bei Thomas von Aquin und Martin Luther* (Göttingen, 1965), 231 f. (against Deman, ibid.).

10. See H.A. Oberman (ed.), *Luther and the Dawn of the Modern Era. Papers to the Fourth International Congress for Luther Research* (Leiden, 1974).

11. G. Ebeling, "Luther and the Beginning of the Modern Age" in: *Luther and the Dawn of the Modern Era*, ed. by H. Oberman, 11-39, here: 39. For the following see also G. Ebeling, *Theologie zwischen reformatorischem Sündenverständnis und heutiger Einstellung zum Bösen*, in: id., *Wort und Glaube*, vol. III (Tübingen, 1975), 173-204; O.H. Pesch, *Theologie der Rechtfertigung bei Martin Luther und Thomas von Aquin. Versuch eines systematisch-theologischen Dialogs* (Mainz, 1967; reprint 1984), 77-122; 468-552.

12. See Thomas Aquinas, *Summa Theologiae*, II-II 1, 1-2; 4, 1; and the famous definition of faith by the *First Vatican Council*, DS 3008.

13. See for instance K. Rahner, Art. *Sünde, V. Dogmatisch*, in: *Lexikon für Theologie und Kirche* 9 (1964), 1177-1181, here: 1179; L. Scheffczyk, Art. *Sünde*, in: H. Fries (ed.), *Handbuch theologischer Grundbegriffe*, vol. 2 (München, 1963), 597-606, here: 601; for the Catholic references, cf. O.H. Pesch, *Theologie der Rechtfertigung*, 534 f.

14. Cf. Thomas Aquinas, *Summa Theologiae*, II-II 34, 2; 162, 6; cf. I-II 73, 4 ad 3; II-II 201 ad 1; 162, 7 ad 4; O.H. Pesch, *Theologie der Rechtfertigung*, 480-482.

15. WA 10 I 1, 508; LW 52, 152.

16. BSLK 560; BC 365.

17. Cf. O.H. Pesch, *Theologie der Rechtfertigung*, 85-87.

18. See n. 16.

19. Cf. for instance WA 39 I, 531 and 581; WA 40 I, 399; LW 26, 253; WA 40 III, 343.

20. Cf. Rom 6:6, 16, 20; 7:23.

21. References and literature in G. Greshake, *Gnade als konkrete Freiheit. Eine Untersuchung zur Gnadenlehre des Pelagius* (Mainz, 1972), 193-274; also in B. Lohse, *Epochen der Dogmengeschichte* (5th ed., Stuttgart, 1983), 115-121; O.H. Pesch - A. Peters, *Einführung in die Lehre von Gnade und Rechtfertigung* (Darmstadt, 1981), 16-25. Augustine's understanding of sin is evident since his *De diversis quaestionibus ad Simplicianum* (396): PL 40, 101-148; CChr 44 (Augustinus XII/1), that is to say: already **before** his controversy with Pelagius.

22. Cf. Thomas Aquinas, *Summa Theologiae*, I-II 1,6.

23. WA 7, 212; PE 2, 364.

24. WA 6, 244; LW 44, 73.

25. See n. 16.

26. BSLK 561; BC 366.

27. Cf. WA 18, 742; LW 33, 225.

28. Cf. for instance *Tract. in Joh.* 5, 12: CChr 36,
    40: *Nemo habet de suo, nisi mendacium et peccatum*
    (quoted by the II Synod of Orange in 529, [DS
    392]); also *De gestis Pelagianorum* 34: CSEL 42,
    89f; *De civitate dei* 5, 19; 14, 28; 19, 4: CChr
    47, 156; 48, 452; 664 ff.; further references in
    W. Geerlings, *Christus Exemplum. Studien zur
    Christologie und Christusverkündigung Augustins*
    (Mainz, 1978), 183-189.

29. WA 1, 359; LW 31, 48.

30. WA 7, 438; LW 32, 86.

31. WA 18, 600-787; LW 33, 15-295.

32. WAB 8, 98f; LW 50, 171-174.

33. For the following see O.H. Pesch, *Theologie der
    Rechtfertigung*, 106-109; 377-382; id., *Hinführung
    zu Luther*, 176-188; and id. "Freiheitsbegriff und
    Freiheitslehre bei Thomas von Aquin und Luther,"
    in: *Catholica*, vol. 17 (1963), 197-244, where the
    most important literature of the recent discussion
    is listed. For the American public, the most
    extensive analysis of Luther's doctrine is H.S.
    McSorley, *Luther Right or Wrong?* (New York -
    Minneapolis, 1969).

34. Cf. WA 18, 638; 672; 752; 781; LW 33, 70; 118 f.;
    240; 285.

35. Cf. WA 18, 669; 676-677; LW 33, 114 and 126.

36. Cf. WA 18, 634-635; 675; 684; 698; 709-710;
    742-743; 750-751; LW 33, 64 f; 124; 138; 158;
    175f; 225; 237ff.

37. Cf. WA 18, 635; 750; LW 33, 65f; 237.

38. Cf. WA 18, 628; 679; 766; 767; 776; LW 33, 55;
    130; 261 f; 263; 277.

39. Cf. WA 18, 671-683; LW 33, 117-138.

40.   Cf. WA 18, 709-711; LW 33, 175 ff.

41.   WA 18, 635; 750; LW 33, 65; 237.

42.   Cf. WA 18, 634-635; 693; 720-721; LW 33, 647; 152; 192 ff.

43.   See n. 33.

44.   Cf. WA 18, 744; LW 33, 227.

45.   Cf. H.-J. Iwand, *Um den rechten Glauben. Gesammelte Aufsätze* (München, 1959), 14 f.; 248.

46.   See n. 16. At this point we enter into Luther's extensive reflections on the "new human being," frequently undervalued particularly by the German Lutherans. See, for instance, O.H. Pesch, *Theologie der Rechtfertigung*, 51-76; 109-122; 283-322; id., *Hinführung zu Luther*, 154-175, and the literature listed there. Among the Lutherans, it is especially P. Althaus and A. Peters; among the Catholics, it is P. Manns and E. Iserhoh, who emphasize this important line of Luther's thinking. But we cannot deal with it extensively because of our concentration on Luther's anthropology.

47.   Compare WA 6, 209; LW 44, 30; WA 7 26; B. Woolf, ed., *Reformation Writings of Martin Luther* (London, 1952), I, 364; WA 39 I, 91; 98; LW 34, 160 and 167 f.; WA 39 I, 202; with WA 5, 394.

48.   It would be necessary here to refer to almost the whole of medieval philosophical and theological anthropology. See, representing a large discussion, R. Heinzmann, *Die Unsterblichkeit der Seele und die Auferstehung des Leibes. Eine problemgeschichtliche Untersuchung der frühscholastischen Sentenzen- und Summen-literatur von Anselm von Laon bis Wilhelm von Auxerre* (Münster, 1965); Th. Schneider, *Die Einheit des Menschen. Die anthropologische Formel "anima forma corporis" im sogenannten Korrektorienstreit und bei Petrus Johannis Olivi. Ein Beitrag zur Vorgeschichte des Konzils von Vienne* (Münster, 1973); G. Ebeling, *Disputatio de homine. Erster Teil: Text und Traditionshintergrund, Luther-Studien*, II/1 (Tübingen, 1977); *Zweiter Teil: Die philosophische Definition des Menschen, Kommentar zu These 1-19, Lutherstudien*, II/2 (Tübingen, 1982).

49. Cf. Thomas Aquinas, *Summa Theologiae*, I 85, 4; 86, 1. 3-5.

50. See G. Ebeling, *Disputatio de homine*, and id., "Das Leben - Fragment und Vollendung. Luthers Auffassung vom Menschen im Verhältnis zu Scholastik und Renaissance," *Zeitschrift für Theologie und Kirche* 72 (1975), 310-336.

51. Cf. WA 40 II, 328; LW 12, 328.

52. Cf. the 32nd thesis of the *Disputatio de homine* (1536), WA 39 I, 175-180; LW 34, 137-144, in the critical edition by G. Ebeling (*Lutherstudien*, II/1, 15-24): "*Paulus Rom. 3. Arbitramur hominem iustificari fide absque operibus, breviter hominis definitionem colligit dicens: hominem justificari fide.*"

53. See theses 20-40. I urgently hope that G. Ebeling will soon be able to publish the third part (commentary to theses 20-40) of his monograph mentioned in n. 48; for the moment, his article mentioned in n. 50 must suffice.

54. Relevant texts are WA 42, 45-46; 122-125; 166-167; LW 1, 60 f.; 162-167; 222 ff.; WA 14, 111; WA 24, 51; WA 39 I, 175-180; LW 34, 137-144 (see n. 52). A summary of Luther's doctrine on the "image of God" in the framework of the tradition before and after him is found in A. Peters, *Bild Gottes. IV. Dogmatisch*, in: *Theologische Realenzyklopädie* VI, 506-515; for a theological evaluation see G. Ebeling, *Dogmatik des christlichen Glaubens I* (Tübingen, 1978), 376-414.

55. So G. Ebeling, "Das Leben", 320.

56. See first of all the famous essay by J.P. Sartre, "Ist der Existentialismus ein Humanismus?", in: id., *Drei Essays* (Frankfurt - Berlin, 1961), 7-36; on the background and on the "variations" of this thesis see now the comprehensive summary in: W. Kasper, *Der Gott Jesu Christi* (Mainz, 1982), 41-67, under the heading: *Der Atheismus im Namen der Autonomie des Menschen.*

57. Cf. BSLK, 563; BC 366.

58. See above, I.

59. See M. Hoffmann, "Reformation and Toleration," in this volume.

60. Cf. O.H. Pesch, *Theologie der Rechtfertigung*, 183-186; see an analysis of the traditional Catholic manuals of dogmatic theology from this perspective in: A. Hasler, *Luther in der katholischen Dogmatik. Darstellung seiner Rechtfertigungslehre in den katholischen Dogmatikbüchern* (München, 1968), 65-73; 147-174.

61. Cf. for instance WA 7, 66; LW 31, 367; WA 11, 440 f.; LW 36, 440 f.; WA 15, 504; also 10 III, 223; 10 I 1, 100.

62. Cf. for instance BSLK 516; 704, 30; BC 349, 445; WA DB 7, 10; LW 35, 370.

63. For a summary of the meaning of this famous formula in Luther's theology see: O.H. Pesch, *Hinführung zu Luther*, 189-202.

64. Cf. J.B. Metz, "Der Unglaube als theologisches Problem", in: *Concilium* 1 (1965), 484-492, here: 487-489.

65. Cf. n. 37 and 38.

66. Cf. WA 56, 356; LW 25.

67. WA 18, 754; LW 32, 243.

68. Cf. WA 18, 695; LW 33, 155.

69. Cf. Thomas Aquinas, *Summa Theologiae*, I-II 110, 2-4; 112, 2-4; 113, 3-8.

70. See the references in n. 46.

71. See the summary in: O.H. Pesch, *Frei sein aus Gnade. Theologische Anthropologie* (Freiburg, 1983), 356-360.

72. See n. 46.

73. WA DB 7, 10; LW 35, 370.

74. Cf. Thomas Aquinas, *Summa Theologiae*, I 79, 12-13.

75. WA 8, 606; LW 44, 298. On Luther's understanding of "conscience" see G. Ebeling, "Theologische

Erwägungen über das Gewissen," in: id., *Wort und Glaube* I (Tübingen, 1962), 429-446; B. Lohse, "Conscience and Authority in Luther," in: *Luther and the Dawn of the Modern Era*, 158-183.

76. WA 5, 525.

77. Once more we touch an immense medieval and yet patristic discussion. Historical information is found in: H. Reiner, *Gewissen*, in: *Historisches Wörterbuch der Philosophie* III (Basel, 1974), 574-592; for a summary of the extremely complicated history of the notion "synteresis" see: O.H. Pesch, *Das Gesetz. Kommentar zu Thomas von Aquin: Summa Theologiae, I-II 90-105, Deutsche Thomas-Ausgabe* 13 (Graz, 1977), 489-492.

78. G. Ebeling, "Theologische Erwägungen über das Gewissen," 440.

79. WA 1, 372; LW 31, 67.

80. See M. Brecht, "Divine Right and Human Rights in Luther," in this volume.

81. WA 7, 838; LW 32, 112.

82. WA 10 III, 18.

83. WA 15, 219; LW 40, 57.

84. Cf. O.H. Pesch, *Hinführung zu Luther*, 48-115; and my research report: "Neuere Beiträge zur Frage nach Luther's 'reformatorischer Wende'," in: *Catholica* 37 (1983), 259-287; 38 (1984), 66-133.

85. This has become self-evident since that true "break-through" in the Catholic Luther-research inaugurated by J. Lortz, *The Reformation in Germany*, 2 vols. (London - New York, 1968), 6th ed. in one vol. with an Afterword by P. Manns (Freiburg, 1982). Further information in: O.H. Pesch, *Hinführung zu Luther*, 18; see also my presentation: "Luther and the Catholic Tradition," in: *Lutheran Theological Seminary Bulletin*, Gettysburg, Pennsylvania (Winter 1984), 3-21.

86. See particularly the structure of the argumentation in *Wider Hans Worst* (1541), WA 51, 469-572; LW 41, 185-256.

87. Cf. WA 6, 455; LW 44, 196; WA 11, 268 f.; LW 45, 114.

88. See M. Hoffmann, "Reformation and Toleration," in this volume.

89. Cf. B. Lohse, "Conscience and Authority," 172; cf. id., "Was heisst Reformation?," in: id., *Luther-deutung heute* (Göttingen, 1968), 5-18; id., *Martin Luther. Eine Einführung in sein Leben und sein Werk* (München, 1982), 96-101; 180-190.

90. Two significant examples are 1 Cor. 13:2 and 1 John 4:17a; cf. P. Althaus, *The Theology of Martin Luther* (Philadelphia, 1966), 429-458.

91. See n. 85.

92. In this sense I totally agree with the so-called "political theology" and the "theology of libera-tion."

93. Cf. WA 40 III, 352; commentary in: O.H. Pesch, *Theologie der Rechtfertigung*, 152-159; id., *Hinführung zu Luther*, 264-271; and most recently O.H. Pesch - A. Peters, *Einführung*, 119-130.

94. J. Lortz, *The Reformation in Germany* I, 199, 451.

95. Precisely that is the analysis by a German atheist psychologist: H.E. Richter, *Der Gotteskomplex. Die Geburt und die Krise des Glaubens an die Allmacht des Menschen* (Reinbek, 1979).

Martin Brecht

DIVINE RIGHT AND HUMAN RIGHTS IN LUTHER

The term **divine right** (*ius divinum*) occurs seldom in Luther; that of **human rights,** of course, not at all. But we do find the content of these terms and several catch-words containing their meaning, though in contexts other than those familiar to us today. Our topic is, therefore, not out of line but lends itself to articulating what is peculiarly characteristic of Luther's thought.

I. THE GOSPEL IN CONTRAST TO HUMAN LAWS

Luther's opponents soon turned the controversy concerning indulgences into a clash over ecclesiastical authority and norms by justifying indulgences with the unquestionable legislative power of the pope. Luther, on the other hand, found it impossible to reconcile the indulgence decrees with the Bible. That led him in 1518-1519 to question whether the papal institution and authority were sanctioned by divine right. On the basis of his exegetical, canonical, and historical studies, he came to a negative conclusion and consequently could acknowledge the pope at most as a secular authority. For Luther the power of the keys, that is, the power to loose and to bind, was given to all church officials, in case of emergency even to all baptized Christians. The commission to tend the sheep did not

carry with it the privilege of sovereignty. The pope
was not the head of the universal church; the Greek
churches attested to that. But the most incisive
objection arose from the contradiction between the
elaborate judicial system of the Roman church, which
was felt to be oppressive, and the principles of the
gospel. The ecclesiastical government exercised such a
tyranny that Luther was led to the terrifying conclusion that the Antichrist had established his seat in
the midst of the church. Luther criticized the fact
that the faithful were being leashed, regimented,
frightened, and oppressed by countless human laws,
although in the church, according to the will of
Christ, there was to be only one law, that of love for
one another.

However, the matter involved more than an unjust
system of government that burdened, exploited, and
abused its subjects. In return for observing its laws
the church promised salvation. But for Luther salvation could be only a gift of God, since human beings
were not of themselves able to fulfill the divine
demands. The good works required by the church competed
in an impossible way with Christ's unique work of
salvation. That was a relapse into the false way of
salvation of Jewish legalism which, in line with the
Apostle Paul, had to be absolutely criticized and
rejected. The new orientation of faith, thus made
necessary, concentrated on the acceptance of the gospel
of the Christ who became human, suffered, died, rose
from the dead, and ascended into heaven, as the only
ground of salvation. The conduct of the believers was
to correspond solely to that of Christ. They were free
from all other demands. This overcoming and abrogation
of ecclesiastical or "human" laws meant, at that time,

an extraordinary liberation and relief which exceeded by far the elimination of particular, onerous regulations. Luther brought again to prominence the truly revolutionary message of the gospel, namely, that salvation is a gift, not to be produced by one's own achievement and effort. This emancipation was made possible by challenging the papacy's claim to God-given authority. In his counter-argument Luther did, of course, not formulate a general bill of rights for the believers. The gift of freedom is of a markedly different kind, in that it has been given from the beginning rather than having to be claimed.[1]

II. THE EQUALITY OF CHRISTIANS IN THE PRIESTHOOD OF ALL BELIEVERS

Specific and lasting elements of Luther's thought on the gift of freedom can be illustrated by certain consequences to which he came during the following period. In his work *To the Christian Nobility of the German Nation*[2] Luther formulated a program of reform for church and society to address concrete complaints and grievances. Since the ecclesiastical office time and again rejected reform and had indeed immunized itself against it, reform was to be carried out by the Christian secular authorities which were in possession of the necessary political power. This was possible on the basis of the theory of the priesthood of all baptized Christians - a theory that denied the superiority of a special priestly class in the church. As a matter of principle, all who are baptized have the same rights in the church and, therefore, the duty in case of necessity to bring about order. Luther had come to a significant principle of equality regarding the

baptized, which no longer allowed for hierarchical
privileges.

As we know, Luther did not extend the application
of this principle to the political sphere, and this can
be taken as one of his limitations in light of modern
developments. It was always his view that in the
world, as opposed to the Kingdom of Christ, there had
to be differences regarding power, gender, ownership,
and vocation. This, however, was not due to inconsis-
tency or a lack of progressiveness on his part but was
a matter of a different world view. In the fallen,
sinful world there are no ideal conditions; rather
there is only a relatively ordered communal existence
within which Christians are to make their contributions
in whatever situations they have been placed. The
equality of God's children is a promise to the faithful, and it will not be fully realized until the
Kingdom of God.

III. CHRISTIAN FREEDOM AND SERVITUDE

The famous double thesis of Luther's treatise on
freedom describes the same contradictory state of
affairs: "A Christian is a perfectly free lord of all,
subject to none. A Christian is a perfectly dutiful
servant of all, subject to all."[3] Even until most
recent times Luther has been severely blamed for
isolating the freedom of the inner, spiritual person
from all external circumstances, and he has been
accused of ignoring the necessity for real political
and social freedom. But for Luther all that is required for life, for justice, and freedom is the gospel of
Jesus Christ which promises salvation and can be
received only by faith. Works have nothing to do with

the attainment of the gift of freedom. Human beings must simply recognize that freedom cannot be obtained by their own effort; rather, Christ bestows that freedom on them which overcomes human lostness. In an utterly unequal marriage contract Christ gives to the soul his own righteousness and takes in return the soul's uncleanness unto himself. With Christ the Christian becomes king and priest. Christians certainly do not have dominion over other people. Like Christ they remain ever tempted by the powers of corruption, while at the same time retaining the upper hand over them. The right of the common priesthood consists in the immediate access to the merciful God. We can hardly imagine today what a relief from religious rules, efforts, and anxieties Luther's concept brought to his contemporaries. Inasmuch as it deals with the ultimate existential questions of life and death, of salvation and damnation - questions that today are mostly repressed, it has lost none of its importance for us.

On the other hand, Luther placed the relationship to one's own body and, above all, to one's fellow human beings under the rubric of servitude and service, thereby rejecting all personal claims and self-assertion. Christians no longer have such needs. They have already achieved everything; they conduct themselves once again as in paradise. The example for their service is none other than the incarnate Christ himself. And from him their service receives its incomparable dignity in that it represents him to their fellow human beings. Therefore, what we have here is something other than a social ethic simply conformed to the contemporary patterns of authority. From the gospel and from justification Luther derived an alternative to all other claims and expectations. Differences in

terminology should be carefully noted. The freedom of
the Christian willed by God cannot be sued for as a
right but is a gift provided by God. There remains a
condition of dependence and reliance that is particularly offensive to modern sensitivities. No one can be
the maker and creator of his/her own salvation but must
leave it entirely to God. That was Luther's deepest
religious experience. Liberated Christians are under
the obligation of serving love to their fellow human
beings - an obligation which is comparable to the
concept of civic duties, not to human rights. Christians do not thereby acquire their being; rather they
çonform to the being already given them. Herein lies a
significant beginning for humane action and for a
corresponding world formation which should not be
criticized as failing to give human beings their due.

IV.   THE APPEAL TO THE CONSCIENCE BOUND BY GOD'S WORD

Luther's appeal to his conscience at the Diet of
Worms has become famous.[4] As we know, he did not
thereby postulate a general freedom of conscience;
rather he refused to recant because his conscience was
"bound to God's word." To act against this bond would
have meant for him an ultimate danger and loss of
salvation, inasmuch as he was not confuted by Scripture. His additional appeal to evident arguments of
reason is clearly subordinate to the appeal to Scripture. Here, too, Luther seems to fall short of advocating the human right of freedom of conscience as such.
For him the person with a conscience was not his/her
own absolute court of appeal but rather was oriented in
God's will as announced in the Bible. The conscience
could be certain and healthy only when in harmony with

this norm. Popes and councils, on the other hand, could never function as the last resort, for their fallibility had been demonstrated time and again.

In his pamphlet written at the Wartburg *On Confession, Whether the Pope Has the Authority to Command,* Luther accused both the pope and canon law with encroaching upon the rule over the consciences, which God had reserved for God's self, whereas all secular legislation did not do so. That is a satanic rebellion which God cannot tolerate:

> That God will not permit. Here he is a zealot, for in the conscience he wants to be alone and he will allow his word to rule alone. Here there should be freedom from all human laws.[5]

Divine right sets the limits for human laws and thereby guarantees freedom. This important aspect will be further developed later. The pope, however, proves to be the Antichrist by his incursion into the sphere of divine authority. Private confession and celibacy are matters of choice and as such are quite good. Yet they are perverted when they are turned into compulsory institutions whereby consciences are deformed. Then confession and celibacy no longer rely on Christ's work but on a papal precept that is incompatible with Christ's work. There can be freedom of conscience only where there is freedom, inner freedom at least, from the tyranny of papal law.

V. THE CONCRETE PROBLEM OF MONASTIC VOWS

A short time later Luther discussed more extensively and forcibly the contrast between human laws and divine right in his large treatise *On Monastic Vows (De*

votis monasticis).[6] Its basic argument is still of
interest. Its starting point was exactly the same as
in the treatise on freedom: Luther understood himself
to be so liberated by Christ from his monastic vows
that he, although a servant to all, was subject to none
save Christ alone. Christ was his immediate bishop,
abbot, prior, lord, father, and master. And that meant
freedom from all human institutions.[7] Six large
sections contain the very comprehensive arguments for
this thesis. First he points out that monastic vows
are not based on God's Word, but rather that they are
in contradiction to it. That alone means already that
such vows are annulled, forbidden, and condemned by
divine authority because they arbitrarily go beyond the
will of Christ. Freedom from human laws is won by
appealing to the highest court, the last resort. In
fundamental expositions Luther demolished the system of
the elitist and privileged monastic ethic with its
distinctions between law and counsel, as well as
between the states of perfection and imperfection. The
foundations of monastic vows are judged by him to be
counter to the gospel and, therefore, ungodly and
blasphemous.

After examining the vows with regard to the divine
norm Luther turns to the question of their correspondence with the principle of faith. For this Luther
draws on Romans 14:23: "Whatsoever is not of faith is
sin." With monastic vows one relies on works instead
of faith. For Luther this is a fall from faith to a
doctrine of the demons. In the context of our topic
the third section is the most important, for it lays
out the opposition of the monastic vows to the freedom
of the gospel. Whatever is not necessary for salvation
and righteousness must remain free. The conscience

must not allow itself to be seduced away from Christ,
its bridegroom, by trust in works. It lives on a gift
given, not on a reward earned.

This exposition reaches its climax in the Pauline
argument that Christians are called to freedom. That
is the content of the gospel over against which every
other alternative is anathematized. Then follows a
crucial sentence which Luther deliberately also placed
at the top of the second list of the earlier *Themata de
votis*:

> This freedom comes from divine right. God
> ordained it and never revoked it. He can
> neither accept anything that runs counter to
> it, nor allow anyone to violate it even by
> the most insignificant ordinance.[8]

This freedom extends not only inward to the conscience
but with this freedom the entire body of human commandments is superseded. "Everything not specifically
commanded by God is abrogated and made a matter of free
choice." To violate this divinely instituted freedom
is sin. By implication, then, the vows must be revoca-
ble, for the believers are free lords over the vows.
In the case of marriage vows (which Luther's opponents
used as a point of contention) there is a difference
insofar as they are made not to God but made in love to
another person and thus they belong into the category
of Christian service. However, the relationship
established by God in baptism is a covenant of freedom.
With the statement "Christian freedom is of inalienable
divine right," Luther formulated as it were a "bill of
rights for the Christian." Characteristically, this is
not an independent statement about Christians but
anchored in divine right. To be sure, the human right
to freedom cannot be derived directly from Luther's

statement. Nevertheless, it is a fundamental Christian declaration concerning the destination of humankind. It took on its first tangible form in connection with the opening of closed precincts, the unlocking of the cloisters.

The next two sections deal with the incompatibility of the vows with the commands of God, including love, and with the rationale of monasticism. At this point Luther already takes up the argument against celibacy. A "final attack" speaks, among other things, of the characteristic reversal of the vow. Persons actually do not make vows to God; instead, in baptism God makes a vow - that is, God pledges God's faithfulness to us, whereby grace is again shown to be a gift and not a reward. In conclusion Luther remarked that what he intended was less to silence his opponents than to lift up the consciences to God and to make them certain. Of course, in the face of so many authorities, rules, and misunderstandings it is a difficult task to convince the consciences of such a joyous freedom after they had despaired and been lost in hell for so long. And yet freedom is the only foundation on which one could withstand the devil and stand the judgment of God. Luther was not talking about a superficial release from the monastery, which could not be sustained against the doubts and scruples of the conscience. The freedom of the gospel is not libertinism. Rather, it is the paradoxical freedom of the servants of God who follow Christ in discipleship. Immediately after Luther's theses on monastic vows had reached Wittenberg, Johann Bugenhagen said: "This work will bring about a transformation in the public order," something which the Wittenberg discussion on vows had not until then been able to attain. And Melanchthon spoke about the "beginnings of the freeing of the monks."[9]

During the ensuing period it did not fail to happen that Luther had to come back several times to this theme, now in order to justify the withdrawal of monks and nuns from the monasteries and convents. His 1523 writing *Why Nuns May, in All Godliness, Leave Their Convents: Ground and Reply*,[10] was prompted by the escape of nine nuns from the convent at Nimbschen, among them Katharina von Bora. Luther asserted among other things that vows can be only voluntary; God does not desire any forced service. Woman is not created for virginity but to bear children. We will have to investigate further this divine mandate for human procreation. The annoying breach of prevailing convention caused by the flight from the monasteries was not regarded by Luther as a valid argument against it. When one's own soul is in peril, one need not show consideration for one's neighbors. Rather, one is right in expecting consideration from them. "Need breaks iron." There are elementary human needs which cannot be suppressed by rules and regulations.

In this context Luther made an equally unconventional proposal which later was put into practice. The convents served frequently as residences for daughters of the nobility for whom no suitable marriage could be arranged. Luther proposed that these young women should marry commoners; he could also imagine the marriage of a nobleman to a woman of the citizen class. His reasoning is related to our topic:

> If we are unequal in the eyes of the world, we are nevertheless all equal in God's eyes as children of Adam, God's creature; each person is valued like the next.[11]

Luther's *Exhortation to the Knights of the Teutonic Order That They Lay Aside False Chastity and Assume the True Chastity of Wedlock*,[12] written in 1523, had considerable political implications, for it was related to the secularization of the *Ordensstaat* Prussia. According to the creator's will woman is to be the helpmate of man. Marriage, therefore, cannot be taken, as the pope takes it, for a hindrance to serving God. The divine institution of marriage stands against human ordinances and traditions. They cannot and must not alter it. The reliance on God's word, in this case for the divine institution of marriage, invalidates human regulations and has thereby again the effect of emancipation. Similarly Luther repeatedly invoked the Fourth Commandment of the Decalogue to argue against monastic vows. For him there was no doubt that God was given honor by marriage, not by celibacy.

VI.   THE GOD-WILLED SEXUAL CONSTITUTION
OF HUMAN BEINGS FOR MARRIAGE

A few weeks before his own marriage Luther wrote to the Antonite Preceptor Wolfgang Reissenbusch in Lichtenberg his *Christian Writing to Wolfgang Reissenbusch, That He Give Himself Over to Marriage*.[13] He declares quite sharply that chastity, when defined as celibacy, is not a possibility at the disposal of human beings, and that they therefore cannot find it praiseworthy. God in God's word of creation made and equipped human beings for marriage. That is "God's word and work." Thus, the negation of sexuality negates the human being as such. No one can escape from it. Reissenbusch's marriage could not possibly have a better foundation than God's Word, and therefore he should not be concerned about possible slander. As early as 1522 Luther had labeled the prohibition against marriage for priests "a devilish thing opposed to God's order."[14] Such a vow of celibacy is invalid.

The foundations for this view can be found already in Luther's treatise *The Estate of Marriage* written in 1522.[15] God's order in Gen. 1:28 "Be fruitful and multiply" is more even than a command or divine law. It is

> a divine work which it is not our prerogative
> to hinder or ignore. Rather it is just as
> necessary as the fact that I am a man, and
> more necessary than sleeping and waking,
> eating and drinking, and emptying the bowels
> and bladder. It is a nature and disposition
> just as innate as the organs involved in
> it.[16]

Human sexuality is rooted even deeper than in God's law, namely, in God's creational word and work, and, therefore, every vow contradicting it is at once invalid and no more binding than a "spider's web." In the introduction of *A Sermon on the Estate of Marriage* from 1525[17] Luther praised the manifold glory of the holy order of marriage which the triune God instituted even in paradise and protected with a special command-ment in the Decalogue and which, therefore, is above all other orders.

Johann Fabri, who was the General Vicar of Con-stance at that time, cited I Cor. 7 as a counter-argu-ment against Luther's criticism of celibacy. That challenged Luther to an exposition of this chapter.[18] The unmarried state favored by Paul demands a special gift, without which the vow cannot be made. Anyone who cannot live as a celibate is commanded by God to marry.

"Necessity commands you to marry": this is true also
for Christians in their corporeality. Chastity is not
something like "taking your shoes on and off." Wherever that is not taken into consideration, as in the
constraints of the monasteries, one is guilty before
those persons who are affected. Before God there is no
preference of celibacy over marriage; both are of equal
value to God. To be sure, marriage with its divinely
ordained toil and labor for the family livelihood is
much more dependent on faith than the well provided for
life in a cloister. In faith no higher religious worth
is placed on any estate or nation. Here Christian
freedom as well as equality prevail.

VII.   THE PROBLEM OF SERFDOM

Already in this interpretation of I Cor. 7 Luther
also met with the problem of serfdom.[19] The mutual
duties of any relationship of service are treated as
analogous to those of marriage partners; that is, they
are to be fulfilled. The equality of believers is not
affected by social inequalities. Before God the slave
is free, and the free person is a slave. Again, it is
human doctrines that threaten Christian freedom. Like
Paul, Luther affirms the possibility of emancipation
from slavery. However, it must happen rightfully,
i.e., without a breach of the service relationship.
Yet this is something else than social conservatism.
The obligations to one's neighbor, which are to be
fulfilled in love, remain, for that is a part of the
Christian "servanthood." One must distinguish between
freedom before God and servanthood in relationship to
one's fellow human beings.

> In sum: we owe nobody anything but to love
> and to serve our neighbor through love. Where
> love is present, there it is accomplished...

Luther's evaluation of the servant relationship between persons corresponds exactly with the basic idea in his treatise on freedom. What is interesting in his rebuke against monasticism is that it has changed the Christian freedom into a hellish prison, and loving service into a hostile freedom.

Likewise, in his sermons of 1522/23 on I Peter,[20] Luther had to discuss the relationship between masters and servants as found in I Peter 2:18-23.[21] As Christians and before God, servants are equal to everyone else. However, the behavior prescribed for them is obedient service according to the instructions of their masters, even if the masters are evil, angry, or rude. This is the way for the servants to practice Christian servanthood. The servant is actually serving Christ and therefore does not question the master's strange or uncouth behavior. According to Luther's understanding, I Peter 2:18-23 speaks to serfs who were at the mercy of their masters but should accept this cross as followers of the suffering Christ.

Even in Luther's time such an ethic of suffering was hardly acceptable to persons sensitive to social justice. The pamphlet *To the Assembly of the Common Peasantry*, written in 1525 in southwest Germany and perhaps influenced by Müntzer's thought, sharply protested against Luther's interpretation that the text demands obedience even to a "scoundrel." By "rude master" (Greek *diskolos*) the writer of the pamphlet understood only a person who occasionally had an outburst of bad temper.[22]

We see that it was long before the Peasants' War
that Luther rejected the peasant's demands for the
elimination of serfdom based on the liberation of
Christians by Christ.[23] Of course, Luther's 1525
statement that the patriarchs and prophets of the Old
Testament also had had slaves (in his *Admonition to
Peace, A Reply to the Twelve Articles of the Peasants
in Swabia*) was a theologically weak argument, but it
was not his decisive point. Inner Christian freedom
and the equality of Christians could exist next to
social dependencies and differences. The Christian's
right to freedom and equality was not extended into a
human right. Luther did not even hint at a tendency or
preference in this direction, as such conceivable. An
optimizing of conditions in this transitory world was
not within his horizon of interest.

VIII.   THE DISTINCTION BETWEEN
THE TWO KINGDOMS (*REICHE*)

The 1522/23 sermons on I Peter were the occasion
for Luther to achieve exegetically a new understanding
of his political and social ethic in general. This
subsequently provided the theological basis for the
important treatise *Temporal Authority: To What Extent
It Should Be Obeyed.*[24] Christians affirm secular
authority along with its coercive power as a means of
securing peaceful communal life. Motivated by love to
their fellow human beings, they participate in the
functions of temporal government, although they themselves do not have need of it. At the bottom of this
view lies the concept of God's two rules (*Regimente*).
Inwardly, Christians are ruled by the word of God.
Temporal authority, on the other hand, regulates the

affairs of the external communal life. Although
political authority has nothing to do with the inner
authority of Christ, there nevertheless exists no
opposition between the two. In Christ's kingdom there
is no coercive power - a fact which proves the papal
legal system to be corrupt. Nonetheless, for all their
freedom, Christians subject themselves in love to the
human laws of civil authority. Their freedom does not
aim at wrongdoing but in benefaction toward the neighbor. Differences of class and gifts have no validity
before God. Therefore, everyone, whether high or low,
should meet all other persons with respect. The
believer does not allow salvation to be dependent on
conditions imposed by anyone, not even the pope. On
the other hand, the Christian submits to public political directives, even if they are tyrannical and unjust,
because the Christian ought not resist evil. However,
any intrusion of secular power into the affairs of
faith is clearly rejected. Religious freedom was for
Luther of incomparably greater importance than political freedom.

Based on evidence from the Old and New Testaments,
Luther believed that secular authority constituted an
order ordained by God and that, to that extent, it was
of divine right. As just mentioned, Luther developed
his ideas in his work written in 1523: *Temporal
Authority: To What Extent It Should Be Obeyed.*[25]
Secular authority receives the same high esteem as
marriage, agriculture, or a trade - orders which God
likewise has instituted. Just as these, civil authority is coordinated with the realm of human common life
in this world, and from this assignment it derives its
competent authority as well as its limits. As members
of the human community Christians participate with

their service of love also in political tasks of common
life and do not withdraw from them. Further, it is
important to note that government is bound by laws
which, however, are not to be applied rigidly but with
equity. Luther appreciated the constitutional state,
although Christians were the very ones who could give
up all claim to vindicate their rights.

IX.   FREEDOM OF CONSCIENCE

Interestingly, the treatise on temporal authority
was occasioned by the problem of the extent and limits
of political power, after Luther's books and his
translation of the New Testament had been banned in
some of the territories and had to be handed over to
the authorities. Just as the pope had extended his
religious laws into the secular realm, now the secular
authorities were meddling in spiritual affairs. In
both cases human laws were impinging upon the freedom
of faith. The responsible authorities overstepped in
each case the limits of their jurisdiction. As far as
spiritual thought is concerned, the state has no
perception. Further, no one can be forced into faith.
Thought is free. At most, the state can force its
subjects to deny their beliefs, but that would be
certainly far more immoral than any possible error on
the subjects' part. The state, ordained by God, is a
"human order" insofar as it must not interfere in the
relationship of the soul to God. Encroachment on
spiritual matters would amount to a satanic rebellion
against God and a tyranny which is not to be obeyed but
to be resisted. Originally Luther denied any obligation of the state to take care of the correct belief,
and he rejected the laws against heresy. The only

weapon against heresy is the word of God. Paul already
knew that sects would arise along side of the church
(I Cor. 11:19). Sects could not be opposed in any
way except with the word. In principle Luther adhered
to this understanding also in dealing with Thomas
Müntzer[26] and the anabaptists. But later when their
conduct and activities became criminal he narrowed his
position down. Luther was not advocating the human
rights of freedom of conscience and religion, although
this would not have been impossible given his understanding and was, in fact, claimed by some of his
followers. What he accomplished, however, was that he
set limits to political power at this point, which
constituted an important step in the development of the
modern concept of tolerance.

X. DIVINE NATURAL LAW

When the so-called *Schwärmer* opposed the traditional law of the church with the law of the Bible and
understood this Biblical law categorically as literal
law, Luther felt compelled once again to clarify his
position:[27] The Christian is not bound by the law of
the Bible; it is merely a "Jewish *Sachsenspiegel*,"
i.e., a law only for Jewish people. That is even true
of the Decalogue. However, with the exception of the
prohibition against graven images and the law of the
sabbath, the Ten Commandments are at the same time a
compilation of natural law given by God in the hearts
of all human beings. Its epitome, as far as human life
in community is concerned, is the Golden Rule (Matt.
7:12).[28] Every tool teaches the user to direct his/her
behavior toward fellow human beings according to the
law of love. The divinely given norm appears to be

radically reduced to its humane principle. But Luther
knew also that people in their egotism are completely
unable to meet this obligation of themselves unless the
gospel frees them to a consistently humane behavior.

CONCLUSION

Only conditionally can Luther be called a standard
bearer of human rights. He advocated freedom and
equality, not in general but only in the religious
realm. Thus, freedom of conscience was the only
element in his position which to a certain extent
amounted to general significance. Yet it is important
to recognize that even in Luther the divine right
mostly functions as a advocate for the vocation of
human beings to freedom, equality, and the realization
of their creational constitution, and therefore as an
advocate against human laws. To that extent divine
right intends the welfare and salvation of persons and
not their restriction. The absolute bondage to God
does not stand in contradiction to humanity. Civil
authority is divinely ordained, necessary to the
regulation of communal life in a fallen world. Therefore, it is still legitimate, even if it violates
justice. The limits of obedience to the civil government appear where it demands something against God's
command or intervenes in the realm of the conscience,
which God has reserved for God's self. Luther knew
full well that these limits set by God were often
violated, and he had an explanation for these trans-
gressions. In a *Table Talk* of 1531 he said boldly:

> The world is not ruled by religion and
> equity, but rather by superstition and
> tyranny, because it is under the devil. And

> if we preach that faith makes free, it wants
> to be free in every way, but in a freedom
> which is of the flesh. Thus it perverts the
> true religion into superstition or rather
> into the lies of the devil.[29]

Luther had no illusions about the fact that the freedom brought about by the Reformation was subject to misunderstanding.

It goes without saying that Luther, with his political and social views, was a product of his time. Just the same, we cannot dismiss without further ado the significance of his insight. Above all it should be amply clear that all his ideas concerning human rights are integrated into the context of the always inopportune and paradoxical double thesis of the Christian's freedom and servitude at the same time. This context insures the freedom of the individual person against all earthly powers. The weakness of Luther's position appears to lie in the legitimation or nonlegitimation of the demand for equality. On the other hand, it fully understands the realization of human solidarity, which otherwise can only be declared, as a duty willed by God and as the meaning of action in a world in which differences have not yet been abolished. This attitude of service to one's fellow human beings owes no apology to the postulates of human rights. This service of love is made possible by the freedom which is already given by God and which, therefore, covers far more than the alleged interiority of human beings.[30]

Luther's relation to **freedom, equality,** and **fraternity** amounts to a complex result: on the one hand Luther can be called an advocate of freedom against all totalitarian systems. In this way for instance he was

quoted by Roger Williams in Massachusetts against the
repression of the Calvinist authorities.[31] On the
other hand, Luther obviously was not interested in
political freedom in a modern sense. He did accept the
social differences as a reality of the world, although
he principally insisted on the **equality** of all Christians in the church. Perhaps the most interesting
point is **fraternity**. Luther rejected the many pious
fraternities because of the unique fraternity of all
Christians. Up to today the fraternity of all humankind remains only a scarcely realized demand. Strange-
ly enough, the loving serfdom of the Christians toward
their neighbors could be a radical alternative and a
new possibility, a new chance for a more humane
society.

NOTES

1. Cf. M. Brecht, "Der Zusammenhang von Luthers reformatorischer Entdeckung und reformatorischem Programm als oekumenisches Problem," in: *Luthers Sendung für Katholiken und Protestanten*, ed. K. Lehmann (München - Zürich, 1982), 11-30, esp. 23 ff.

2. WA 6, 407-410; LW 44, 115-217.

3. WA 7, 20-38, 49-73; LW 31, 333-377.

4. WA 7, 838; LW 32, 112-113.

5. WA 8, 151-152, 164, 170-173.

6. WA 8, 573-669; LW 44, 243-400; cf. also *Themata de Votis*, WA 8, 323-335.

7. WA 8, 576.

8. WA 8, 613; LW 44, 309; cf. WA 8, 330.

9. WA 8, 317.

10. WA 11, 394-400. Cf. *Against the Spiritual Estate of the Pope and the Bishops, Falsely so Called*, WA 10 III, 105-158; LW 39, 247-299; *How God Rescued An Honorable Nun*, WA 15, 86-88; LW 43, 85-96; WA 15, 595; and *An Answer To Several Questions On Monastic Vows*, WA 19, 287-293; LW 46, 145-154.

11. WA 10 II, 157; LW 39, 298.

12. WA 12, 232-244; LW 45, 141-158.

13. WA 18, 275-278.

14. WA 10 II, 152-153; LW 39, 293.

15. WA 10 II, 275-304; LW 45, 17-49.

16. WA 10 II, 276; LW 45, 18.

17. WA 17 I, 12-29.

18. WA 12, 92-142; LW 28, 1-56.

19. WA 12, 128-133; LW 28, 42-47.

20. WA 12, 259 ff., esp. 327-341; LW 30, 3 ff., esp. 72-86.

21. WA 12, 336-338; LW 30, 81-84.

22. K. Kaczerowsky, ed., *Flugschriften des Bauernkrieges*, Rowohlts Klassiker der Literatur und Wissenschaft, Deutsche Literatur 33 (Hamburg, 1970), 143-168, esp. 154.

23. WA 18, 326f; LW 46, 37 f.

24. WA 11, 245-281; LW 45, 75-129.

25. Ibid.

26. WA 15, 210-221; LW 40, 49-59.

27. WA 16, 361-393, esp. 380.

28. WA 32, 493-499; LW 21, 234-241.

29. WA Tr 2, Nr. 2148.

30. For further background on this subject, see: M. Lienhard, "Luther und die Menschenrechte," *Luther* 48 (1977), 12-28.

31. Cf. L. Moore, "Religious Liberty: Roger Williams and the Revolutionary Era," *Church History* 34 (1965), 57-76.

Manfred Hoffmann

REFORMATION AND TOLERATION

Throughout the history of Christianity the **Parable of the Wheat and the Tares** (Matt. 13:24-30) has served theologians to test and validate their attitude toward religious toleration. It became over the centuries some kind of *locus classicus* for a milder stance.[1] There were, of course, other Biblical texts serving to justify severe repression of heretics. For instance Luke 14:23: *compelle intrare* ("force them to come in") was taken to authorize the coercion of heretics into the true faith. And Deut. 13:1 ff. was understood to stipulate the killing of false prophets along with the eradication of entire villages aiding and abetting such abominations. But the parable of the wheat and the tares took another tack: *sinite utraque crescere*. Let the evil seed furtively sown by the devil grow up together with the good seed until the judgment day when the angels will harvest and separate good from evil, true from false. During the Reformation era it was above all Erasmus of Rotterdam who espoused a concept of toleration solidly based on this parable, and he held on to his moderate position in all the controversies that embroiled him against his will and better judgment.[2]

Luther, too, expounded this parable. In fact, he preached and commented between 1525 and 1546 five times on this lectionary text.[3] While he occasionally

referred to the parable also in other contexts, it is
his exegetical and homiletical exposition that attracts
our special attention, for by carefully tracing the
development and alteration in his interpretation one
can determine changes in his attitude toward toleration
under different historical conditions.[4] Such an
approach might shed new light on the vexing problem of
how and why Luther changed his attitude. Interestingly
enough, while Erasmus' interpretation of the parable
never underwent any significant alteration, Luther felt
compelled to apply the same word of God differently in
varying historical circumstances.[5]

Analyzing this material, even the most sympathetic
interpreter cannot fail to discover Luther moving from
a relatively tolerant stance toward harsh intolerance.[6]
To be sure, already in his earlier years he was anything but sanguine toward the Roman church while
expecting, quite naively, its tolerance of his own
teaching.[7] Totally convinced of the rightness of his
cause as he was, he was willing to receive what he was
not able to give.[8] All the same, he later hardened
into a more rigid intolerance especially toward the
so-called "false brethren" on the Left Wing, the
anabaptists and revolutionaries, and even the spiritualists and passivists, all allegedly his own offspring.[9] However, this change in attitude was based on
the constant conviction, a conviction he had come by so
painfully hard, namely, that he and his followers
represented the wheat, the good seed, the true word of
God. Anyone not in line with this truth was bluntly
tagged as tares, whether they were papists or sectarians. Luther had no qualms to condemn generously to the
right and to the left.

Our texts give evidence that Luther's change in attitude took place sometime after the beginning of 1525 when he interpreted Matt. 13:30: "Let wheat and tares grow together" with reference to Titus 3:10: "A heretical person avoid" (*haereticum hominem devita*), whereby *devitare* was subtly changed from the passive meaning "avoid" to an active "reject."[10] Unlike Erasmus and many of the Left Wing theologians who read this text as advising merely to "shun" the heretics and to "let them be like heathens and publicans" (Matt. 18:17),[11] Luther increasingly opted for active measures against false doctrine and worship. Indeed, at least by 1530 he had let himself be persuaded to agree on the civil government's duty of *cura religionis*, the state's foremost obligation to take care of the true religion, including the right to impose the death penalty on heretics in extreme cases of malicious obstinacy.

Luther always interpreted "Let both grow together" (Matt. 13:30) in the light of I Cor. 11:19: *Opportet et haereses esse* ("for there must be heresies among you, that they which are approved may be made manifest among you"). In fact, the admixture of heretics in its ranks was for him a mark of the true church. But Luther never connected "there must be heresies among you" with Matt. 5:39: *Non resistere malo* ("do not resist evil"). To be sure, he taught non-resistance to evil, but only in the civil area, i.e., in relation to secular government: the Christian must patiently bear the injustice of evil government.[12] Insofar as religion is concerned, however, he did not yield to any tendency toward passive endurance of error and heresy, as it was indeed advocated by most Left Wing congregations, and also by Erasmus. On the other hand, Luther never drew on *compelle intrare* (Luke 14:23: "compel

them to come in") - a text which served Augustine to
have the Donatists coerced,[13] or on Deut. 13:5: "The
(false) prophet shall be put to death" - a text which
served Calvin to justify the execution of Servetus.[14]
On the whole, then, Luther avoided the extremes of
passivity (do not resist evil) and of unconditional
coercive action (the heretic shall be put to death).
Rather, his seemingly reluctant progression from
relative toleration to a pronounced intolerance remained within the context of the notion of "rejection"
(*wehren*) which while it included both passive and
active elements was nonetheless increasingly imbalanced
toward active suppression. What remained constant was
not only Luther's unshakable conviction that he represented the truth, but also his inordinate aggressive-
ness toward both fronts of, in his view, false teaching, the Roman Catholic establishment and the Left Wing
proliferation of sects.

I

The complex idea of "rejection" (*wehren*) needs to
be clarified more in detail. If synchronically compared, Luther's five explanations of the parable of the
wheat and the tares revolve around five *topoi* which are
suggested by the Biblical text itself and remain constant over the 20 year period: the **mixture** of true and
false teaching in the church; the **enemy** sowing evil
seed on good ground; the **sleep** at night of the servants; the **admonition** not to pluck out the tares but to
let them grow; and the **harvest** in the end time. Most
important for our purposes are the mixture motif and
the admonition to let them both grow. And we are
concentrating primarily on the alterations between the

first sermon of early February, 1525 and the rest of the expositions.

But before trying to indicate the prevailing modifications, it is interesting to note the tenor of each writing in order to get a sense of the drift in Luther's homiletical and pastoral intention. 1525: Do not be **surprised** and **frightened** by the mixture of wheat and tares among the Christians. 1528: Do not be **offended** or **scandalized** by the tares but recognize the true church. 1531/34(?): In the true church Christ **comforts** against despair by giving reasons for the presence of evil. 1546: Christ **consoles** us not to be terrified, to despair, or to be scandalized, but to bear offenses with the patience of the saints without, however, allowing false teachers to rule. So, between 1525 and 1528 there is obviously a move from a marginal position in the old church to a central focus on the new church. The apprehension of the little flock had given way to a confidence in its own establishment as the true church.

A look into the **mixture motif** shows that wheat and tares symbolize first of all true and false teaching; the matter is one of conscience not of the fist. This emphasis prevails in all five texts. But after 1525 true and false are also seen as good and evil in the conduct of the people so that the consequential connection between faith and works, tree and fruit, doctrine and ethics comes to the fore: one acts as one believes. Furthermore, subsequent to 1525 the kingdom of heaven is no longer identified with individual believers but with the church. Thus the problem of true and false, respectively, good and evil, turns into a question of the purity of the church. No doubt, the puritan aspirations of the Left Wing congregations

caused this turn from the individual to community and
organization. For Luther the church in this world
never can be completely pure. Indeed, impurity is a
sign of the true church which, like a sound body,
excretes filth whereas a corrupt body, like a false
church, no longer discharges dross. After 1530 the
focus shifted to ecclesiastical discipline and excommunication. Strict discipline without preaching grace
and subsequent readmission of penitent sinners brings
the church to naught since even the saints are falli-
ble. This switch to the infirmity of the true Christian is condensed in the 1538 statement that the church
itself confesses to be a *peccatrix*. Conversely, an
excess of sanctity renders the church a sect of the
devil. In 1546 the issue of the true Christian's
infirmity is so much up front that it is couched in a
full-blown saint-sinner dialectic. The preoccupation
with the degeneration of his own body leads the old
Luther to take a person's physical condition as a
paradigm for spiritual life - and for dealing with
heretics. As the Christian must reckon with the
continued presence of sin in spite of forgiveness, so
the church with false teaching in spite of the truth.

With this concentration on the church Luther
introduces also the teaching on the **two kingdoms**.
After 1525 the church's dealing with heretics is seen
as running parallel to the civil government's duty of
punishing public offenders in the secular realm,
including the death penalty for capital crimes.
Furthermore, the threat of political disturbance,
sedition, and revolution is mentioned in connection
with heresy. And although Luther insists on the
sword-word duality as marking the distinction between
the kingdom of Christ and the kingdom of the world, the

authority of civil government is extended to the duty
of making sure that there is but one true proclamation
of the word in the land to prevent discord and upris-
ing. The 1531/34(?) sermon goes one step further,
indeed farther even than the subsequent statements, by
maintaining that both kingdoms work "hand in hand."
Luther had moved from the distinction of the two
kingdoms to their cooperation. As the church upon
examination and admonition punishes false preachers
with excommunication, so the state is called upon not
only to inflict the death penalty on capital criminals
but also, and foremost, to turn to the sword for
protecting and promoting Christ's honor by doing away
with heretical doctrine and false worship. The traditional crime of irreligion, blasphemy, is mentioned
here, so that the text makes it clear that Luther was
thinking in terms of the state's *cura religionis*.[15]
The 1546 sermon, finally, defines the church more as an
external institution with emphasis on the governing
authority of official ministers. The church and its
function of maintaining order within its precincts is
placed side by side with God's other orders of creation, civil authority in the political realm, and
parental authority in the family. However, this sermon
does not stress the punishment of evil in church,
state, and house so much as the need for persons in
public office in all three areas to choose the lesser
of two evils for the sake of preventing more harm.[16]

All sermons are constructed according to a simple
division into two parts: "What the word **says**" and
"what are we called to **do**." For Luther proclamation
involved a double orientation, the speaking and hearing
of the word in faith, and the doing of the word in
obedience. It seems that the mixture motif pertains

more to the **instruction** by the word, whereas the admonition not to pluck up the tares has more to do with the **application** of the word. Not surprisingly, then, we find the passive element more in the first section where Luther has no way of changing the text, and the increasingly active element in the second section where Luther introduces the notion of *wehren*.

We are turning now to the second part: "**Let them grow.**" The emphasis on suffering and bearing the evil of heresy pervades all sermons. Thus an element of passivity continues throughout. Clearly in line with the intention of the parable, Luther's theology of the cross stresses the patience of the saints. Another theme also runs through all texts: since heresy is a matter of heart and spirit, the word of God alone is the weapon for this spiritual warfare. And it is the church, not the state, to which this arm is entrusted. Consequently, the servants must preach the pure gospel, must not judge before the harvest time but rather commend the cause to God. Unlike the papists and Left Wing radicals who, though being themselves the tares, pull out, strangle, and kill others as tares, the servants of the householder are called to have compassion on the seduced souls. Although heresies spring up from the true church, their eradication makes things worse, for pulling one out in one place make two grow up in another. Moreover, wheat might be destroyed and the possible conversion of misled folk prevented. Finally, not to judge before God's time is right because, after all, the heretics have already condemned themselves (Titus 3:11). This tolerant attitude is eloquently expressed in Luther's 1525 sermon:

> Notice what raging people we have so long
> been. We wanted to force the Turks to the

faith with the sword, the heretics with fire,
and the Jews with death. We wanted to root
out the tares with our own power as if **we**
were the ones to rule over hearts and spirits
and make them pious and good - which God's
word alone must do. But by death we separate
them from the word, so that it can no longer
work on them. Thus we bring upon our heads
two deaths in one... We destroy at once the
body temporarily and the spirit eternally...
Therefore, the inquisitors and murderers...
should be rightly terrified by this parable,
even if they had real heretics before them.
But now they burn true saints and are themselves heretics. What does this mean other
than that they root out the wheat and call it
tares?[17]

Does the parable then commit the Christian to
passive toleration of heresy except for the preaching
of the gospel? Luther's answer: "Not to eradicate the
tares does not mean not to '*wehren*.'"[18] The catch-word
wehren connotes a whole range of meanings from "guard-
ing against" and "warding off" over "preventing" and
"forbidding" to "defending" and "resisting," but also
to "rejecting" and "punishing."[19] The notion of *wehren*
comes into play after 1525 and runs through the rest of
the texts with a strong impetus, opening up as it does
an avenue for active resistance against heretics.
Particularly the texts from the 30's and 40's raise the
question, whether to suffer the heretics means to
tolerate them, in such a way that Luther can dialecti-
cally relate passive suffering with active resistance.
Similarly, the earlier understanding of judgment,
meaning that preachers are not to judge but to leave

the execution to God since the heretics have already
judged themselves, undergoes a subtle modification
implying active judgment and punishment. Civil government is instructed to examine and discriminate heretical preaching on the basis of God's word. After
hearing and judging by the criteria of the gospel two
opposing kinds of proclamation, secular authority
should "let go," i.e., expel from the country, the
obstreperous false preachers because of the potential
danger of sedition on their part.[20]

There is an evident connection between the rejection of heresy and the **publicity** of the heretical
preaching. The Left Wing evil seed springing off from
the good field cannot be recognized and dealt with
until it grows leaves and thereby shows its true
colors, i.e., until it goes public in preaching and
teaching. Catholic doctrine, on the other hand, is
already known to be false and evil and therefore must
be hindered from being planted in broad daylight. And
if established, it must be abrogated together with its
worship, the mass. The *wehren* notion thus includes two
aspects: prevention by prophylactic measure before the
fact, and prohibition *ex post facto*.[21]

Titus 3:10: "A heretical person avoid" receives
in the 30's an increasingly active interpretation to
mean arguing, speaking up against, reproving, and
rebuking their license to sin. This verbal rejection
goes hand in hand with the church's ban and excommunication. With the 1546 emphasis on the official governance of the church an additional element comes in: "do
not let them rule, reign, or govern, neither in the
church nor state nor home." Even though the physical
body, the body politic, the household, and the institutional church remain infirm and therefore must suffer

the lesser of two evils within them, they yet constitute vessels from which God raises God's kingdom.
Consequently, the God-ordained institutions of external
authority are empowered not to tolerate any usurpation
in office or take-over of ruling functions. As to the
church, heretical public preaching and administration
of the sacraments must be prevented or prohibited in
order that the true doctrine of faith, now understood
as a formal creed to be confessed by all who live in
the land, remain pure.[22]

The notion *wehren* thus moves toward an emphasis on
separation and exclusion. Introduced after 1525 along
with the Titus 3:10 f. reference, it likewise turns
from passive avoidance to active rejection. For purist
reasons the heretics separate themselves from the body
of Christ and, on account of their excessive holiness,
form their own sects of the devil.[23] But later there
is an active sense of separation as Ps. 1:5 and 2 Tim.
2:19 are drawn upon to justify rejection: the false
must be separated from the true; true Christians must
"depart from iniquity." The emphasis "they separate
themselves" from us has given way to "we separate
ourselves" from them as we dismiss them to go their way
as incorrigible ones, and as rejected by the community
of faith.[24] Apparently, the separation which Luther
earlier so carefully had left to the eschatological
harvest is now anticipated by the exclusion of the
church.

Yet this exclusion, i.e., ban and excommunication,
is not yet the ultimate punishment. In the church's
realm abandonment is a penultimate action. But in the
political arena civil government has received the sword

> to cut off (*abkoppen*) offenses lest they gain
> ground and do harm. Now, the most dangerous

and abominable offense is the spreading of wrong teaching and false worship. Therefore, a Christian government should be foremost concerned with this offense since it always involves disorder of civil rule... Now, where civil government determines pernicious error by which Christ's honor is blasphemed and salvation hindered, and the erring preachers do not let themselves be directed and refuse to desist from their preaching, civil government should confidently repel (*wehren*) them and know that by authority of its office it ought to be no other than that it turns the sword and all its power to the effect that the teaching be preserved pure and the worship clean and unadulterated. Thus one side works into the hand of the other. Those in spiritual government help with the word and ban, but civil government with sword and violence that the people become pious and all offense is removed (*gewehret*). Then things go well and God will give prosperity to both governments. As for those evil scoundrels who are left over, who do not care for the word and also are not punished by secular authority they will find their punishment in the last day.[25]

On the whole, one can notice in Luther's interpretation of the parable of the wheat and the tares a significant shift in focus: from the **wheat** among the tares to the **tares** among the wheat; from individual Christians in the kingdom of God to the church as a community of believers, and eventually to the governance of the institutional church as a public order;

from the preaching of the pure word to the word as true doctrine, and to the public articles of faith to be confessed by all inhabitants in a territory; from preaching the word to judging preaching on the part of secular authority; from shunning heretics to public rebuke and reproach; from permitting to let them go to making them go; from passive suffering of heresy to its prevention, prohibition, and punishment; from the distinction between the kingdom of Christ and the kingdom of the world to a cooperation between their distinct functions implying the civil government's foremost duty of *cura religionis*; from a passivity toward heretics in the light of the ultimate judgment to a penultimate activity of rejection and separation, i.e., excommunication from the church and expulsion from the land; and finally, from mere restraint of heretics by civil government to their possible execution for blasphemy and sedition.

II

This shift in Luther's attitude took place sometime after early February 1525. To pinpoint the actual date and to identify the reasons for the change, we have to bring in additional supportive documentation.

Luther's position before 1525 seems clear and without major modifications. His dialectic kept the two kingdoms, the kingdom of the world and the kingdom of Christ, distinct, despite the ultimate unity of their rule and authority in God's will.[26] The emphasis on **distinction** in unity prevailed: there must be no interference by civil authority in religious affairs, as long as the proponents of deviant beliefs do not propagate and put into action seditious ideas. Thus,

Luther never identified with the Catholic coordination
between spiritual and secular authority as historically
manifest in medieval Christendom, nor with Melanchthon's correlation of the political and ecclesiastical domain on the basis of an underlying universal
natural and moral law. The early Luther seems to lean
toward Left Wing sectarianism with his insistence on
the individual's freedom of conscience, though he did
not share the Left Wing's dualistic presuppositions.[27]

Luther's 1523 treatise on political ethics,
*Temporal Authority: To What Extent It Should Be
Obeyed*, makes that point clear beyond the shadow of a
doubt: civil government may coerce and punish only in
matters of civil disobedience.

> Since belief or unbelief is a matter of every
> one's conscience... the secular power should
> be content and attend to its own affairs and
> permit their subjects to believe one thing or
> another, as they are able and willing, and
> constrain no one by force. For faith is a
> free work, to which no one can be forced.
> Indeed, it is a divine work, done in the
> spirit, certainly not a matter which outward
> authority should compel or create.

Therefore, to fight false doctrine is the bishops'
business not the princes'. Heresy is a spiritual
matter; it cannot be subdued by iron, fire, or water,
but only with spiritual weapons, the word. After all,
persecution of heretics will only intensify their
obstinacy. Moreover, if civil government suppresses
religious error by force it acts without a just cause
and against the right (*Recht*). For even in secular
affairs punishment is illegal unless a crime has been
first judged by the law (*Recht*). How much less, then,

is it legitimate to take violent action in spiritual
matters without right and without God's word. As there
are no legal grounds for religious persecution, civil
government has no right to punish heretics. Sword and
word perform different functions, because they function
in different realms. Consequently, the prince's
conscience must be instructed (*Gewissensunterricht*) to
act in their domain according to the right and let the
word of God take its own course. The word alone will
overcome the heretics.[28]

Luther did not renege on this stance until after
the Peasants' War. Even when Thomas Müntzer came
forward with his portentous, potentially seditious
teachings, Luther advised the Saxon princes at the end
of July 1524, not to interfere with the office of the
word. Let Müntzer preach what he will and against
whomever he wishes. If his spirit is right, it will
not be afraid of us and will remain right:

> Is our spirit right, then it will neither be
> afraid of him nor anyone else. Let the
> spirits collide and fight it out. If mean-
> while some are led astray, all right, such is
> war.

However, if the Müntzerites resort to insurrection, the
princes must take violent measures and banish them from
the country.[29]

Shortly before the war, on February 4, 1525 (and
probably at the same time as his first sermon on the
parable of the wheat and the tares), Luther wrote in
the same vein to Lazarus Spengler in Nürnberg:

> I do not yet consider them (viz., the
> Müntzerites) blasphemers, but take them for
> heathens and apostate Christians whom civil

government must not punish, particularly not
with punishment of the body.

But were they to renounce their political loyalty, they
surely have revolution and murder on their mind so that
the magistrate must intervene.[30]

And even at the beginning of the war, Luther
reiterated his view in his *Admonition To Peace* at the
end of April 1525:

No ruler ought to prevent anyone from teaching and believing whatever they please,
whether it is the gospel or lies.[31]

Hence, Luther maintained during the Peasants' War
a strict distinction between heresy and sedition.
However, after the horrible defeat and massacre of the
Thuringian peasants under Müntzer's inept military
leadership, Luther's thinking took an ominous turn.
This change became evident in the application of the
concept **blasphemy.**

He had, of course, earlier used this term frequently to rail against what he considered a public
religious abomination, the Roman mass, and he had
instructed temporal authority to perform its duty by
abolishing false worship in favor of the evangelical
teaching. Moreover, he had advised the punishment of
obdurate priests in line with the penalty for other
public offenses like manslaughter, theft, murder, and
adultery. And he must have known that the punishment
for such crimes (including the religious crimes of
blasphemy, idolatry, and perjury) was on the books:
the law of the land stipulated the death penalty in
extreme cases.[32] However, even though Luther could in
rash moments make inconsidered remarks to the effect
that fighting the Roman blasphemy cannot turn out
without bloodshed,[33] he did not exhort civil authority

to impose the death penalty on recalcitrant priests. And his reference to the *cura religionis* of the secular government emphasized the elimination of blasphemy much more so than the protection by the sword of the evangelical faith.

Nevertheless, all this changed between the end of 1525 and the beginning of 1526. While Luther's letter to Spalatin on November 11, 1525 continued his previous understanding, his February 9, 1526 letter to Elector John added a second reason to that of blasphemous worship being wrong and damnable:

> ... a secular ruler must not tolerate that his subjects are led by obnoxious preachers into disunity and dissension from which sedition and revolution are finally to be expected. Instead, in one place there must also be only one kind of preaching

- which, needless to say, was to be the Protestant proclamation.[34] Clearly, the tide had turned. Luther had come around to agreeing that religious unity guaranteed political unity - an idea as old as civilization. In line with the ancient and still existing heresy laws, Luther now linked heresy as blasphemy with potential sedition and high treason. All the same, he never could quite shake off his earlier more tolerant stance so that his attitude was marked till the end by a certain ambiguity.[35]

Once this connection between heresy and sedition via blasphemy had been established, there was no way to halt further rapid development. Electoral Saxony issued mandates against the anabaptists on March 31, 1527 and on January 17, 1528. On April 23, 1529 the imperial edict of the Diet of Speyer condemned the anabaptists to capital punishment without prior interrogation by church authorities.[36] And Luther's trend toward intransigence can be grasped in three cases of hardening the line, the publicity-privacy issue, the increasing severity of punishment, and the indirect coercion to religious practices.

In his 1526 letter, though already linking heresy with potential sedition, he nonetheless maintained the heretics' right to private religious practice; they should merely be condemned to silence:

> Public offense alone is forbidden them. They may stay in the land, and in the privacy of their homes pray to as many gods as they like.[37]

Yet in 1530 he insisted that Christians must report the *Winkelprediger*, the shady, clandestine, and unlicensed preachers who propagate false doctrine and conduct secret ceremonies in houses and corners. If church members fail to come forward with such denouncements to civil as well as ecclesiastical authorities, they are guilty of civil disobedience as much as they become culpable before God.[38] Luther had thus drawn a parallel between religious error as being potentially seditious and private false teaching and worship as being potentially public, because they are bound to be cast abroad so that their proponents encroach upon the public office of the Protestant ministry.

As for the measure of punishment to be meted out for heresy by civil authority, Luther wrote in April 1526:

> If they don't want it (viz., the word of God), we let them go and separate ourselves from them... but we let them live among us.[39]

Yet when the elector decreed banishment Luther was in full accord.[40] The same happened also with regard to the death penalty. After the edict of Speyer 1529 Luther in late February 1530 stated:

> ... because they (viz., the anabaptists) are not only blasphemers but also highly seditious, let the sword by right be used against them.[41]

Luther had moved from the notion that blasphemy is potentially seditious to equating blasphemy flatly with sedition - a conviction that Melanchthon held at least three years earlier[42] and that St. Thomas More had advocated all along.[43] Among the Lutheran reformers only Johannes Brenz in Swabia held on to Luther's earlier teaching and continued consistently to keep heresy and sedition apart as not necessarily consequential. And it was in the Free City of Nürnberg where a point of view was proposed which came close to the modern concept of toleration, namely, that there is in fact no link between false religious opinion and civil disobedience.[44] On the other hand, Thomas Müntzer, the self-proclaimed apocalyptic prophet who cast himself in the role of Daniel, preached that the end time was at hand and that the true Christians are the angels at the harvest who must separate the wheat from the tares by killing all ungodly people.[45]

Regarding coercion in religious matters Luther in 1529 was no longer content with having the heretics condemned to silence and their books confiscated. Rather, he wanted them forced to attend the evangelical services in order that they learn civil obedience and economic obligations, for the Decalogue and the catechism teach also political and economic matters. If they want to live among a people, they must adhere, even against their will, to the civil rights and duties of this people (*Stadtrecht*). This is by no means forcing them to faith, Luther strenuously insists as if to convince himself, but preventing blasphemy and insurrection for their own and other people's sake.[46] Such restrictive measures leave no doubt that the cooperation in the Protestant territory between the state's and the church's coercive power, the "working hand in hand" of civil and ecclesiastical government, had finally been effected.

So, by 1530 and within a span of less than five years, Luther had reached the final stage of intolerance. One finds him, now justified by civil legislation, agreeing to the whole range of punishments from silencing, forbidding books, and voluntary emigration, to forced exile, imprisonment, life sentence, and execution by fire and sword.

His harshest statement against the heretics, the *Exposition of Psalm 82* 1530,[47] expresses his views more comprehensively than ever before. Civil government, i.e., the divinely ordained princes as "gods," is first and foremost obliged to honor God's word and to control all godless teachers. Luther had elevated the *cura religionis* to the top of his definition of political authority, so that its obligation to social welfare received a secondary, and to law and order a tertiary place. He had made the care of religion the primary concern of temporal government and thus aligned himself, to a large extent, with Melanchthon's position which, later, was also taken by Calvin.[48]

Above all, says Luther, secular government must see to it that justice is done to the truly God-fearing people. This justice is a civil right of the Christians. In contradistinction to *Temporal Authority* 1523, where the right of the state was separated from the right of the gospel to take its course independently, Luther here insists that the preaching of the true word is a right of the believers.[49] He had moved from the emphasis on two distinctly different dispensations, the secular administration of justice and the spiritual proclamation of righteousness, to the claim that, precisely by **right** of the Christians, secular government must not only protect, sponsor, and advance the free and open preaching of the word, but also support the evangelical ministers, guarantee their livelihood, and protect their public office. Insisting that the **religious right** of the Christians is to be administered by temporal authority as a **civil right**, Luther had come to embrace the *cuius regio eius religio* principle of the territorial church, or state-church, concept.

This Christian right to the protection of the word of God includes, on the other side, the protection against false teaching and worship. Luther calls on civil government to coerce and punish the heretics because they are seditious. Violent action taken against them is indeed legitimate, for they commit the crime of high treason which as *lèse majesté* does not merely assail the authority of the state but, at bottom, that of God. Their disrespect for civil government, private property, and marriage in fact undermines the divinely ordered institutions of public life: state, economy, and family. But what is more, the sectarians offend against the organized church because they do not confess the public articles of Christian faith but teach against them. In the privacy of their home, heretical persons may secretly and without communication believe what they wish. Yet publicly the truth must be preached and taught in churches and houses, affirmed by confession of faith, and protected by the state - and that for the common good and public welfare.

Consequently, heretics must be punished for both sedition and blasphemy, since they not only desecrate God's name but also insult the honor of their neighbors. They violate both tables of the Ten Commandments. After all, if they wish to enjoy the benefits of civil rights (*Stadtrecht*)[50], i.e., the protection and community offered in the city, they must also fulfill their civic duties in complying, like everyone else, with the municipal laws - which prominently include injunctions against blasphemy, the injury of God's and the neighbor's honor. Should they find themselves unable to do so, they are free to go to a non-Christian community rather than snatching away word and teaching from God and God's people.

III

The external, i.e., historical, political, and sociological reasons for Luther's change between 1525 and 1530 can be indicated in broad lines. There was, of course, the continued and increasing presence of the Left Wing heretics despite the disastrous end of the Müntzer movement in the Peasants' War. Further, with the accession of John to power after the death of Frederick the Wise in May 1525, a sovereign took over the helm in Electoral Saxony who was eager forcefully to promote the Protestant cause as, for instance, his program of church visitations indicates. Also, the Lutheran movement had flourished since the interim of the first Diet of Speyer in 1526. Evangelical churches had been established and consolidated in different territories to such an extent that institutional

structures had to be arranged, ecclesiastical constitu-
tions provided, and the church's relation to the
territorial government regulated.[51] And this establishment of the new church gave rise to questions of
the office and governance in the church, in short, of
the *ordo ecclesiasticus*. After the visitations in
Saxony revealed the deplorable state of religious
knowledge among people and clergy alike, catechisms
needed to be published to give them a pedagogical
foundation for the word preached and believed. However, the favorable climate for Protestant expansion
changed toward the end of the decade when Emperor
Charles V finally had his hands free to deal with the
Lutheran cause in Germany. Protestant princes and
their lawyers drew the Wittenberg theologians into
negotiations about a military alliance and consulted on
the question of armed resistance against the emperor
and the Catholic forces in *causa fidei*. Reluctantly
convinced as he was by legal argumentation and the
proof from natural law, Luther was led to accept the
notion of *cura religionis* for Protestant princes also
in political and military terms.[52] Moreover, with the
Augsburg Confession the Lutheran movement had developed
public articles of faith which could function as a
common doctrinal denominator in Protestant territories.
Last but not least, Melanchthon's influence on Luther
must not be underestimated. The younger reformer held
all along that civil government is the custodian and
defender of the first table of the Decalogue as much as
of the second. This *cura religionis* enjoined secular
authority actively to enforce the public confession of
faith in the land. Conversely, civil government was
authorized to prohibit, coerce, and punish public
blasphemers, idolaters, and perjurers, or anyone else

found in manifest outrageous insult against God's honor and glory.[53] For Melanchthon the equation of heresy, blasphemy, and sedition was always a matter of course.

Melanchthon's was a hard-line position which Luther never fully endorsed or completely avowed. Compared with his own earlier stance Luther indeed had moved toward severe intolerance. But compared with Melanchthon's position Luther had retained elements of a more lenient view. The last two documents we have to consider make this evident. They are two *Gutachten*, i.e., professional theological opinions, solicited by secular rulers from the Wittenberg theologians. The first *Gutachten* was drafted by Melanchthon in 1531 for Elector John of Saxony, signed also by Luther but with a handwritten addendum. The second was composed by the Wittenberg theologians in 1536 for Landgrave Philipp of Hesse - but, again, with a postscriptum in Luther's hand. Both *Gutachten* address the question of whether the ruler is by duty bound to punish the anabaptists with the death penalty.

In his 1531 *Gutachten* Melanchthon swiftly comes to the point: the anabaptist articles are seditious. Already the mere fact that they have organized conventicles amounts to breaking the law of the land which decreed the death penalty for such an offense. Further, they teach: civil government is unchristian; Christians must not swear an oath (of loyalty to secular authority); must not possess private property, nor pay taxes; the church must be reformed to a pure primitive condition, with the implication in some quarters (Müntzer's) that all ungodly people must be exterminated.

But even if their articles would not contain such seditious ideas, their separation from the church and

their setting up their own congregations make for
blasphemy and insurrection against the *ordo ecclesiasticus*. They condemn on principle the public ministry
of the word, draw people from the official church, and
form pure assemblies of true believers. However,
revolution against the church is to be punished the
same way as revolution against the state. Therefore,
the initiators and receivers of the conventicles are to
be put to death without further ado. The adherents, if
they obstinately persist in error after interrogation,
instruction, and admonition, are to share the same
fate. Only the innocuous should be received into the
church upon repentance; but in case they relapse,
banishment or some other milder penalty is indicated.
As if Melanchthon had not been harsh enough, he concludes:

> Even if secular authority deals with one or
> another of them too swiftly, it is right in
> doing so, for the law and punishment in God's
> commandment must be executed *per se* and *in
> genere*, as long as law and punishment are
> rightly intended and right (*Recht*) is done in
> the majority of the cases.

Yet Luther adds:

> Although it is cruel to punish with the
> sword, it is more cruel to condemn *minister-
> ium verbi*, to preach uncertain doctrine, to
> suppress correct teaching, and to that end to
> want to destroy the *regna mundi* (the kingdoms
> of the world).[54]

Luther's hand in drawing up the 1536 *Gutachten* is
clearly evident. It was composed under the fresh
impact of the revolt in Münster. While in agreement
with the substance of Melanchthon's argument, it

differs in tone, in the arrangement of points argued, and, above all, in the instruction of the prince's conscience.

The main body of this *Gutachten* deals with the anabaptist articles concerning temporal affairs and spiritual matters. Their unequivocal rejection of secular government, oath, private possessions, and marriage, leads to the destruction of civil rule. Adherents of such views must be punished, yes, even with the sword, but with careful consideration of extenuating circumstances. Secular power does not thereby force anyone to faith, nor does it punish the secret opinions of the heart, but hinders the spread of illegitimate teaching by which others are being seduced. As the anabaptist teachings on temporal government are seditious, so their articles of faith are blasphemous. Inasmuch as civil authority is by duty bound to establish the true doctrine and correct worship, it must, according to Lev. 24:16 ("the blasphemer shall surely be put to death"), punish public religious offense. But - a significant proviso - government must first submit to the right instruction in order that it judges rightly, not on the basis of conventional uses but according to God's word and the understanding of the old and pure church.

Still more, not only are the anabaptists' secular teachings seditious and their religious doctrines blasphemous, they dare to separate from the church and begin their ministry apart from the *ordo ecclesiasticus*. That is against the word of God. Where there is the true church, people have to stay with the official ministry of that church. Disobedient sectarians fall under the law of the *Theodosian Code* and are to be put to death. Yet the document ends with an admonition to

the sovereign: moderation should prevail; instruction
and exhortation should be given to the perpetrators.
Simple followers who are not obstinate should be identified and punished with milder penalties. The
instigators and pertinacious ones, however, if they
continue their conspiracy, must be dealt with severely
and treated as revolutionaries because they go pregnant
with Münsterite insurrection. Still, as if this softer
line had not been obvious enough, Luther adds in his
own handwriting:

> This is the general rule, yet our Gracious
> Lord (viz., Philipp) may at all times let
> grace go besides the penalty, according to
> the occasion of circumstances.[55]

Ironically, while Melanchthon, who appeared to be
the flexible negotiator at Augsburg so much so that
Luther called him a *Leisetreter* (pussy-footer),
insisted on the principle of the strict enforcement of
the letter of the law, Luther, who has come down to us
as an opinionated and assertive quarreller, advised
equity in judgment and consideration of reasons of
expediency in deference to the principle: *summum ius,
summa iniuria* (the strictest enforcement of the law
amounts to the severest injury). Melanchthon taught
the unmitigated rule of extreme justice, no matter
whether injustice should occur, as long as such injury
is unintended and happens within the general parameter
of the law. Luther, on the other side, admonished that
extreme punishment should occur only in the last resort
to avoid injustice intended or unintended - and therefore it is always better to show mercy (*Gnade für Recht
ergehen lassen*).

IV

The change of Luther's attitude toward toleration seems to be due to a shifting emphasis within the dialectic of his thought. The stress moved from the distinction to the cooperation between civil and spiritual authority. Concomitantly, the focus shifted from the community of faith as a spiritual communion to the church as a social institution which precisely as an *ordo ecclesiasticus* found itself next to the other major social institution, the state. Regarding religious dissent, then, blasphemy came into view as a religious crime which fell into the jurisdiction of both the church and the state. Under the rubric blasphemy, the religious offense heresy and the political crime sedition could be judged as being one and the same. Furthermore, since legislation against the religious crimes of blasphemy, idolatry, and perjury existed in positive law, and new decrees had extended it to include the anabaptists, Luther saw himself justified to call upon civil authority to do away with religious dissent in the Protestant territories.

No matter how intolerant Luther had become in the face of the public dissemination of heresy, he continued to allow for the individuals' right to hold in private whatever religious opinions they chose. And he also went on with counseling both civil and religious authority not to violate the consciences of the weak in faith, and to adjust the measure of punishment to the degree of malice. All the same, what Luther was primarily concerned with was the unity of the public expression of the one evangelical truth. The right to private conviction could be tolerated as long as the

public preaching of the Protestant word was guaranteed.
Luther was, quite naively, persuaded that the word of
truth will put itself through once the heretic was
exposed to the proclamation, instruction, and exhortation of the true church.

Salvation is, of course, a matter of the individual's relation to God through Christ. The freedom of
conscience bound by the word is therefore an individual
right, whereas the right to correct public preaching is
a communal and thus a civil right. The **personal
religious right** is the right to the free and immediate
access to God through the gospel of Christ, not to be
interfered with by any church law, sacerdotal or
hierarchical power, or civil constraint. The **civil
religious right**, on the other hand, is the right to the
public accessibility to the gospel preaching. Consequently, freedom of conscience as freedom of faith
meant for Luther the free access to God through Christ,
the word. However, for this free access to be available for all, the public proclamation of the word had
to be secured, protected, and promoted by civil government. The personal freedom of faith received its most
poignant expression in the teaching on the common
priesthood of all believers - indeed, a revolutionary
innovation within the spiritual realm of the communion
of saints. The public freedom of the faith, however,
was a matter of the organized church as a social
institution in cooperation with the secular rule. The
"democratic" impetus in Luther's concept of the spiritual rule unfortunately did not spill over into his
understanding of the secular realm.

It is ultimately pointless to argue whether Luther
was more medieval or more modern. That is neither here
nor there.[56] He did not even stand above the times.

One things is clear, however: he was not a champion of
the modern concept of religious liberty.[57]   Nor was
Erasmus, for that matter - although his thought was
more amenable to be used by modern liberal sensitivities.   To call Luther the "standard bearer of modern
times" and to hail the Reformation as "the sun after
the medieval darkness" (Hegel) is to miss the point as
much as to see him essentially as a representative of
the Middle Ages (Troeltsch), or worse, as hindering the
emancipation of the modern mind (Burckhardt), or even
as reintroducing medieval obscurantism (Nietzsche).[58]

Luther was hardly the proponent of a subjectivity
which by its inherent right is entitled to be free from
external power, and which liberates itself by virtue of
its own authority.   To understand the modern era as the
unfolding and completion of the Reformation legacy,
i.e., of Luther's claim to subjectivity, conscience,
and freedom, is as skewed an interpretation as to
portray him as the blind leader of the blind guiding
humanity backward into the bondage of supernatural
forces.   Freedom meant for Luther the freedom of the
children of God wrought by Christ on the cross.
Equality signified for Luther the equality of all human
beings **before** God (*coram Deo*), rather than the elimination of differences **among** human beings. Living in a
princely territory instead of in one of the emerging
democratic communities, and enjoying rather cozily the
protection and favors of his *Landesvater*, Luther did
not break out of the traditional Christian patriarchal-
ism with its paternalistic "ideology of good will,"
i.e., the *respublica Christiana* with its feudalistic
structure of super- and sub- ordination, and its ideal,
though never actualized, dynamic of care, love, and
obedience.[59]   Luther had no conception of a liberty and

equality founded on natural law and reason, and realized as a human right within the horizontal dimension
of the world. Where he saw freedom and equality
triumph was in the vertical dimension of the human
being's relation to God in Christ. Therefore, it was
in his theology, not in his political, social, and
economic ethics that Luther took the historic step into
the direction of human emancipation: the human being's
relation to God was liberated from any human authority
and power because it was bound by God's revelation in
Christ alone. And that emancipation was, indeed, a
giant step forward. But Luther's anthropology was so
much a **theological** anthropology that his emphasis on
the freedom of faith and on the equality among God's
children is hardly akin to the modern right of freedom
of religion as an expression of freedom of thought, and
to the modern right of freedom of assembly and worship
as an expression of the freedom of speech.

Instead of Luther's idea of toleration, certain
elements in the Humanist and Left Wing spiritualist
conception of tolerance proved eventually conducive to
being used in the transition to modern thought. Not
that such elements *per se* pointed to the future.
Rather, developing modern thought and ethical sensitivity could link up with them by modifying them into
current usefulness.

Humanists like Castellio and Coornhert functioned
as middle-men to pass Erasmus' concept of toleration on
to modern application though, of course, not without
serious alterations.[60] Advocating the notion that
individual (and therefore relative) expressions of the
transcendent unity of truth yet contain parts of that
absolute truth and consequently are in part true, these
humanists and subsequent humanistic rationalists

anticipated a legitimate pluralism of religious convictions. They applied, like Erasmus, the principle:
"the one unites, the many divide" by reducing the
individual parts of the truth to their ultimate common-
ality in a minimum of shared *fundamenta* which are held
in common by all rational human beings (*consensus*) and
which should be articulated only so far as they express
their transcendent unity rather than their divisive
particularity. This development in thought brought
with it the emphasis on the freedom and equality of all
thinking beings and thus in a way helped usher in the
transition to the Enlightenment, where toleration of
differing religious sentiments relied on the assumption
that one single and basic religious knowledge underlies
as unity all individual religious convictions. These
fundamenta were seen as a source of division only when
they were exclusively defined, their absoluteness
limited to one particular expression, and thus their
unity particularized and relativized. To be biased,
opinionated, or dogmatic meant to claim for oneself
what belonged to all. Instead, one had to hold on to a
fundamental religious unity in the diversity of different religious commitments. Religion and rationality
had entered into an alliance.

It is rather surprising to discover that the
development of the concept of toleration by means of
rationalism is structurally analogous to the non-ra-
tional approach of certain Left Wing spiritualists like
Sebastian Franck whose influence on the modern mind was
much more subconscious. In this line of thought the
transcendent unity of truth is understood, or better,
intuited in terms of pure mystical spirituality. From
the perspective of the unity of human spirits in the
Spirit, the different religious parties could be viewed

with impartiality (*unparteiisch*).[61] So, whether as a transcendent mystery of the spirit or as an equally transcendent yet common-sensically based rational *consensus omnium*, the truth had to remain a lofty set of ideas and ideals, and the variety of its forms had to be kept from claiming universality and finality. Precisely this need to safeguard the unity of truth by keeping its forms relative called for toleration, whether for reasons of spiritual impartiality or rational necessity.

Another development shaping our modern conception of toleration also went far beyond Luther. In political theory the state was increasingly seen as based on the contractual arrangement between free, equal, and rational human beings. Proceeding from the people's sovereignty instead of the ruler's, humanistic rationalists eliminated the thought of the divine ordination of external life and of the divine sanction of existing political power (*etsi deus non daretur*). From Althusius to Grotius to Locke there is a development of thought that would by and large make do without the premise of the state's necessary religious basis. Therefore, any insistence on the unity of the public expression of religious truth became pointless. And that meant conversely that the state was to tolerate and protect from persecution any and every religious conviction, whether held in private or communicated in public. As Frederick the Great said: *"Jeder soll nach seiner eigenen Façon selig werden"* (each person may be saved according to his/her own fashion). Freedom of thought and freedom of religion had entered into an alliance.

Our modern sense of religious toleration is predicated on the assumption that the personal choice

of religion is a human and civil right, and that
private religious commitments can by right be publicized. The end effect of this enlightened attitude is
religious pluralism. In contrast, Luther maintained
that the public expression of the truth must correspond
to the absoluteness of its unity, universality, and
finality. He had to learn, however, that such a
uniform public expression of the truth could not be had
without severe repression by secular government. For
Luther, truth never could be relativized, whereas
falsehood by definition and nature is relative and
therefore dissentious, i.e., blasphemous in its religious, and seditious in its political effect: *"Ein
Lügner muss auch ein Mörder werden"* (a liar will
necessarily become also a murderer).[62] Consequently,
while one may hold falsehood privately, it must not be
publicized since going public implies claims to universality and finality, i.e., to truth. For Luther the
point was clear: either - or, either truth or lies,
either God or the devil. A compromise between the
unity of truth and the diversity of its actual expressions never occurred to him.

NOTES

1. Cf. R. Bainton, "The Parable of the Tares as the Proof Text for Religious Toleration to the End of the Sixteenth Century," *Church History* 1 (1932), 67-89.

2. Cf. M. Hoffmann, "Erasmus and Religious Toleration," *Erasmus of Rotterdam Yearbook Two* (1982), 80-106.

3. Sermon in the *Fastenpostille* 1525 (WA 17 II, 123 ff.); sermon in Roerer's *Hauspostille* 1528 (WA 52, 828 ff.); sermon in Dietrich's *Hauspostille* 1531/34 (?) (WA 52, 130 ff.); *Annotationes in aliquot capita Matthaei* 1538 (WA 38, 558 ff.); sermon 1546 (WA 51, 174 ff.).

4. Though the second and third source are transcripts of sermons (cf. WA 52, XIV f.), their content corresponds largely with that of genuine Luther texts from the same period. Supportive evidence adduced later will show that the 2 sermons in question are generally trustworthy (cf. below n. 34 ff.).

5. This is noteworthy in view of the habitual cliché of the "shifty" Erasmus vs. the "steadfast" Luther.

6. Cf. R. Bainton, "The Development and Consistency of Luther's Attitude to Religious Liberty," *Harvard Theological Review* 22 (1929), 107-149; J. Lecler, *Toleration and the Reformation*, tr. T. L. Westow (New York - London, 1960), I, 147 ff.

7. Cf. for instance N. Paulus, *Protestantismus und Toleranz im 16. Jahrhundert* (Freiburg, 1911), 1-25.

8. As a case in point, compare his 1519 and 1531 (1535) *Commentary on Galatians* (WA 2, 599 ff.; LW 27, 283 ff. and WA 40 II, 134 ff.; LW 27, 104 ff.). For a selection of texts on toleration, see M. Hoffmann, ed., *Toleranz und Reformation*, Texte zur Kirchen- und Theologiegeschichte 24 (Gütersloh, 1979).

9. Cf. M. Edwards, *Luther and the False Brethren* (Stanford, 1975), particularly 82-126.

10. WA 52, 835 ff.

11. For instance, Erasmus, *Supputatio errorum Beddae
     1527, Desiderii Erasmi Roterodami opera omnia*, ed.
     by J. Clericus (Lugduni Batavorum, 1703-1706), IX,
     582; Balthasar Hubmaier, *Von Ketzern und ihren
     Verbrennern 1524, B. Hubmaier Schriften*, ed. by G.
     Westin und T. Bergsten, <u>Quellen</u> und <u>Forschungen</u>
     <u>zur</u> <u>Reformationsgeschichte</u> 29 (Gütersloh, 1962),
     97.

12. WA 11, 248 ff.; LW 45, 86 ff.

13. *Contra Gaud. Don.* I 25, 28, *Corpus Scriptorum
     ecclesiasticorum Latinorum* 53, 226.

14. *Corpus Reformatorum Ioannis Calvini Opera*, ed. by
     G. Baum, E. Cunitz, & E. Reuss (Braunschweig,
     1863-1900), *Defensio orthodoxae fidei* (1554),
     VIII, 452 ff.; and four sermons on Deut. 13: 1-18
     from 1555, XXVII, 225-274.

15. WA 52, 134 f.

16. WA 51, 174 ff.

17. WA 17 II, 125.

18. WA 52, 835.

19. In the 1536 *Gutachten, wehren* had unequivocally
     assumed the meaning *strafen* (to punish), cf. WA
     50, 9.

20. WA 52, 838.

21. WA 52, 834 f.

22. WA 52, 836; 51, 180 ff.

23. WA 52, 130 ff., 829 ff.

24. WA 38, 560 ff.

25. WA 52, 134 f.

26. For an analysis of Luther's *two kingdom* teaching,
     the *cura religionis* and *ius reformandi*, see E.
     Wolgast, *Die Wittenberger Theologie und die
     Politik der Evangelischen Stände*, <u>Quellen</u> und

Forschungen zur Reformationsgeschichte 47 (Güters-loh, 1977), 40 ff.

27. See E. Troeltsch, *The Social Teachings of the Christian Church*, tr. by O. Wyon (London, 1931), II, 491 ff.

28. WA 11, 246 ff.; LW 45, 108 ff.

29. WAB III, 764; LW 40, 49 ff.

30. WAB III, 824.

31. WA 18, 298-299; LW 46, 22.

32. *Corpus Iuris Civilis* C. 1, 6, 2; 11, 1-6; *Codex Theodosianus* 16, 10.

33. For instance, WA 6, 229.

34. WAB IV, 978.

35. Cf. for instance, WAB IV, 1138, 1213; WA 26, 145 f.; LW 40, 230 f.

36. *Reichstagsakten* 8 VII, 1325 ff.; cf. H.-J. Goertz, "Der Zweite Speyerer Reichstag und die Täufer," in: *Gewissensfreiheit als Bedingung der Neuzeit. Fragen an die Speyerer Protestation von 1529*, by R. Wohlfeil and H.-J. Goertz, *Bensheimer Hefte* 54 (Göttingen, 1980), 25-46.

37. WAB IV, 978.

38. WA 31 I, 210; LW 13, 64.

39. WA 19, 263.

40. WAB IV, 1215, 1294.

41. WAB V, 1532; cf. K. Voelker, *Toleranz und Intoleranz im Zeitalter der Reformation* (Leipzig, 1912), 85 ff.

42. WAB IV, 1145.

43. *A Dialogue Concerning Heresies and Matters of Religion* 1528; excerpts in: M. Hoffmann, *Toleranz*, 12 ff.

44. Cf. M. Hoffmann, *Toleranz*, 49 ff., 53 ff.

45. Ibid., 63 ff.

46. WAB V, 1467; cf. BSLK, 504; BC 339.

47. WA 31 I, 189 ff.; LW 13, 42 ff.

48. Cf. M. Hoffmann, *Toleranz*, 41 ff., 80 ff. For Melanchthon as well as Calvin civil government was the guardian of the first table of the Decalogue. This was a final conclusion drawn from the *cura religionis* which Luther yet rejected (cf. WA 7, 66 f.; LW 31, 367 f.; WA 51, 558; LW 41, 248).

49. See n. 27.

50. WA 31 I, 208; LW 13, 61. Cf. E. Wolf, "Toleranz nach evangelischem Verständnis," in: *Zur Geschichte der Toleranz und Religionsfreiheit*, hg. H. Lutz, Wege der Forschung CCXLVI (Darmstadt, 1977), 138.

51. See the pertinent portions in: H. Bornkamm, *Luther in Mid-Career 1521-1530* (Philadelphia, 1983); see also his article "Das Problem der Toleranz im 16. Jahrhundert," in: *Das Jahrhundert der Reformation* (Göttingen, 1966), 262-291.

52. Cf. E. Wolgast, *Die Witttenberger Theologie*, 85 ff.; M. Hoffmann, "Martin Luther: Resistance to Secular Authority," *The Journal of the Interdenominational Theological Center* XI (1985), forthcoming.

53. Cf. n. 48.

54. *Corpus Reformatorum Philippi Melanchthonis Opera*, ed. by C.G. Bretschneider (Halle, 1834-1860), IV, 737 ff.

55. WA 50, 9 ff.

56. See for instance, B. Lohse, *Martin Luther, Eine Einführung in sein Leben und Werk* (München, 1982), 210 ff.; H. F. Geisser, "Martin Luthers Anteil an Mittelalter und Neuzeit," in: *Weder Ketzer noch Heiliger* (Regensburg, 1982), 33 ff.

57. Cf. R. Wohlfeil, "Bedingungen der Neuzeit," in: R. Wohlfeil - H. J. Goertz, *Gewissensfreiheit*, 7-24.

58. Cf. G. Ebeling, "Luther and the Beginning of the Modern Age," in: *Luther and the Dawn of the Modern Era*, ed. H. Oberman (Leiden, 1974), 11-39; and id., "Die Toleranz Gottes und die Toleranz der Vernunft," *Zeitschrift für Theologie und Kirche* 78 (1981), 442-464.

59. Cf. E. Troeltsch, *Social Teachings*, I, 78 ff.; II, 491 ff.

60. See R. Bainton, *Castellio, Concerning Heretics* (New York, 1935); id., *The Travail of Religious Liberty* (Philadelphia, 1951); H. Lutz, ed., *Zur Geschichte der Toleranz*, especially H. R. Guggisberg, "Wandel der Argumente für religiöse Toleranz und Glaubensfreiheit im 16. und 17. Jahrhundert," 455 ff.

61. Cf. M. Hoffmann, *Toleranz*, 66 ff.

62. WA 30 II, 124-126; LW 46, 179-181; WA 30 II, 490; LW 40, 356.

Lewis W. Spitz

THE CHRISTIAN IN CHURCH AND STATE

Christians have lived and learned to live under a great variety of forms of church government and political structure. Neither is of the essence. This statement I believe to be true to Luther's understanding of the place of the Christian in church and state, the understanding of Luther in his early reformatory years and of his so-called mature years. What this means can be grasped only through a close examination of Luther's own expressions on church and state, against the background of his times, and by venturing a surmise on the relevance of his understanding for our own times.

All attempts to change the church by political means through a criticism of its material possessions and power drive, through faint-hearted attempts at renewal or through frank anticlericalism, were frustrated by the sacrosanct and firmly established thousand year old tradition. Only from within was the church to be shaken by a basic attack on its dogmatic foundations. Therefore the decisive blow did not come from the humanists and their world-renowned leader Erasmus of Rotterdam, from whom his contemporaries had expected it, but from a monk, until then virtually unknown, Martin Luther. He led the

attack and established through his new
understanding of the relation between man and
God - the justification of man before God
alone through faith - a new understanding of
the concept of the church, which prevailed
over the foundations of the old Church and
questioned its structure and power practices.
He tied in his criticism of the church based
on the Bible with political, social and
economic demands.[1]

This is Thesis I of the *Thesen über Martin Luther. Zum
500. Geburtstag* prepared by a group of social scientists of the *Akademie der Wissenschaften* of the DDR and
of East German universities. They have come upon the
historical insight that true revolutions come from
within a system and attack its fundamental presuppositions. It is a sensitive thought for those living
within a system so vulnerable as is any Marxist ideolo-
gically constructed state supported by force for the
most part. The statement does open up for us the
questions that concern us here, understanding Luther
and understanding our own situation. As R. G. Colling-
wood put it so well, the purpose of history is human
self-understanding. Questions of church and state are
as urgent now as they were then and a retrospective
look will also improve our vision as we peer into the
future.

Luther's teaching concerning the two kingdoms,
church and state, is certainly one of the most discussed aspects of his theology.[2] The break-up of
medieval church structure necessarily precipitated a
crisis in organization and a new theory to replace the
old assumptions and to justify the Protestant innova-
tions. Luther addressed himself to the problem of

church and state in the early years of the Reformation and continued to write about the application of his teaching as real problems developed during the next three decades. He wrote not as a theoretician or political philosopher but addressed the issues as a theologian with his usual direct and dynamic concreteness. Passionately political in his concern for the evangelical cause and the welfare of the people, he was personally involved in advising city councils, the princes, and the *Reichstag*, admonishing the emperor himself. His final journey through icy storms in the dead of winter was to make peace between the counts of Mansfeld, who were engaged in a fratricidal controversy. From beginning to end in his sermons he admonished rulers for their sins and urged them to obey the laws of God. Later editions of Luther's works were systematically bowdlerized by omitting his sharp attacks on the folly of princes.

Luther began with political realities involving specific people rather than with some abstract social contract theory or notion of subjective rights. The term "state" in a modern sense, in fact, seems to have come into use only in the last half of the sixteenth century, when French jurists drawing on Italian thought about the state (*il stato*) developed a definition of the state as a corporate reality, a kind of real *persona*, even though an abstract concept. Luther usually referred to government as *Obrigkeit* or worldly authority. For him church and state were not passive associations of people or externally structured institutions, but they were the dynamic, positive, active realms in which the immanent God works through people for good in two different ways. In the church God works through the preaching of the gospel and

administering of the sacraments to bring people to
faith in Christ the redeemer, reconciling them to
himself. "For this reason," he wrote, "the church is
and is called the kingdom of God, because in it God
alone rules, commands, speaks, acts, and is glori-
fied."[3] In the state the immanent God is at work
through real people in the natural political order in
order to restrain evil doers, to help people through
education and charitable programs, and by working for
peace and prosperity here in this world. "For there is
no power which is not ordained," he wrote following St.
Paul, "since, as he says here (Rom. 13:1), there is no
power which is not of God..."[4] Although Luther used
the term two-kingdoms (*Zweireiche*), a more appropriate
expression is that of two rules or authorities (*Regimente*) of God, the spiritual and the temporal authorities. In any truly revolutionary situation when
liquidation is underway and fluidity the order of the
day, concepts shift and time is required for the new
definitions to firm up.

Upon which sources did Luther draw in developing
his "two-kingdoms" doctrine? Scholars have varied in
their response to that question. Some have stressed
St. Augustine as the major source of the thought of
Luther the Augustinian, associating the church with
Augustine's *civitas dei* and the worldly kingdom with
the *civitas terrena* or earthly state.[5] The idea is
appealing, but most studies of this kind fail to
appreciate the complexity of Augustine's schema which
involved five cities, *civitas caelestis, civitas dei,
civitas permixta, civitas terrena*, and *civitas diaboli*.
Augustine never associated the *civitas dei* with the
ecclesia as an institution nor turned over the world or
saeculum to the devil.. His conceptions were

transcendent and had to do with grace and lack of
goodness. Moreover, a thousand years of medieval
history had intervened, so that some scholars have
stressed the influence of other patristic and medieval
authorities, such as Marsilio of Padua and especially
William of Ockham, the Franciscan nominalist, whom
Luther called "my dear master."[6] Luther separated
secular and spiritual powers the way Ockham had done.
Nevertheless, when one of the two powers failed, that
is, in an emergency, the one power should help the
other to manage its task received from God. Thus in
1520, for example, Luther thought it appropriate for
the secular authority to keep the pope from suppressing
evangelical preaching and allowed the princes to direct
the visitation program.[7] Ockham, of course, cited
Augustine extensively and it takes great care to
distinguish the difference in perspective.

While these intellectual forebears must be taken
into account both for their contribution to the historical situation as well as to the formulation of theory,
another very obvious source was far more important for
the development of Luther's thought on church and
state, the Holy Scriptures. The New Testament was the
basic influence: the words of Jesus on the place of
believers in the Roman state, the implications of the
Sermon on the Mount, the historical account of the Book
of Acts, and the epistles of St. Paul, especially the
injunctions in Romans 13.[8] Luther lived for many years
as an exegete of the Old Testament in the world of the
Israelites, was influenced by the example of sacerdotal
kingship, and had to struggle free of that background
and the proprietary church arrangement still present in
much of the medieval church. The question of the place
of the Old Testament in Luther's ecclesio-political

thought needs much more study than it has received so far as a source of Luther's ideas.[9] The Scriptural, patristic, and medieval background must be taken into account, but should not obscure the radical nature of Luther's own thought and contribution on the questions of church and state, yes, his contribution to a modern view as distinct from medieval assumptions. The term *Zwei-Reiche-Lehre* or two kingdoms theory is a relatively modern theological concept which has been enormously complicated by the attempt of the dogmaticians to incorporate it into systematic theology and heavily burdened by the weight of modern political debate as to its implications for the twentieth century history of western Europe and America.[10] Luther did not suddenly arrive at clarity on questions of church and state anymore than he came to understand the gospel and its implications. Seen from the vantage point of his basic theological understanding, his definitions of church and state and his perceptions as to how they should relate in concrete historical circumstances are not only perfectly comprehensible but seem almost natural and nearly inevitable.

"Thank God," wrote Luther in the *Smalcald Articles*, "a child of seven knows what the church is, namely, the holy believers and lambs who hear the voice of their Shepherd; for the children pray in this way: 'I believe in the holy Christian Church.'"[11]

The age of seven was already in the Middle Ages considered to be the diacritical or discretionary age for children. In his later writings such as *Against Hanswurst* (1541) Luther continued to assert that a child of seven could understand what the church is.

A seven year old child, indeed, a silly fool,
can figure it out on his fingers - although
that stupid ass, the pope, together with his
damned Harrys [Henry VIII and Henry of Braun-
schweig-Wolfenbüttel (hence Jack-sausage)]
cannot understand anything - that the worthy
emperors, princes, lords, and pious people of
former days undoubtedly neither intended nor
desired to give their property for the purpose of adorning and honoring nothing but the
devil's whores and idolatry, much less to
educate and to support murderers of men's
souls, robbers of churches, Harrys, and ar-
sonists. On the contrary, they desired to
support good churches and schools, that is to
say, the holy word of God, the office of
preaching and other services, theologians,
ministers, preachers, in addition to the
poor, the widows, the orphans, and the sick -
all this to the praise and glory of God.[12]

That seven year old child is like Jesus at twelve
confounding the elders, for many scholars have seen but
have not understood these things.

Luther restored the New Testament understanding of
the church as the communion of saints, the *communio
sanctorum*, as the apostolic creed has it, *die Gemeinde
der Gläubigen*.[13] In 1520 he wrote:

I believe that there is on earth, through the
whole wide world not more than one holy,
common, Christian Church, which is nothing
else than the congregation or assembly of the
saints, that is, the pious, believing men on
earth, which is gathered, preserved, and
ruled by the Holy Ghost, and daily increased

by means of the sacraments and the Word of
God.[14]

In the 1539 treatise *On the Councils and the Church*
Luther explained:

> Setting aside various writings and analyses
> of the word 'church', we shall this time
> confine ourselves simply to the Children's
> Creed, which says, 'I believe in one holy
> Christian Church, the communion of saints.'
> Here the creed clearly indicates what the
> church is, namely a communion of saints, that
> is, a crowd or assembly of people who are
> Christians and holy, which is called a
> Christian holy assembly, or church. Yet this
> word 'church' [*ecclesia*) is not German and
> does not convey the sense or meaning that
> should be taken from this article.[15]

The church is created by the Holy Spirit through the
preaching of the good news of salvation, for when faith
in Christ enters a person's heart, he or she becomes a
member of the only holy Christian church on earth.
"The church does not make the Word, but rather it comes
into existence through the Word," Luther wrote.[16] "Oh,
the church is a lofty, deep, hidden thing which nobody
can perceive or behold, but can only grasp and believe
in Baptism, Sacrament [Lord's Supper], and Word," he
exclaimed.[17] The church is the spiritual kingdom in
which faith comes by hearing the Word (*fides ex audi-
tu*), and it is the Word of God, too, which preserves
the church.[18]

The church is hidden in the sense that only God
knows those who belong to it. It is not invisible in a
Platonic sense but rather by virtue of being abscon-
dite, within the hearts of human beings. It is,

properly speaking, not a building, or an external institution, made up of a hierarchy and laity, but it is a spiritual congregation, one with the saints in heaven. In 1521 he responded to the taunts of clerical opponents such as Hieronymus Emser:

> When I called the Christian Church a spiritual congregation, you ridiculed me as if I wished to build a church as Plato a city which nowhere exists...[19] No, the church exists in real people such as Peter, John and Amsdorf, and yet in the church there is neither Greek nor Jew but Christ alone.[20]

There are three signs or *notae* by which the assured presence of the true church can be known, the preaching of the Word and the celebration of the dominical sacraments, Baptism and the Lord's Supper, for the word of God is not preached in vain and does not return again void. In his treatise *On the Councils and the Church* Luther discussed the signs of the true church.[21]

Where even a small number of Christians are gathered together around the word and sacraments they possess the rights of the church, for Christ had promised, "Where two or three are gathered together in my name, there am I in the midst of them." In 1520 Luther first used the phrase "the priesthood of believers." Every congregation of Christians has the right of church government, to call or ordain, and also to depose its ministers. The congregation is responsible for the administration of the sacraments, determining the order of worship and exercising the office of the keys.[22] Luther preferred to use the word *Gemeine* or *Gemeinde* for "congregation" rather than the more abstract term *Gemeinschaft* or the ambiguous term *Kirche* (*ecclesia*). In 1523 he wrote *That a Christian Assembly*

*or Congregation Has the Right and Power to Judge All
Teaching and to Call, Appoint, and Dismiss Teachers,
Established and Proven by Scripture.*[23]   The *ius vocan-
di*, right of calling, and the *potestas clavium*, power
of the keys, belong to the Christian congregation. The
church is built in the Spirit on the rock Christ, and
not on the pope nor on the Roman Church, for the pope
and bishops are idols, not ministers. The "rock" to
which Christ referred in Matthew 16:18 is Christ
himself and not Peter, who was not holy and sinless.[24]
In 1526 in his *German Mass and Order of Service* he went
the farthest in describing the ideal of the church as a
voluntary assembly of committed Christians.[25]   In *A
Christian Sermon on the Power of St. Peter*, June 29,
1522, based on Matthew 16:13-19, he declared:

> A pastor exercises the office of the keys,
> baptizes, preaches, administers the sacra-
> ment, and performs other functions not for
> his own sake, but for the sake of the congre-
> gation. For he is a servant of the whole
> congregation, to whom the keys have been
> given, even though he himself is a knave.
> For if he does it in place of the congrega-
> tion, the church does it. If the church does
> it, God does it.[26]

He opposed enforcing uniformity in liturgy on all the
congregations, for the church operates voluntarily with
love in the spiritual sphere. Whether it is in his
Large Catechism 1529, and his extremely popular *Personal Prayer Book* 1522, or a late treatise such as *Against
the Roman Papacy - An Institution of the Devil* 1545, he
opposed associating the church with the Roman clerical
hierarchy.[27]   In his *Great Confession Concerning*

Christ's Supper 1528, he expressed his faith in the
true catholicity of the believers' church:

> I believe that there is one holy Christian
> Church on earth, that is, the community or
> number or assembly of all Christians in all
> the world, the one bride of Christ and His
> spiritual body of which He is the only head.
> The bishops or priests are not her heads or
> lords or bridegrooms, but servants, friends,
> and - as the word 'bishop' implies - superin-
> tendents, guardians, or stewards. This
> Christian Church exists not only in the realm
> of the Roman Church or pope, but in all the
> world, as the prophets foretold that the
> gospel of Christ would spread throughout the
> world, Ps. 2:8; Ps. 19:4. Thus this Chris-
> tian Church is physically dispersed among
> pope, Turks, Persians, Tartars, but spiritu-
> ally gathered in one gospel and faith, under
> one head, that is, Jesus Christ.[28]

The church, then, was the company of all believers
who trust in Christ the Savior. It is therefore
present locally in the Christian congregations and
exists universally wherever, God knows where, Christians are to be found. The nature of church polity
remained for Luther a secondary consideration. While
he considered the confessing congregational form of
church government to be ideal, he was forced by circumstances to accept a form of state-church in which the
church was an independent spiritual authority but the
state as the secular authority assumed responsibility
through the consistories for such "external matters" as
buildings, moral deportment, and salaries. Even these
functions carried on by the state, city councils and

princes, he viewed as the work of Christians in authority who were serving as "emergency bishops" until a better day when better educated people would make a more ideal form of church government possible.[29]

"Since the time of the apostles the secular sword and authority has never been so clearly described and grandly lauded as by me, which even my enemies must acknowledge," declared Luther.[30] So, then, Luther was an advocate of an authoritarian state? Quite the contrary, for what he meant was that on the one hand the state was not to be subjected to the papacy, which had no business running an earthly princedom like the papal states or trying to subordinate princes, kings, and emperors to its power, and on the other hand the state was not to be condemned or civil society abandoned to the realm of Satan as some of the radical sectarians were doing. Rather, the state, too, belongs to God's rule and as the kingdom of God's left hand had a legitimate and very important role to play here in this world.

Luther held with St. Augustine that secular authority was divinely established and exists by reason of sin (*de ratione peccati*) to wield the sword against evildoers. But beyond that Luther believed that the state served a positive function, working for the good of society and performing certain functions which had been wrongly usurped by the medieval church, which had become a power-mad institution. The state is based on natural law, the law of love (*lex charitatis*), which is fundamental to all moral and social laws. To be considered legitimate the state must function as the servant of the people and as an instrument of God's love on this earth. The state should govern with equity, applying justice tempered with mercy. The

government must not wage unjust war such as a crusade
or a war of conquest, but only defensive war in order
to protect the subject, just as the police protect the
citizens within the borders of the state.

Luther did not, like Aquinas, write a formal work
On the Governance of Princes, but he wrote instead
against "the foolish princes."[31] Some seven of his
treatises are especially concerned with secular authority (*Obrigkeit*). Three of these are especially important for his teaching on government, *Temporal Authority: To What Extent It Should be Obeyed* 1523; *Against
the Heavenly Prophets in the Matter of Images and
Sacraments* 1525; and *On War Against the Turk* 1529.[32]
The writing *On War Against the Turk* concludes with a
characteristic flair:

> With this I have saved my conscience. This
> book shall be my witness concerning the
> measure and manner in which I advise war
> against the Turk. If anyone wishes to
> proceed otherwise, let him do so, win or
> lose. I shall neither enjoy his victory nor
> pay for his defeat, but I shall be innocent
> of all the blood that will be shed in vain.
> I know that this book will not make the Turk
> a gracious lord to me should it come to his
> attention, nevertheless, I have wished to
> tell my Germans the truth, so far as I know
> it, and to give faithful counsel and service
> to the grateful and the ungrateful alike. If
> it helps, it helps; if it does not, then may
> our dear Lord Jesus Christ help, and come
> down from heaven with the Last Judgment and
> strike down both Turk and pope, together with

all tyrants and the godless, and deliver us from all sins and from all evil. Amen.[33]

If the loving God works in the spiritual kingdom through the gospel in a way that only faith can perceive, the just yet loving God also works in the temporal kingdom through the instrument of secular authority. Neither the *corpus iuris*, with which Luther was familiar from his law-school days (and he read a substantial number of important ancient jurists as well as Cicero) nor the New Testament conceived of the state as an institution or as a community of citizens but as a rule, authority and power. In Romans 13:1 St. Paul admonished: "Let every soul be subject to the higher powers." God did not withdraw from the scene after creation and lapse into indifference (*deus otiosus*), turning worldly affairs over to the sovereignty of autonomous human beings.[34] No, the rulers in authority are themselves but instruments of God's governance even though God is hidden and disguised in them as behind an actor's mask (*larva*). There is, therefore, nothing absolute about the power of any legal order or regime, for every ruler and regime stands under the judgment of God and makes but a transient and historically conditioned contribution. God established three governances against Satan: the church, government, and the family. In the *Large Catechism* writing on the fourth commandment (Thou shalt honor thy father and thy mother), Luther described family and governmental authority as the foundation of the secular orders, political and economic, and pointed out that this commandment follows immediately upon the first table of the law which is concerned with God's honor. Luther often spoke of a ruler as a "father and helper," "gardener and caretaker," and "God's official."[35]

Secular government may also be called God's kingdom. For He wants it to remain and desires that we should be obedient to it. But it is only the kingdom of God's left hand. His proper kingdom, where He himself rules and where He appoints neither father nor mother, emperor nor king nor policeman, but where He is Lord himself, is this - where the Gospel is preached to the poor.[36]

In his monastic years Luther often reflected the pejorative medieval ecclesiastical view of the state as, in Augustine's phrase, a "great robbery" (*magna latrocinia*). From 1520 on, however, he stressed the positive good that government can do for society. He came to believe that next to service to the word as preacher and teacher, service in government was the best contribution a citizen could make to the common good.[37] Worldly government is a divine ordinance and an excellent gift of God who established and maintains it for the safety and welfare of the people.[38] If, however, the government makes demands contrary to the love of neighbor, the Christian must in good conscience follow the apostle's counsel to obey God rather than a human being and to withhold obedience to such a government (Acts 5:29). Luther advocated passive disobedience rather than active disobedience except for such "wondermen" or "heroes" who have a special divine calling and a sure commission to undertake a revolution against injustice, as, for example, Samson did in the Old Testament account. But anyone who wants to act like a Samson must first become a Samson, for to act without a call from God to act is to become "the devil's monkey."[39]

The question of resistance to government, difficult in the days of Nero and St. Peter, remains an
acute problem in the twentieth century. Luther's
position on the question has remained a formative and
guiding principle for many Christians down to the
present. His separation of the two kingdoms was
perverted into the notion that God rules the church and
Satan the world, so that even a demonic ruler must be
obeyed.[40] Despite his repeated and forthright criticism of princes (and one of his preferred texts was
Psalm 146:3, "Put not your trust in princes"), Luther
was temperamentally conservative in political matters.
It is sometimes said that it was his eschatological
expectation that made a radical change seem to be
futile, since he anticipated the early end of the
world. But this hysteria-hypothesis is much overdone,
for like St. Paul he knew that the Christian lives in a
state of tension between the seeming permanence of the
present life and yet its transiency, a feeling reinforced by the expectation of the imminent second coming
of Christ in judgment. But that did not prevent Luther
from having a family and from long range educational
planning and church reform. Rather, it was a certain
political realism which attenuated any expectation of
radical improvement by revolution which involves
bloodshed. For, as he frequently observed, "changing a
government is one thing, but improving it is another."
At Worms in 1521 he had deliberately avoided rabble-
rousing which might have precipitated a bloodbath.[41]
But if the government tyranically interferes in questions of faith, the Christian must for the sake of
conscience admonish the ruler and disobey.[42] He long
felt that it is better for the Christian to suffer

persecution than to rebel or to inflict harm or death on the ruler.

Luther only gradually came to accept a theory of active resistance to temporal authority. Lutherans such as the preacher at the City Church in Wittenberg, Johannes Bugenhagen, the reformer at Strasbourg, Martin Bucer, and Prince Philipp of Hesse developed a theory of a "constitutionally-based resistance" to the emperor. He had not only declared Luther an outlaw but had condemned him to death and was organizing powerful armies to suppress the Protestant Estates. Luther opposed the organization of Protestant armies and defending the gospel by force of arms. Until late in 1530, in fact, he refused to sanction the resistance of Elector Johann of Saxony to the emperor and then only reluctantly acquiesced to a theory of resistance, when the jurists convinced him that the rule of law required the estates to resist an emperor who was threatening to act contrary to the traditional imperial law and constitution. Luther supported the Protestant League of Gotha and Torgau in the hope that the princes would be able to restrain the emperor from attacking and precipitating a bloodbath. Once again, Luther opposed using force against Catholic states or to promote the evangelical cause against adherents of the old faith.[43]

Luther's stand on resistance was in large part replicated by John Calvin, although an argument can be made that Luther finally went farther in favor of resistance than did Calvin. As an embattled minority in France, Calvinists such as Pierre Viret, François Hotman, and Philippe du Mornay developed more elaborate theories of resistance to royal tyrants, but their ideas should not be read back into Calvin's thought. Calvin, too, was conservative in his effort to be

Biblical. His idea of resistance to the king by the
lesser magistrates, like the ephors in ancient Sparta,
was analogous to Luther's eventually allowing the
princes to defend themselves against an emperor who was
threatening to violate "the good old law of the Empire"
and to act against natural law, the law of love upon
which positive law and political action should be
based.

If the world were made up of real Christians who
live out the law of love, no rulers, sword or law would
be needed, Luther believed. But most people are merely
nominal Christians and even the best of Christians
while still on earth retain a sinful nature (*simul
justus et peccator*). To the extent that they are not
fully sanctified, Christians, too, need the restraints
of the law.[44] The government is indirectly helpful to
the church by maintaining peaceful conditions so that
the gospel can be preached. The church serves the
government indirectly by developing subjects of good-
will and sound character.[45] Since government performs
useful services, the Christian should be politically
active, serving in government and furthering its work,
for in so doing he or she is also doing the Lord's
work.[46] The Christian owes military service for the
defense of the homeland, a just cause, but never for
aggressive or preventive wars, which can never be
justified. Under no circumstances can a Christian
serve in a war against his or her own conscience.
Never is a crusade for the sake of religion justified,
such as the popes have preached against the Turks.[47]
The law of love (*lex charitatis*) must be the guiding
principle for the Christian citizen and love of neighbor should motivate people to public service.[48]

The law of love should be the guiding principle of those in authority, but the government or state is not of itself a Christian authority. The legitimate rule of non-Christian governments is God's ordinance as well as that of any government within Christendom, just because such a government has nominally Christian rulers. God can use virtuous rational pagans to govern and a smart Turk may make a better ruler than a stupid Christian.

> For we surely see that God scatters the most glorious knowledge and worldly rule and kingdoms among the heathen, just as He does the beloved sun and rain, to serve over and among the godless... So He calls such worldly government among the heathen His own ordinance and creation.[49]

This view marks a distinct break with the medieval papal theory that the legitimacy of a government depends upon its subordination to the spiritual sword as embodied in the pope. Christian rulers should model their behavior after Christ and perform works of service and love toward their subjects.

Luther rejected any conception of the state as representing naked power lacking an ethical base and indifferent to the love of people or responsibility to God. He opposed all purely naturalistic accounts of the origin of government and of its legal foundation, for government is God's creature and ordinance.[50] Good positive laws are rooted in a law which is inherent in human nature, but this law is not merely naturalistic but is theonomic, having a divinely obligatory character. From the Stoics to the end of the 18th century the concept of natural law was generally understood to mean a body of principles which, resting on a divinely implanted endowment of human nature, underlie all good ethical precepts, just laws, and sound political institutions.[51] This natural law (*lex naturae*) for Luther is a natural ethical law present among all peoples in all times, though not to be confused with a rationalistic-Enlightenment or democratic-revolutionary national law concept. There is a certain moral *synteresis* and a sense of the need for equity (*epieikeia*).[52] Luther repeatedly identifies natural law and the law of love: "Thou shalt love thy neighbor as thyself."[53]

> Therefore, when you seek an advantage over your neighbor which you are not willing for him to have over you, there love is done for and natural law torn up.[54] People now are beginning to praise natural law and natural reason to the effect that all written law comes from and flows out of them, and this is quite true enough.[55]

All positive laws (*leges*) and civil rights (*iura civilia*) must be derived from natural law (*lex naturalis, ius gentium*). Luther held the Decalogue to be the best expression of natural law or the law of love. Other law codes such as Roman law, Mosaic ceremonial law, Saxon law, were positive law only and were very imperfectly derived from natural law. Sometimes positive laws reflect the selfishness of the ruling classes, placing property rights over human rights, reflecting power rather than reason. Reason should reign supreme in the realms of *politia* and *oeconomia*.[56]

> Everything runs smoother with wisdom than with force.[57] It is necessary for men to rule with reason and not with power alone, as is already now the case, for sheer power

without reason cannot last long and keeps the subjects in a state of everlasting hatred against authority, as all history loudly testifies.[58]

The best judges are those who can squint between their fingers and do not throw the book at the offender. Anything but a sycophant or Erastian, Luther blasted the princes who believed that they held their office not for the sake of serving their people, but because of their beautiful blonde hair.[59] He took it upon himself to remind the emperor that he was a mere *Madensack*, a mortal bag of worms, who himself would some day stand before the very King of Kings.[60]

One of the perennial problems from the moment when Pontius Pilate asked Jesus of Nazareth: "Art thou the King of the Jews?" to the late 20th century has been that of the proper relation of church and state. In the medieval period Christendom (*corpus christianum*) was conceived of as a religious-metaphysical entity which embraced the church (*ecclesia*) or body of Christ (*soma Christou* or *corpus mysticum*) and the state, that is, the empire (*imperium*). The empire was theoretically conceived of as the supreme political entity comprehending all monarchies and princedoms. This means that the state is a Christian authority. Traces of the *corpus christianum* thinking remained in Luther's thought, but he introduced fundamental changes which contributed to a modern development.[61] In such writings as *To the Christian Nobility of the German Nation Concerning the Reform of the Christian Estate* 1520, he seems still to be speaking of a Christian authority. In other words, both the spiritual and the secular authorities are treated as aspects of one Christian commonwealth. But even in this treatise, it has been

argued, Luther viewed the church as the congregation of
all believers and saw the nobility as Christians in
authority, not as a Christian authority. The hierarchy,
as well as the canon lawyers and scholastics doctors
serving it, naturally had a special interest in fitting
secular authority into an overall church-dominated
unity. Luther took the first step in separating the
two authorities by differentiating the areas of compe-
tence of the two rules. For Luther the bond of unity
was not in a concept of the *corpus christianum*, but
rather God's own direct sovereign rule in grace and
power. The order and power of earthly rulers, too, are
good gifts of God.[62]

What is most striking about Luther's teaching is
his constant stress on separating the functions of
church and state, his insistence upon the essential
dissimilarity of the spiritual and temporal authorities, and his determination to keep them distinct in
practice. "I must always drum in and rub in," he
declared, "drive in and hammer home such a distinction
between these two kingdoms, even though it is written
and spoken so often that it is annoying."[63] Church-
people should not seek in a dictatorial and domineering
fashion to change and correct civil law and secular
princes, and lords should not in a dictatorial and
domineering fashion want to change and correct God's
Word and try to say what is to be preached and taught,
for that is forbidden them as well as the lowest
beggar. In opposition to medieval confusion, when the
papacy constantly intervened in political matters and
secular rulers dominated the proprietary church (*Eigen-
kirche*), Luther sought to separate the spiritual and
secular functions of the two authorities. This ideal
was expressed in the Lutheran Confessions as well.

History played tricks on Luther, as Veronica
Wedgwood once observed, for the development of the
territorial churches during the course of the 16th
century made it difficult to preserve his congregational ideal and the separation of the spiritual and
secular functions of church and state. Predictably,
the city councils in the urban reformation of the early
decades and the territorial princes in the latè reformation undertook the reform and care of the church.
This was true of Catholic as well as of Protestant
territorial states, Bavaria, for example, where Leon-
hard von Eck as early as 1522 received extensive power
over the clergy, church income, defense against heresy,
and preserving external order in the church.[64] It has
been argued that there was practically no alternative
to the development of church organization in evangelical lands and there is much debate as to the extent to
which that development deviated from Luther's ideal.
On the one hand, Luther desired a church of true
believing and confessing Christians (*Bekenntniskirche*).
On the other hand, he did not wish to abandon society
to a purely secular amorality and so favored retaining
an official church for all the people where at the very
least Christian morality could be promoted (*Volks-
kirche*). The anabaptists did, after all, achieve the
separation of church and state, but only at the cost of
turning their backs on the state and consigning secular
society to the rule of the devil. Luther had worked a
great change in the concepts of church and state by
trying to restore the New Testament understanding of
them. He enunciated important new ideas on how the two
kingdoms were to relate and be distinguished.[65] He was
not a political philosopher, but a theologian, and yet

he had a most profound influence on political thought and historical events.

In conclusion, Luther, together with the other Reformers, restored the New Testament understanding of the church as the communion of saints, a community based on love rather than on power of coercion. Christ is the head of the church and all true believers are its members. He drew an absolute distinction between the spiritual and secular authorities. His doctrine of vocation elevated the dignity of service in government just as it did all other secular callings in life. He set in motion resistance theories that were to have important historical consequences, for as he himself had said when he stood alone before emperor and the estates of the empire: "It is neither safe nor right to go against conscience." He developed natural law thinking in a way that contributed in due course to constitutional theory. Above all, Luther along with the other Reformers developed the kind of inner-directed person needed for the great transformation in modern times of subjects into citizens. Luther made an important contribution to these developments, even though he would be the first to declare the limitations of all human achievements and to confess that God had done it all. Surely his religious message made the most important contribution toward stability in these uncertain times, for it implied a certain Christian nonchalance toward the "poor breadbasket of this life" and toward the "rulers of this world."

Luther always admired Emperor Charles V, who had been a mere boy when Luther stood before him in Worms. In fact, Luther included Charles V among the great heroes of history in the company of David, Cyrus, Cicero, and other great figures of the past. Emperor

Charles perhaps unconsciously returned a measure of this admiration, for when his armies had overrun the Protestant armies in the Smalkald Wars and captured Wittenberg, he did Luther a good turn. The Spanish soldiers standing at Luther's graveside in the Castle church screamed out that he should be dug up and his body burned as befitted a heretic. But Charles responded by saying: "I do not make war on dead men!"

NOTES

1. Cited by J. Rogge, "Luthers Kirchenverständnis in seinen Spätschriften," *Zeichen der Zeit* 37 (1983), 195.

2. F. Lau, *Luthers Lehre von den beiden Reichen* (Berlin, 1952), 8.

3. WA 8, 656; LW 44, 379 f. H. W. Krumwiede, *Glaube und Geschichte in der Theologie Luthers. Zur Entstehung des geschichtlichen Denkens in Deutschland* (Göttingen, 1952), 18-38, considers the teachings on the spiritual and temporal governments of God as part of the basic structure of Luther's theology.

4. WA 57, 108.

5. For examples of this kind of Augustine-Luther association see Y. Congar, "'Civitas Dei' et 'Ecclesia' chez S. Augustin. Histoire de la recherche: son état present," *Revue des Etudes Augustiniennes* 3 (Paris, 1957), 1-14; E. Kinder, "Gottesreich und Weltreich bei Augustin und bei Luther. Erwägungen zu einem Vergleich der 'Zwei-Reiche-Lehre' Augustins und Luthers," in: *Beiträge zur historischen und systematischen Theologie. Festschrift für Werner Elert* (Berlin, 1955), 24-42; W. von Loewenich, "Das Neue in Luthers Gedanken über den Staat," in: *Von Augustin zu Luther. Beiträge zur Kirchengeschichte* (Witten, 1959), 210-224.

6. J. Heckel, "Marsilius von Padua und Martin Luther. Ein Vergleich ihrer Rechts- und Soziallehre," *Zeitschrift der Savigny-Stiftung für Rechtsgeschichte* 75 (1958), 268-336; H. Junghans, "Das mittelalterliche Vorbild für Luthers Lehre von den beiden Reichen," in: *Vierhundertfünfzig Jahre lutherische Reformation 1517-1967. Festschrift für Franz Lau zum 60. Geburtstag*, ed. by H. Junghans, I. Ludolphy, K. Meier (Göttingen, 1967), 135-153. Junghans believes that Marsilio was so political that his significance for Luther was limited, but that Ockham reworked Marsilio's teaching theologically and was therefore more important for Luther, 135. See also S. C. Tornay, "Occam's Political Philosophy," *Church History* 4 (1935), 214-223; and A. S. McGrade, *The Political*

Thought of William of Ockham. Personal and Institutional Principles (Cambridge, 1974), part 3, Theory of Institutions: Secular and Spiritual Government, 78-172.

7. H. Junghans, "Wittenberg und Luther - Luther und Wittenberg," *Freiburger Zeitschrift für Philosophie und Theologie* 25 (1978), 104-119, this specific reference, 118.

8. For representative literature on this vast subject see W. Schweitzer, *Die Herrschaft Christi und der Staat im Neuen Testament* (München, 1949); H. W. Beyer, *Der Christ und die Bergpredigt nach Luthers Deutung* (2nd ed., München, 1935); Harald Diem, *Luthers Lehre von den zwei Reichen, untersucht von seinem Verständnis der Bergpredigt aus* (München, 1938); Hermann Diem, *Luthers Predigt in den zwei Reichen* (1947) republished along with his brother Harald's work and an excellent bibliography prepared by J. Haun in: *Theologische Bücherei. Neudrucke und Berichte aus dem 20. Jahrhundert. Systematische Theologie. Zur Zwei-Reiche-Lehre Luthers* (München, 1973); G. Wünsch, *Die Bergpredigt bei Luther. Eine Studie zum Verhältnis von Christentum und Welt* (Tübingen, 1920); P. Althaus, *Paulus und Luther über den Menschen* (Gütersloh, 1938; 4th ed., 1963); P. Meinhold, *Römer 13. Obrigkeit, Widerstand, Revolution, Krieg* (Stuttgart, 1960); G. Hillerdal, "Römer 13 und Luthers Lehre von den zwei Regimenten," *Lutherische Rundschau* 13 (1963), 17-34; G. Scharffenorth, *Römer 13 in der Geschichte des politischen Denkens. Ein Beitrag zur Klärung der politischen Traditionen in Deutschland seit dem 15. Jahrhundert* (Diss. Heidelberg, 1964).

9. See A. Jepsen, "Was kann das Alte Testament zum Gespräch über die Zwei-Reiche-Lehre beitragen?", *Lutherische Rundschau* 15 (1965), 427-440. Four volumes of collected essays provide useful scholarly analyses and texts: U. Duchrow and H. Hoffmann, eds., *Die Vorstellung von den Zwei Reichen und Regimenten bei Luther. Texte zur Kirchen- und Theologiegeschichte* 17 (Gütersloh, 1973); U. Duchrow, W. Huber, and L. J. Reith, eds., *Umdeutungen der Zweireichelehre Luthers im 19. Jahrhundert* (Gütersloh, 1975); H. H. Schrey, ed., *Reich Gottes und Welt. Die Lehre Luthers von den zwei Reichen* (Darmstadt, 1969); G. Wolf, ed., *Luther und die Obrigkeit* (Darmstadt, 1972).

Luther clearly differentiated the "two kingdoms", spiritual and secular, in *Temporal Authority: To What Extent it Should be Obeyed* 1523, WA 11, 245--280; LW 45, 81-129, in his *Commentary on the Gospel of St. John* 1529, WA 28, 70-264, and elsewhere.

10. J. Heckel, *Im Irrgarten der Zwei-Reiche-Lehre* (München, 1957), discusses the complications of the theory and of the scholarly debate about it. I. Iserloh, J. Glazik, H. Jedin, *Reformation and Counter Reformation, History of the Church* 5 (New York, 1980), 217, speak of the "polemical situation [which] resulted in exaggerations and one-sidedness which not even Luther could maintain to the end. This led in turn to contradictions, which make Luther's doctrine of the two kingdoms seem even today to be a 'maze'." This charge is vaguely reminiscent of that made by sixteenth century polemicists who accused Luther of contradictions by comparing his mature views with his youthful views.

11. BSLK 459-460; BC 315.

12. WA 51, 524-525; LW 41, 221. J. Rogge, "Luthers Kirchenverständnis," 197.

13. See the excellent discussion by P. Althaus, "The Church as the Community of Saints (*Communio Sanctorum*)," *The Theology of Martin Luther* (Philadelphia, 1966), 294-322. In *Communio Sanctorum, I, Die Gemeinde im lutherischen Kirchengedanken* (München, 1929), Althaus relates Luther's understanding of "church" with the New Testament's and contrasts it with that of Catholicism with its hierarchical and highly institutionalized definition. See also H. Preus, *The Communion of Saints. A Study of the Origin and Development of Luther's Doctrine of the Church* (Minneapolis, 1948) and F. Kattenbusch, "Die Doppelschichtigkeit in Luthers Kirchenbegriff," *Lutherana* 5, nos. 2/3 (1928), 237, on the church as the holy congregation which is the final purpose of God here in time and in the hereafter.

14. WA 7, 219; PE 2, 373.

15. WA 50, 624; LW 41, 143.

16. WA 8, 491; LW 36, 144.

17. WA 51, 507; LW 41, 210.

18. WA 3, 259; LW 10, 216 f.

19. Wa 7, 683; LW 39, 218. On the visible/invisible nature of the church, see W. Elert, *The Structure of Lutheranism* I (St. Louis, 1962), 255-402, especially 261-267; WA 7, 720: The church indeed lives in the flesh, but "just as the Church is not without food and drink in this life, and yet, according to Paul, the Kingdom of God does not consist in eating and drinking, so also the Church is not without place and body and yet body and place are not the Church nor do they pertain to her," cited in E. Iserloh, et al., *Reformation and Counter Reformation*, 216. See E. Rietschel, *Das Problem der unsichtbar-sichtbaren Kirche bei Luther* (Leipzig, 1932), 33-34.

20. Luther to Amsdorf, 1542, in E. L. Enders and G. Kawerau, eds., *Luthers Briefwechsel* (Leipzig, 1884-1932), 14, 175.

21. WA 50, 629-633; LW 41, 148-172. Besides the three basic signs Luther discusses seven or more indications that the true church is visibly present among Christians in given localities.

22 WA 11, 408-416; LW 39, 305-314. See also J. O. Evjen, "Luther's Ideas Concerning Church Polity," *The Lutheran Church Review* 45 (1926), 207-237, 339-373. WA 6, 564; LW 36, 112: "If the clergy were forced to admit that as many of us as have been baptized are all equally priests, as we truly are, and that only the ministry was committed to them, but with our consent, they would soon know that they have no right to rule over us except insofar as we freely agree to it."

23. WA 11, 408-416; LW 39, 301-314. "Therefore, whoever has the office of preaching imposed on him has the highest office in Christendom imposed on him."

24. WA 7, 709-710.

25. WA 19, 72-113; LW 53, 51-90.

26. WA 10 III, 215-216.

27. E. F. Klug, "Luther on the Church," *Concordia Theological Quarterly* 47, no. 3 (July, 1983),

193-207, presents an excellent summary of Luther's understanding of the church and points out that the Lutheran Confessions parallel these definitions very closely.

28. WA 26, 506; LW 37, 367. E. F. Klug, "Luther on the Church," 198.

29. Cf. L. W. Spitz, "Luther's Ecclesiology and his Concept of the Prince as *Notbischof*," *Church History* 22 (1953), 3-31.

30. WA 19, 625; LW 46, 95 f.

31. WA 11, 246; LW 45, 83 f.

32. WA 11, 245-280; LW 45, 75-129; WA 18, 62-125, 134-214; LW 40, 73-223; WA 30 II, 107-148; LW 46, 155-205. G. Rupp, *The Righteousness of God. Luther Studies* (London, 1953), 288, n. 4, gives a list of seven treatises specifically concerned with *Obrigkeit*. A similar list of key passages on the distinction between the spiritual and secular authorities is to be found in G. Hillerdal, *Gehorsam gegen Gott und Menschen* (Göttingen, 1955), 18, n. 2. See the excellent collection of contemporary essays in G. Wolf, ed., *Luther und die Obrigkeit* (Darmstadt, 1972).

33. LW 46, 204-205.

34. See J. Binder, *Luthers Staatsauffassung* (Erfurt, 1924), 7. H. Jordan, *Luthers Staatsauffassung. Ein Beitrag zu der Frage des Verhältnisses von Religion und Politik* (München, 1917; repr. Darmstadt, 1968), traces the development of Luther's view of the state from his still medieval perspective before 1517 through the periods 1517-1521, 1521-1526, and 1527-1546, with his increasing involvement in political developments. G. Törnvall, *Geistliches und weltliches Regiment bei Luther* (München, 1947), 9, writes: "With the doctrine of the two rules Luther wants to make clear for the worldview of faith the fact that God rules the world in two different ways, namely on the one hand the rule with the Word and on the other the rule with secular power or authority." Törnvall suggests that more is to be gained by dealing with the problem in terms of the twofold aspect of God's own rule than from the level of human institutions. E. Brandenburg, *Martin*

Luthers Anschauung vom Staate und der Gesellschaft
(Halle, 1901) maintains Luther's social and
political conservatism. See also E. Walder,
"Reformation und Moderner Staat," *Archiv des
historischen Vereins des Kanton Bern* 65/66
(1980/81), 445-583.

35. H. Bornkamm, *Luthers geistige Welt* (2nd ed.,
Gütersloh, 1953), 267. F. Lau, *"Äuszerlich
Ordnung" und "weltlich Ding" in Luthers Theologie*
(Göttingen, 1933), 59, asserted that family,
vocation, and government are bulwarks against the
chaos that Satan seeks to create.

36. WA 52, 26; WA 36, 385. E. Brandenburg, *Martin
Luthers Anschauung vom Staate und Gesellschaft*,
2-8, interpreted Luther's stress on the negative
function of the state as part of his medieval
inheritance, but it is also clearly Biblical.

37. W. Elert, *Die Morphologie des Luthertums* II
(München, 1953), 46.

38. WA 30 II, 554-556.

39. WA 11, 261; LW 45, 104. See R. Hermann, *Die
Gestalt Samsons bei Luther* (Berlin, 1952); E.
Kohlmeyer, "Die Geschichtsbetrachtung Luthers,"
Archiv für Reformationsgeschichte 37 (1940),
150-169; H. Zahrnt, *Luther deutet Geschichte.
Erfolg und Misserfolg im Licht des Evangeliums*
(München, 1952), 191-192.

40. See the study of the evolution and inversion of
Luther's doctrine which developed during the 19th
century, U. Duchrow, *Two Kingdoms: The Use and
Misuse of a Lutheran Theological Concept* (Geneva,
1977). Inevitably in the 20th century Luther's
Zwei-Reiche theological concepts were perverted to
the political and ideological purposes of nation-
alists and national socialists. During the First
World War the two powers were viewed as the church
in its place and the Kaiser's sword. Interestingly enough Luther's dedicated defamer Hartmann
Grisar, S. J., wrote a little noticed book, harsh
but to the point, entitled *Der deutsche Luther im
Weltkrieg und in der Gegenwart* (Augsburg, 1924).
The Nazis went even further, of course, not
allowing the church even a merely "harmless
spiritual" role, but through the "German

Christians" using the institutional church for
their wicked purposes.

41.   WA 10 III, 19; LW 51, 78.

42.   WA 28, 286; LW 37, 185 f. W. Günter, *Martin
      Luthers Vorstellung von der Reichsverfassung*
      (Münster, 1976), 177-179, relates that after the
      failure of the Diet at Augsburg 1530 Luther was
      convinced by Philipp of Hesse and the jurists that
      the empire was a *regnum politicum* in an Aristote-
      lian sense, that the emperor was therefore under
      the law as an elected official, and could be
      called to account by the lesser magistrates, the
      estates. In later years Luther used not only
      arguments from imperial custom and the good old
      law of the empire, but even some "natural law"
      arguments justifying resistance to imperial
      aggression. H. Angermeier, *Reichsreform und
      Reformation* (München, 1983), 74-76, concludes that
      the Reformation had a tremendous impact upon the
      efforts to reform the empire, aiding the territo-
      rial estates at the expense of the Catholic church
      and encouraging them toward the goals set already
      at the time of Maximilian I of liberty, compe-
      tence, institutionalism, and general welfare. See
      also H. Angermeier, "Reichsreform und Reformation
      in der deutschen Geschichte," *Säkulare Aspekte der
      Reformationszeit*, H. Angermeier and R. Seyboth,
      eds. (München - Wien, 1983), 1-26.

43.   C. Shoenberger, "The Development of the Lutheran
      Theory of Resistance 1523-1530," *The Sixteenth
      Century Journal* 8 (1977), 61-76. W. D. J. C.
      Thompson, "The 'Two Kingdoms' and 'Two Regiments':
      Some Problems of Luther's 'Zwei-Reiche-Lehre',"
      The Journal of Theological Studies 20 (1969),
      164-185, emphasized the theological source of
      Luther's political perspective. On princely
      resistance to the emperor, see K. Müller, *Luthers
      Äusserungen über das Recht des bewaffneten Wider-
      stands gegen den Kaiser* (München, 1915); J.
      Heckel, "Widerstand gegen die Obrigkeit? Pflicht
      und Recht zum Widerstand bei Martin Luther,"
      Zeitwende 25 (1954), 156-168. Some of the politi-
      cal interplay between the Protestant princes and
      the emperor is described by A. J. Dueck, "Religion
      and Temporal Authority in the Reformation: The
      Controversy Among the Protestants Prior to the
      Peace of Nuremberg, 1532," *The Sixteenth Century
      Journal* 13 (1982), 55-74. Philipp of Hesse argued

that the emperor could expect obedience on the part of the estates only when he did what was "right", a decisive step in the direction of active resistance. See W. Becker, *Reformation und Revolution* (Münster, 1974), 75. See also H. Scheible, ed., *Das Widerstandsrecht als Problem der deutschen Protestanten 1523-1546* (Gütersloh, 1969).

44. WA 11, 249-253; LW 45, 88-94; WA 10 I, 454; WA 16, 353; WA 22, 69; WA 31 I, 192; LW 13, 43 f.

45. WA 6, 408-409; LW 44, 129 f.

46. WA 31 I, 436; LW 14, 114.

47. WA 30 II, 115; LW 46, 155-205; WA 19, 623-662; LW 46, 87-137.

48. WA 11, 260-261; LW 45, 103 f.: "Here you ask further whether the policemen, hangmen, jurists, counselors, and lesser officials can also be Christians and have a blessed estate. I answer: If the government and its sword are a divine service... then also that must be divine service which the government needs to wield the sword.... Therefore, when [the authorities] do this, not with the intention of seeking their own ends but only of helping to maintain the law and power with which the wicked are restrained, there is no peril in it for them, and they may follow it like any other pursuit and use it as a means of support.... For... love of neighbor seeks not its own, considers not how great or small but how profitable and how needful for the neighbor or the community the actions are."

49. WA 11, 260-261; LW 45, 103 f.; WA 51, 238; LW 13, 193: "For God is a mild, rich Lord who scatters much gold, silver, riches, principalities, and kingdoms among the heathen as if they were chaff or sand. So He also scatters among them lofty reason, wisdom, languages, rhetoric, so that His dear Christians look like plain children, fools, and beggars next to them."

50. WA 31 I, 191-192; LW 13, 44-51, on Psalm 82:1: "God stands in the congregation of God and is Judge among the gods."

51. J. T. McNeil, "Natural Law in the Thought of Luther," *Church History* 10 (1941), 211-227. See also F. Gogarten, *Die Lehre von den zwei Reichen und das natürliche Gesetz* (1935) and M. Schloemann, *Natürliches und Gepredigtes Gesetz bei Luther* (Berlin, 1960), on the unity of Luther's concept of the law and opposition to the antinomians. Theologians have divided on whether Luther had a "natural" natural law doctrine or rather one derived from revelation. Similarly some have tried to unite the two kingdoms in his teaching by declaring that both are under the royal kingship of Christ. But in the words of Francesco Petrarch at least sometimes "truth is lost through overmuch discussion."

52. F. X. Arnold, *Zur Frage des Naturrechts bei Martin Luther* (München, 1936), 87-91, 111-116. Arnold is critical of Karl Holl for "overmodernizing" Luther's understanding of natural law, 25, 85-86. G. Wingren, *Luther on Vocation* (Philadelphia, 1957), 44-45,. holds with H. M. Müller that for Luther the *lex naturae* and the law of love were identical, and that the real line of distinction is to be drawn between the universal law of love (*lex charitatis*) which makes demands on all human beings and the spontaneous love of the Christian which springs from his/her new life in Christ.

53. WA 18, 80; LW 40, 96 f.

54. WA 6, 60; LW 45, 307. WA 11, 279; LW 45, 127 f. Luther declares that one should always act so "that love and natural law always prevail. For when you judge according to love, you will easily decide and judge all things without any lawbooks. But when you ignore love and natural law, you will never manage to please God, even though you have devoured all the lawbooks and jurists."

55. WA 51, 211; LW 13, 159 f. See also J. Heckel, *Lex Charitatis. Eine juristische Untersuchung über das Recht in der Theologie Martin Luthers* (München, 1953).

56. WA 30 II, 562; LW 46, 242: "All temporal government and bodily existence are subjected by God to man's reason."

57. WA 28, 527.

58.	WA 19, 440.

59.	WA 19, 648-649; LW 46, 121-123.

60.	WA 15, 278.

61.	K. Mathes, *Das Corpus Christianum bei Luther im Lichte seiner Erforschung* (Berlin, 1929), rehearsed the historiography of the problem. R. Sohm, the historian of church law, gave the classic formulation to the *corpus christianum* concept, *Kirchenrecht*, I (Leipzig, 1892), 548 ff. E. Troeltsch, the sociologist of religion, did almost irreparable damage to historical truth by accepting the idea that Luther was still entrapped by *corpus christianum* thinking, by misinterpreting Luther's natural law concept, and by asserting that Luther accepted a "double morality" for the two kingdoms, *Die Soziallehren der christlichen Kirchen und Gruppen* (Tübingen, 1912), 466 ff. It is not possible to rehearse the vast bibliography on this subject, the works of K. Rieker, R. Wolff, K. Müller, F. Meinecke, and many lesser scholars, but a more recent intelligent treatment meriting special mention is that of H. Bornkamm, *Luther's Doctrine of the Two Kingdoms in the Context of his Theology*, trans. by K. H. Hertz (Philadelphia, 1966). Bornkamm describes Luther's two-kingdom teaching as three dimensional, retaining something of the medieval relationship of church and state, the relationship of the spiritual and secular kingdoms of Christ and of the world respectively, and the Christian's activity for oneself and others.

62.	WA 56, 123.

63.	WA 51, 239-240; LW 13, 194-196. J. Tonkin, *The Church and the Secular Order in Reformation Thought* (New York - London, 1971), compares Luther's dialectical approach with Calvin's stress on salvation history and with Menno Simons' thoroughgoing dualism. Among the magisterial reformers Ulrich Zwingli went the farthest in the direction of state-churchism, a form of theocracy. Calvin sought to free the church from government control following Luther in asserting the difference in function and competences of church and state. In recent times H. H. Brunner, son of the famous Zürich theologian E. Brunner, wrote a kind of utopian description of what the church in

Switzerland would be like when freed from all
dependence upon the state, *Kirche ohne Illusionen.*
Experimenteller Report aus der Zeit nach dem 7.
Juli 1983 (Zürich, 1968).

64. See A. Seifert, *Weltlicher Staat und Kirchen-
     reform. Die Seminarpolitik im 16. Jahrhundert*
     (Münster, 1978). A good picture of Luther's
     active involvement with secular governments in
     promoting the Reformation can be gathered from a
     reading of K. Trüdinger, *Luthers Briefe und
     Gutachten an weltliche Obrigkeiten zur Durch-
     führung der Reformation* (Münster, 1975), and the
     outstanding work of E. Wolgast, *Die Wittenberger
     Theologie und die Politik der Evangelischen Stände*
     (Gütersloh, 1977).

65. The two kingdoms teaching of Luther remains a much
     discussed theme in modern theology, R. Ohlig, *Die
     Zwei-Reiche-Lehre Luthers in der Auslegung der
     deutschen lutherischen Theologie der Gegenwart
     seit 1945* (Bern, 1974); C. Walther, "Hat die Lehre
     von den zwei Reichen noch einen Sinn?," *Luther.
     Zeitschrift der Luther-Gesellschaft* (1978), 15-24.
     Walther concludes that "the double-aspect of the
     two kingdoms not only has the call constantly to
     reaffirm the ground of faith and its reality, but
     with the certainty of faith again and again to
     take the step into the uncertainty and inconclu-
     siveness of human life." Two essays by E. Wolf
     underscore the continued relevance of Luther's
     thought on the two kingdoms, "Königsherrschaft
     Christi und lutherische Zwei-Reiche-Lehre,"
     207-229, and "Kirche, Staat, Gesellschaft,"
     261-283, in: *Peregrinatio, II, Studien zur
     reformatorischen Theologie, zum Kirchenrecht und
     zur Sozialethik* (München, 1965). Luther's two
     kingdoms' approach, for it was not a "doctrine",
     is relevant also to the American scene, both now,
     with a benign government, and in the future,
     should our democracy ever give way to hostile
     tyranny. Not only German Lutherans, but also
     German Methodists such as W. Nast were interested
     in maintaining the separation of church and state,
     but held both to be under God's rule. See C. F.
     W. Walther, *Die Kirche frei vom Staate. 66
     Leitsätze mit biblischen Beweisstellen entnommen
     aus D. C. F. W. Walthers Referat: "Die rechte
     Gestalt einer vom Staate unabhängigen Ortsgemein-
     de"*, O. Willkomm, ed. (Zwickau, 1919); L. W.
     Spitz, *Life in Two Worlds. A Biography of William*

Sihler (St. Louis - London, 1968), 152-171; and C. Wittke, *William Nast, Patriarch of German Methodism* (Detroit, 1959).

Jürgen Moltmann

REFORMATION AND REVOLUTION

I. MARTIN LUTHER AND THOMAS MÜNTZER

Martin Luther and Thomas Müntzer - these are not
simply names of historical personages out of the 16th
century, but also symbols for different fronts in a
battle which embroils the world even today. Because of
this, the images of these two remain fluid in history
and controversial, needing to be defined anew for each
succeeding age. The names, themselves, stand for
certain confessional stances, summoning one to judge
for or against. What do they stand for?

Martin Luther: this name, brilliant and universally recognized, stands for the Reformation of the
church in the 16th century, for the courageous confession of a single man before the Emperor and the German
nation at the Diet of Worms in 1521, for the free and
unadulterated proclamation of the gospel, for the
justification of sinners by grace alone, for freedom of
faith and freedom of conscience - and also for the
narrow limits of the Protestant princely territory.

Thomas Müntzer: this name, repressed and largely
unknown, stands for the linking of the reformation
message to the liberation struggle of the downtrodden
and exploited peasants throughout Europe in the 16th
century, for the right to revolt against brutal despot-
ism, for the judgment of history against those in

power, for the liberation of the poor, for "divine justice" in all things - and also for the apocalyptic illusions and shoddy organization which led to the terrible defeat of the peasants on May 15, 1525, at Frankenhausen.

The memory of **Martin Luther** has been cherished and celebrated in Protestant churches since the beginning: each Reformation Festival on October 31st recalls his posting the *Ninety-Five Theses* on the door of Castle Church in Wittenberg, every 10th, 50th, and 100th anniversary of his birth and death calls for a celebration. Many Protestant churches are named "Lutheran" churches after him.

The memory of **Thomas Müntzer,** on the other hand, has been imperiled and suppressed from the start. Immediately after his torture and execution at the hands of the Catholic Count Ernst of Mansfield, a pamphlet containing the purported *Confession of Thomas Müntzer*[1] appeared in support of the claim that after acknowledging his crimes, Müntzer had returned penitent into the bosom of the Catholic church. Luther, Melanchthon, and the other reformers who had come out in support of the princes and against the Peasants' Revolt, portrayed Müntzer as the "agitator against God and authority" *par excellence*, a revolutionary who received his proper due, who could not stand law and authority, but who attacked and fought against it, wanting to crush it and instead establish himself as the lord and law-giver. His writings were outlawed and destroyed in the Protestant lands and cities to such an extent that even today it is difficult to locate many of them.

Interest in Müntzer was first reawakened in connection with a renewed interest in the liberation

struggle of the peasants themselves. This occurred at
the time of the German bourgeois revolution in 1848, a
revolution inspired by the ideas of the French and
American Revolutions, fighting against the sovereign
rule and spirit of subjugation. With this common
connection, the old story of the peasants, of the
"early bourgeois revolution" (*frühbürgerliche Revolution*), was brought back to life. The peasants became
"forerunners" of the freedom-fighters of 1848 who also
adopted the earlier ideas of the "common man", of
"*Bundschuh*" and "confederacy", as well as the vision of
a "free people on free land." In 1848/1849, Friedrich
Engels understood the "German Peasants' War" to be the
first of three decisive battles waged by European
commoners against feudalism.[2] The sad parallel he also
found was that in both 1525 and in 1848 the insurgent
people were left in the lurch by a half-hearted mid-
dle-class and thus perished through lack of leadership.
For Engels, reformation and revolution go together; the
Reformation and the Peasants' War in the 16th century
were united phenomena: revolution begins with reformation and reformation is fulfilled in revolution. The
true inheritance of the peasants' unsuccessful liberation movement had passed over to the new socialism of
the workers and commoners.

Ever since Engels' analysis in the revolutionary
year of 1848, Thomas Müntzer has also been honored, not
by the churches of the Reformation, but by the socialist movement. As the "theologian of revolution", a
title given to him by Ernst Bloch in 1921, he has found
his proper place in the revolutionary tradition of
German history.[3] Wilhelm Pieck, then president of the
German Democratic Republic, noted this fact in his

speech on democratic land-reform in East Germany on
September 2, 1945, when he said:

> The centuries-old dream of the peasants and
> farm workers to take the land of the petty
> nobility into their own hands must now be
> realized... I would have you remember the
> great Peasants' War of 1525... where under
> the leadership of Thomas Müntzer the destruc-
> tion of feudalism, the equality of all
> people, and the institution of a true democ-
> racy was demanded....[4]

However, this history of freedom in Germany does
not only aim at socialism, but also at democracy.
Müntzer did not dream of a "dictatorship of the proletariat," nor of the party claiming to represent the
proletariat, but rather of the equality of the people
under the "sole rule of divine justice."[5] Thus it is
not proper to use Müntzer's legacy one-sidedly. Though
East German Marxism always regarded the Reformation and
the Peasants' War as the unified expression of the
"early bourgeois revolution" and never saw Luther and
Müntzer in contrast, but as two representatives of the
same cause, there has nevertheless been a decided
preference for the "people's rebel" Müntzer over
against the "princes' vassal" Luther. The communist
parties have up to now never celebrated any Reformation
festivals, but have annually remembered the Peasants'
War. In 1925 Ernst Thälmann wrote: "Jubilees are not
empty commemoration days for communists and the class-
conscious part of the proletariat, but guiding principles for the class struggle, guidelines for action."[6]
And in 1975 one reads: "The legacy of the revolutionaries of the 16th century is being, and will be fulfilled in the German Democratic Republic."[7]

In 1983, this attitude seems to have shifted. The East German government has decided officially to celebrate the 500th anniversary of Martin Luther's birth. A special Luther committee, led by the head-of-state, Erich Honecker, has been set up to plan the event. Luther is welcomed back into the history and tradition of the first socialist state in Germany. East Germany, being the homeland of the Reformation, celebrates him as "one of the greatest sons of the German people" and as "one of the most important humanists": "By taking up the struggle and declaring that 'the church stands in need of reformation' Luther precipitated also a movement which led to social progress," declared Honecker.[8]

Is Luther, then, no longer a "betrayer of the peasants" and "vassal of the princes," but rather a spiritual revolutionary whom Müntzer, the political revolutionary, was bound to follow? Are we no longer to think in terms of "revolution contra reformation," but of "revolution and reformation"?[9] If it is said of Luther that he was not a "betrayer of peasants," but that he acted as a bourgeois intellectual of his century, what can then be said of Müntzer? - that he was a "deviation toward the left," an "agitator" who "aimed at great things at a time when the general development of history was not yet ready for them?" - a development that "progressed toward bourgeois circumstances rather than to a utopian classless society," as the East German historian Gerhard Zschäbitz put it in his book on Luther.[10] If this assessment of Müntzer becomes official, doesn't it put him and the peasants' rebellion close to Lech Walesa and the democratic socialism of the people from below - "Solidarity" - against the dictatorial "socialism from above?" And supposing this historical parallel comes too close for comfort, would not then Luther, the supporter of the state, once again be considered a more convenient partner for the ruling "authorities," even within the socialist state than the prophet and rebel Müntzer?

Müntzer's image has changed according to the whims and interests of history. What do we really know of him historically? Who was he and what did he want?

II.   THE RAPID RISE AND FALL OF THOMAS MÜNTZER

Thomas Müntzer was presumably born around 1468 as the son of an artisan family in Stolberg/Harz. Until 1520 there is nothing remarkable to be reported about his life, but then he entered the limelight of history and in only five years became, next to Luther, the most independent, original, and influential thinker of his time.

His development was quite straightforward and normal: he entered the Augustinian order in Quedlinburg, studied in 1506 as a monk in Leipzig, and in 1512 in Frankfurt/Oder where he received his Master of Arts degree. On the side he worked as a "collaborator" (assistant) in the service of both church and school, became a teacher in Halberstadt and a prior for the convent Frohse near Aschersleben. Like many others in his time, Müntzer tried to make a quick ecclesiastical career for himself. And then in 1518/19 it so happened in Leipzig that, through a personal encounter with Luther, he was seized by the Reformation spirit.

He joined the "Wittenberg Circle" and became himself a Reformer with the full passion of his soul. Called to preach in the city of Jüterbog in 1519, he was considered a "follower of Martin," as the first

Lutherans were then called. He preached the Scripture,
the Scripture alone, liberated from accretions of
centuries of tradition. He proclaimed the faith,
liberated from ecclesiastical laws and customs. He
called for the formation of a general council in order
to reform the entire body of the church. This provoked
at once a vehement quarrel with the Jüterbog Francis-
cans. Luther was notified of the situation and came
down on Müntzer's side. "Müntzer recognized in Luther
the course-setting pioneer of the evangelical truth,"
while "Luther saw in Müntzer an open mind, emphatically
committed to his cause."[11] There arose between them a
solidarity of fighting spirits based on mutual trust.
Müntzer was also present at Luther's *Leipzig Debate*
with Eck, so important in Luther's progression from
reform to a reformation of the church. There Müntzer
probably came to see that it was not enough to criticize the church's shortcomings, but that it was necessary to put Christ's gospel above everything: God's
word and will alone!

When in 1520 the preaching position at St. Cather-
ine's in the up-and-coming industrial town of Zwickau
opened up, Luther himself recommended his trusted
follower for the position. Müntzer's preaching was
acute, lively, and inflammatory, provoking agreement
and opposition, *pro* and *con*. He was sure of Luther's
protection in any conflict. 1520 was the year in which
Luther's great Reformation writings appeared: *On the
Freedom of the Christian*,[12] *The Babylonian Captivity of
the Church*,[13] and *An Appeal to the German Nobility*.[14]
His criticism of the church fell on fertile soil with
Müntzer who defended it and spread the message abroad.

Then, however, he came into contact with a completely different reformation group in Zwickau: the

so-called "anabaptists" or "fanatics," led by their
"prophet," Nikolaus Storch. Over against much malicious polemic one must keep in mind that this anabaptist movement represented basically nothing more than
an early pietistic brand of community-oriented Christianity on the fringes of the official church - one
fastened upon Holy Scripture, rejecting infant baptism
as unbiblical and involuntary, understanding personal
faith as the coming of the Holy Spirit to dwell in the
heart, and attempting to reform the church according to
the prototype of the primitive Christian community
(Acts 4:32-35). As in Zürich, so also in Zwickau these
"prophets" came from the educated, humanistic strata of
society. Yet their communities were found especially
"among the lower classes." To say, even in the 20th
century, that they "replaced the Bible with inner
illumination, and that they saw the experience of the
cross instead of justification by faith as a new way to
salvation"[15] is nothing less than Lutheran defamation
still today. What Müntzer learned from the Zwickau
prophets was the significance of what he called "the
advent of faith" in the human being.

But Nikolaus Storch also had personal contacts
with the Hussite movement in Bohemia. Through him
Müntzer became acquainted with the pre-Reformation
movement of the Hussites. He came at least to that
conclusion, namely, that there can be no reform of the
church in society without a corresponding reform of the
society itself. The "arrival of the faith" in a person
cannot take place without that person's entering upon
the way of a disciple of Jesus and taking upon oneself
his cross in the battle. Church reform without social
reform is just as half-baked as a correct faith without
an authentic life in the discipleship of Jesus.

Radical discipleship of Jesus, however, means suffering, self-denial, and persecution in the world. Thus,
church and society can be renewed only through a period
of suffering. In Zwickau Müntzer became embroiled in
the controversy with the Lutheran Egranus, out of which
he developed the foundations of his political theology
of the cross. For this reason he was forced to leave
Zwickau in 1522.

It is significant that at this point his hope
turned from Wittenberg to Prague. He lived for several
months in Bohemia, spoke with the elders of the Brethren church, studied the Hussite writings, preached in
the Bethlehem's Chapel and in the Teyn Church at
Prague, and participated in a demonstration commemorating Hus on the seventh of July. He became, one could
say, one of them. On All Saints Day that year he went
public with his *Prague Manifesto*[16] hoping that it would
win the Hussite congregations over to his plan for a
great apocalyptic *reformatio mundi*, a reformation of
the world. It was his reformation creed at this time.
The right way led from the church to Holy Scripture and
from Scripture to an internal faith generated by the
Spirit. Priests and scribes should no longer rule,
since only the true believers, the elect, actually
experience the friendly inner voice of God. The "new
church" is a fellowship of true believers, without
domination by hierarchy of theologians.

Was Müntzer's orientation already political? Had
he become a follower of Hus or a radical Taborite? The
question is superfluous: Müntzer's path from the
ecclesiastical rule of the church to faith in Scripture
and to a personal, inner experience of faith led
necessarily to communal fellowships and communal
democracy, or "basic community" and "basic democracy"

as one calls it today. For God will "shortly" give the
kingdom of this world over to the elect, and God will
destroy the godless who have up to now usurped the
kingdom by force. After his stay in Prague, Müntzer's
criticism and vision were more and more reinforced by
such an apocalyptic expectation.

On Easter, 1523, Thomas Müntzer became the preacher at Allstedt in the electorate of Saxony, a small
town inhabited mainly by farmers. He soon established
himself as the dominating figure in the area. His
sermons were convincing to the town council, the
citizenry, and the peasants from the surrounding
villages. He must have come across with the certainty
of a *nuntius Christi*, convinced that he would bring to
a successful conclusion the work Luther had begun. As
for Luther himself, he was able, upon his return from
the Wartburg, to reestablish peace and order after the
1522 riots in Wittenberg by his famous *Eight Wittenberg
Sermons*:[17] the Reformation should proceed not through
violence but through God's word, and one should take
careful consideration of the consciences of the weak.
This admonition provided his disciple Müntzer with the
clue for his own work; he would carry out what Luther
did not yet dare to do himself. Luther, according to
Müntzer, did not want to put a stumbling-block in the
way of the ignorant ones because they were still just
newborn children in the faith; but these "babes" were
now over a century old! He would not understand at all
why Luther supposed that one must still wait. Christianity has really no more time to waste.

And so he started with the reform of the worship
service, creating in his *German Evangelical Mass* and
German Church Office, the first evangelical liturgy in
the German language.[18] Luther was to follow him in

1526 with his own *German Mass*.[19]   Müntzer's liturgical
writings remained in use in Erfurt and Braunschweig
well into the 19th century. His worship service in the
vernacular and his popular sermons made him known
everywhere. But at the same time, believing as he did
in the imminent coming of Christ, he prepared the
gathering of the elect people for the kingdom near at
hand. He formed a "covenant of the faithful and divine
will," which besides the Allstedt congregation also
included Mansfeld miners and followers from far beyond
North Thuringia. He wanted to collect and to prepare
the true believers: neither can the reign of Christ
come nor the tyrants be overthrown without a re-educa-
tion of the people. In Allstedt Müntzer saw his main
task in preparing the people for this upheaval.

In his theological work *On Fictitious Faith* 1524[20]
Müntzer disengaged himself from the, in his opinion,
inconsequential "justification by faith" position of
the Wittenberg theologians. A critical point had
thereby become acute: Allstedt turned into a
"counter-Wittenberg," a new center of the Reformation.
The people devoted themselves to Müntzer, so that
Luther felt he had to warn the princes about Müntzer's
"rebellious spirit," saying that he was "completely
possessed of the Devil" (1524).[21] Müntzer for his part
attempted to justify himself before Duke John of Saxony
in a sermon on the prophet Daniel's interpretation of
Nebuchadnezzar's monarchy dream by calling upon the
princes to join his "covenant of the faithful and
divine will" in time, for the kingdom of this world
would shortly be destroyed, namely in three-and-a-half
years, with the breaking in of Christ's messianic
kingdom.[22] Should the princes not convert, "the sword
will be taken away from them and given to the ardent

people to bring about the downfall of the godless," he had warned already earlier, on October 4th, 1523 in a letter to the prince.[23] The Duke reacted by demanding an immediate disbanding of the "covenant," a stop to all publishing, and a discontinuation of any rebellious preaching. The town council and officials in Allstedt submitted, and Müntzer was forced to flee, his plans foiled by both the town and the princes. He attempted to publish pamphlets in Nürnberg, among them the *Highly Provoked Defense Against the Ignorant, Easy Living Flesh in Wittenberg,*[24] as he now referred to his former hero and master Luther. Then he joined the rebelling peasants on the Upper Rhine. Finally he found refuge in the free imperial city of Mühlhausen where for a year Heinrich Pfeiffer had already been inciting insurrection against the princes. In March 1525 the two succeeded in getting a new town council elected, dominated by their own people.

At the same time almost everywhere in Germany and in other European countries the peasants' rebellion was underway: the peasants in Allgäu, Tyrol, Swabia, Franconia, Alsace, and Thuringia revolted in order to win back their ancient rights and freedoms, which had been gradually taken from them by the princes over the centuries, and to realize the "freedom of the Christian" over against the rich and propertied churches and cloisters. With surprising harmony the princes organized their forces to suppress the revolt. In April 1525 the people's movement seized Thuringia. Pfeiffer and Müntzer took over the leadership and attempted to organize the loose mass of peasants. They hoped to join up with the peasant groups from Hesse, Franconia, and Swabia. On April 27, 1525, Müntzer published a call to arms:

Take up the cause and fight the Lord's
battle. It is high time. The entire German,
French, and Italian land is at stake, the
Master is ready to play, it's the scoundrels'
turn... Don't let your sword grow cold.
Forge anew, let it ring upon Nimrod's anvil.
Cast down the proud tower at their feet.[25]

Nevertheless, he neither succeeded in mobilizing
the mass of peasants nor in organizing an alliance
between the various rebelling groups. Only around 8000
peasants gathered at Frankenhausen. Müntzer showed up
with 300 men from his "covenant of the faithful and
divine will." Meanwhile, the Protestant Landgrave of
Hesse formed an alliance with the Catholic Count of
Mansfeld and marched on Frankenhausen. The battle took
place on the 15th of May: Müntzer preached, the
peasants sang "to God the Holy Spirit let us pray...,"
and then they all waited for the divine miracle to
occur. Instead, the princes' cannons fired and the
mercenaries fell upon the virtually defenseless peasants: 6000 were slaughtered on the battlefield; 600
prisoners were later executed in the town. Müntzer
himself was able to flee but was soon found and handed
over to Count Ernst of Mansfeld as booty. The count
had him tortured in order to extort desired confessions
before executing him along with Pfeiffer on May 27, and
impaling the corpse as a deterrent for others.

Thus the back of the rebellion in Thuringia was
broken. The revenge of the princes reached horrible
proportions there as elsewhere: after the defeat of
the peasants' movement it is estimated that another
100,000 peasants in Europe were murdered, not to speak
of the thousands of mutilated people. For the rest all
that remained was the submission and lethargy of

enslaved, farm-working bond-servants. The nobility had
won. Is that, however, the end of the story? Had
Thomas Müntzer been forever "refuted" by the massacre
at Frankenhausen? "The silence of the people is an
indictment of the tyrants," reads an old German saying.

III.   LUTHER'S ATTITUDE TOWARD MÜNTZER AND THE PEASANTS

Luther's so-called "teaching of the two kingdoms"
originated from his own overwhelming experience of the
Reformation: by the word alone, not by force. The
teaching was developed, however, in his acute confron-
tation with Thomas Müntzer and the rebellious peasants.
If one returns, therefore, to his "two kingdoms teaching" today, one must inevitably end up speaking about
his attitude toward the Peasants' War.

In 1523, Luther wrote his famous treatise *Temporal
Authority: To What Extent It Should be Obeyed*.[26] Here
his opponents are, on the one side, those anabaptists
and spiritualists who wanted to live without armament
or violence according to the Sermon on the Mount, and
therefore refused governmental offices. On the other
side, he sees himself confronted with the princes who
want to impede or crush the Reformation with force. On
both sides he sees a godless confusion of the kingdoms:
on the one side politics is to be joined to religion,
and on the other religion with politics. His teaching
on the two kingdoms is intended to be a critical
differentiation between the two realms, which are
always intermixed in historical actuality. It is not a
teaching meant to establish a new Christian ethic.
Spiritual and temporal authority (*Regiment*) are distinguished by the word of God, not by political rulers.
That emphasis is often overlooked: since God in the

spiritual realm (*Regiment*) works "through the Word
without force" calling people to faith, the temporal
realm must therefore be restricted to worldly matters.
This is also easily ignored when one supposes that the
two kingdoms teaching establishes an (un)holy respect
for the autonomy of the political domain.

Finally, one must recognize that for Luther both
of God's realms are engaged in the battle against the
kingdom of Satan, and in this regard they have more in
common than their mere distinction and definition over
against each other might lead us to presume. Unfortunately, this partnership of both kingdoms in the battle
against the power of evil is all too often forgotten.

However, Luther and the controversies of his time
are not entirely without blame for the misunderstandings surrounding the two kingdoms teaching. The first
emergency situation and test of the just developed two
kingdoms teaching was not a religious or ideological
dictatorship of civil government, i.e., a perversion of
the "temporal power (*Regiment*)," but rather the upris-
ing of the peasants, which they themselves, and then
Thomas Müntzer in a massive way, saw as motivated and
legitimated by religious demands, Biblical concepts and
apocalyptic hopes - a justification of a cause which,
according to Luther's theology, was a perversion of the
"spiritual power (*Regiment*)."

In 1524, Luther wrote an *Open Letter to the
Princes of Saxony Concerning the Rebellious Spirit.*[27]
He gave them the following counsel for dealing with
Müntzer:

> Let them preach as confidently and boldly as
> they are able and against whomever they wish.
> For... there must be sects, and the Word of
> God must be under arms and fight... But when

they want to do more than fight with the
Word, and begin to destroy and use force,
then your Graces must intervene, whether it
be ourselves or they who are guilty, and
banish them from the country. You can say:
'We are willing to endure and permit you to
fight with the Word... But don't use your
fist, for that is our business, else get
yourselves out of the country.' For we who
are engaged in the ministry of the Word are
not allowed to use force.[28]

With this, Luther had fixed his position on all phases
of the Peasants' War. Is this the application of the
two kingdoms teaching "to the emergency situation of
revolution," as it is called? For who, after all, made
the "revolution" in the Peasants' War, the peasants or
the princes, the people or the tyrants?

Early in 1525, the *Twelve Articles of the Swabian
Peasantry* appeared,[29] a truly moderate program for the
restoration of the former rights, of which they had
been robbed by the princes. The peasants called on
Luther as an arbiter, and he responded with the *Admonition to Peace: A Reply to the Twelve Articles of the
Peasants in Swabia*.[30] In the first section he appeals
sharply to the consciences of the princes and lords.
In the second, he gives the peasants the same admonition he had attempted to address to the princes: they
are mixing the spiritual with the temporal realm as
they try to prove their earthly rights and demands with
the gospel and attempt to put them through by force.
Nevertheless, already in this writing a disparity can
be recognized in Luther's arguments: his view of the
foundation of rights extends only to the rights of
temporal government, not to the rights of subjects. A

civil authority perverted toward tyranny is more tolerable for him than the insurrection of subjects. "The fact that the rulers are wicked and unjust does not excuse disorder and rebellion."[31] In the name of Christ there is no right to violent resistance, only the readiness to patient suffering: "Suffering! Suffering! Cross! Cross! This and nothing else is the Christian law!"[32] Had he spoken with equal weight to both sides, then indeed he would have had to say also that no insurrection and revolt can be used as an excuse for the civil authority being evil and unjust, and that in the name of Christ there is also no right for the violent suppression of the people - and that one must not expect a readiness for suffering on the part of those who in any case are already suffering, but rather from those who oppress them and make them suffer.

Under the immediate impression of a trip through the rebellious land, and on the basis of what happened to him personally on the journey, Luther wrote in 1525 the famous/infamous piece *Against the Robbing and Murdering Hordes of Peasants*.[33] It is directed not to the peasants but to the princes, and encourages them to strike down the peasants' rebellion with every means of force. The language is as immoderate as is obviously his agitation. On that account he offends flagrantly against his own "two kingdoms teaching," when he maintains for instance:

> Thus, anyone who is killed fighting on the side of the rulers may be a true martyr in the eyes of God... On the other hand, anyone who perishes on the peasants' side is an eternal firebrand of hell... These are strange times, when a prince can win heaven

with bloodshed better than other men with prayer![34]

In this pamphlet of religious agitation in a civil war, Luther does not differ in any way from his enemy Thomas Müntzer, only that he is sitting in Wittenberg and not standing on the battlefield at Frankenhausen.

As many of his personal remarks show, Luther suffered for the rest of his life from the guilt which he brought upon himself in the Peasants' War. It is, therefore, certainly improper to search for historical explanations for these inexplicable outbursts in the above-mentioned writing. Were they moments of person- al, emotional excitation? Did he, as one in social upward mobility, have no understanding for the poverty of the peasants? Was it the deep anxiety over the work of the Reformation, that would have been destroyed by the power of the princes, had he expanded it to include the "revolution of the peasants?" We do not know what moved him, but we must know what moves us in comparable situations in which the peoples of the Third World find themselves. Can there be a reformation in spirit without a revolution on the earth? Can there be a renewal of the church in society without a renewal of society? Does not every political revolution itself need in turn a reformation of the hearts as well, so as not to degenerate into a new tyranny?

IV. POLITICAL THEOLOGIES OF THE REFORMATION

The political end of Thomas Müntzer raises first of all the question concerning the political options of the other parties active during the Reformation, for it certainly cannot be claimed that in comparison to Müntzer other theologians at that time were non-political and purely ecclesiastical and spiritual. Secondly, one must ask: what were the concrete political chances for the various political options? Finally, the question is: how do they all stand up against the claims of the gospel to which they all appeal?

The first question can be answered with a short overview: the **Roman Catholic Church** with its princely bishops relied on the Hapsburg universal monarchy. The empire of Charles V was supposed to guarantee the unity of Christendom, defend it against the Turkish threat in the East, and support its missionary work in the newly-discovered areas of America. Rome, therefore, strengthened the development of the Hapsburg monarchy towards absolutism, and Hapsburg returned the favor in the military support of the Counter Reformation.

Luther and the Wittenberg group, on the other hand, allied themselves with the princes and their special interests within the empire. By handing over many church possessions to the sovereigns, they won many of them over to carry out the Reformation in their territories. Thus arose the confessionally united **principality.** According to Müntzer, Luther had at the Diet of Worms in 1521 already come to such an understanding with his elector. In the 16th century, the result of this policy was the "Smalkaldic League" of the Protestant princes, the "Smalkaldic War" against the Hapsburgs and the Catholic princes, and the "Peace of Augsburg," and in the 17th century the "Thirty Years' War" and the peace agreements of Münster and Osnabrück in 1648.

Zwingli, Bucer and **Calvin** linked the Reformation gospel together with the free cities and the imperial cities. In contrast to the reform of the Lutheran princely territories they promoted a bourgeois city reform. For this reason, most of the imperial cities did not turn to Luther but rather to Zwingli, Bucer, and other Reformers. *Religio et libertas*, freedom of faith and the first democratic freedoms in the cities, made for the best combination. But the result of this development was freedom only for a certain elitist and educated segment of urban society, not freedom for all the people. This central European urban reformation became influential in the Puritan reformation in industrialized England and later in North America.

Thomas Müntzer, however, and the so-called "anabaptists" of the Reformation era sought the realization of the evangelical faith in the peasants' movement. Their central idea was not "the one and only saving church," nor "the one and only saving faith," nor even the freedom of religion and of the conscience for the individual, but rather "divine justice in all things." They wanted **popular reform**, reform of the people, by the people, and for the people.

The **peasants' movement** did not originate from the Reformation. It started already in the Middle Ages and represented the reaction of free peasants to the oppression and deprivation of rights forced upon them by the rise of feudalism. It cannot be called a revolution in the modern sense. Rather, it was a resistance movement based on their ancient rights and freedoms and directed against the terrorism from above of the nobility and princes. Müntzer was quite right when he warned in 1524 that the lords and princes were the source and cause of usury, thievery, and robbery, turning peasants into slaves and serfs. It was not until the Enlightenment in the 18th, and the French Revolution at the beginning of the 19th century that the people were able to recover their old freedoms.

The peasant rebellions from the 12th until the 17th century are telling signs of the people's resistance to enslavement. Müntzer thus did not join a "rebellion" or a "revolution," but rather he became a part of the ongoing resistance movement of the people against their subjugation.

Did this liberation movement of the peasants in 16th century Europe have a real chance to succeed? The shining example for all of the European peasant rebellions was the successful freedom fight of the Swiss Confederacy against its enslavement by the Austrian Hapsburg dynasty. The confederate democracy which the Swiss had established might also possibly become a reality for the people of Tyrol, Carinthia, Swabia, Thuringia, Alsace, Hungary, the Hotzen Forest, and the Black Forest!

However, these other people failed apparently because they lacked the protection of the mountains and the military organization. Thomas Müntzer endeavored to organize the loose mass of peasants, but "solidarity" is just very difficult to establish among certain people. Spies, bribery, betrayal, selfishness, and fear crippled the German resistance from the beginning. If any word of Müntzer's forced confessions can be taken as true, then it is that which puts the blame for the catastrophe at Frankenhausen on the "selfishness" of the peasants. Moreover, Müntzer himself was no general, but a theologian and apocalyptic prophet. He had more sense for apocalyptic visions than military strategy. He was able to inspire the liberation movement with the messianic hope, but beyond that he was not practical at all. This made for the difference between him and the leader of the democratic movement in 17th century England, Oliver Cromwell. Cromwell was skilled in both the religion of hope and in military organization. Therefore, he was successful where Müntzer failed.

Nonetheless, the absolutistic self-glorification of the princes who defeated Müntzer and the peasants was only to be of short duration. Within a century the minor princes were swallowed up by the major princes, who in turn were swallowed up by the kings, until the French Revolution in 1789 prepared the way for the realization of the dreams of the oppressed people: **Freedom - Equality - Fraternity.** In the long run, democracy, i.e., social democracy, prevailed in Europe. This is what the peasants' movement of the 16th century and the theologian Thomas Müntzer stood for.

Finally, the question whether one party or the other achieved historical success for a shorter or longer period is secondary to the theological issue: What is in accordance with Christ's gospel? If we compare the political options of the Reformation era with the gospel of God's kingdom which Jesus proclaimed to the poor (Luke 4:18 ff.), then it is clear to me that a proclamation of the justification of sinners without a corresponding lifting-up of the poor and a liberation of the oppressed remains incomplete and can easily lead to the justification of sin and of sinful political structures. That means, unless a Reformation theology leads necessarily to a theology of liberation, it is not a real reformation theology. Without the liberation of the poor, oppressed, and forsaken people, Luther's reformation falls short of the mark, is bogged down, and betrays its cause.

Without Martin Luther there could not have been a Thomas Müntzer, but without a Thomas Müntzer there can be no Martin Luther. Without the Reformation there

would not have been a revolution, but without a revolution there can also be no complete reformation. God's
justice must hold true in all things.

V. SYSTEMATIC IMPLICATIONS

In closing, I would like to make a few remarks
concerning the double principle I have presented:
There can be no reformation without revolution and no
revolution without reformation.

1. No Reformation without Revolution

If we understand the word "reformation" not only
as a technical, historical term, but as a theological
concept, then we use it as the Reformers did, in the
sense of a *Reformatio Dei*: it is the work of God to
reform the church into the true church of Christ
through God's word of the gospel. This Reformation
took place, of course, through Luther in the 16th
century, but it did not occur once for all times.
Rather, it must be an on-going process: *ecclesia
reformata et semper reformanda*. To be sure, there were
apocalyptically oriented theologians in the 16th
century who saw the Lutheran Reformation as the beginning of the end and considered Luther to be the angel
of Revelation 14:6 who announced the *Evangelium aeter-
num*. Without this expectation of an imminent apoca-
lypse, however, the Reformation must be understood as a
process of continuous renewal.

As *Reformatio Dei*, the work of the Reformation is
all-embracing and thus is not to be limited to any
single aspect of life, because God cannot be limited.
It is for this reason that the reformation of life must
follow upon the reformation of faith, as it was already

understood in 1563 in the so-called "Second Reformation", the Reformed movement in the Palatinate, because
faith in Christ leads directly into individual and
communal discipleship of Christ.[35]

As the Lutheran and Calvinist Reformation ossified
into the *orthodoxy* of correct doctrine, Pietism and
Puritanism, i.e., the *orthopraxy* of the pure life came
into being. If, however, the **reformation of doctrine**
and the **reformation of life** necessarily belong together, then there can be no isolated reformation of the
church in a society without a simultaneous **reformation**
of that very society. Church and society are too
closely bound together for the church to be reformed
without consequences for society.

With Luther, the consequences are clearly recog-
nizable. His concern for societal reform emerges from
the new "vocation-ethos" (*Berufsethos*) which he developed. Next to **Word** and **Sacrament**, the recognition of
the divine **vocation** of every Christian in his or her
worldly occupation is the third great insight of the
Lutheran Reformation. In fact, the Lutheran "vocation-ethos" has altered the secular world just as much
as the Calvinist-Puritan "work-ethos."

The Western European, English, and American
reformation has gone even farther: the freedom of the
proclamation of the gospel promoted and presupposed the
freedom of speech and of opinion. Freedom of faith
presupposed the **freedom of conscience** from church
authority and the **freedom of religion** from civil
authority. The freedom of the Christian community
required the freedom of assembly and thus presupposed
the freedom of republican and **democratic** polity. There
is a free church only in a free nation, that is, in a
society of fundamental human and civil rights. This

principle should be stated: there can be no
reformation of the church without the revolution of
freedom and human rights in society.

2. No Revolution without Reformation

This second principle is a bit more difficult to
determine. By it I mean that all struggles for freedom
are ambivalent. How can alienated people struggle
against alienation without producing new alienation in
the struggle? How can a revolution of oppressed people
against a dictatorship avoid the dictatorship of those
who have led that revolution and were victorious? In
the modern revolutionary movements of Marxism we have
seen the rise of the alienating and oppressing power of
Stalinism, with millions of people having been victim-
ized. In many liberation movements we have seen the
apocalyptic spirit of the "day of revenge" at work.
One may say that revolution many times swallows up not
only its enemies but also its own children. I am
saying this not to blame the popular revolutions or any
liberation movements. On the contrary, it is the
inherent contradiction in revolutions and in libera-
tions which we have to face here: how can one liberate
oneself for freedom without using force? How can the
kingdom of a free and non-violent community of human
beings be won against oppressive forces without using
violence? And if it is necessary to use "liberating
violence" in order to overcome "oppressive violence"
and "structural violence," how can one overcome the
alienating effect this course of action has on one's
own mind and one's whole people?

Karl Marx was right with his formulation that the
critique of religion leads to the "revolutionary
imperative:" "to overthrow all circumstances in which
humans are humiliated, enslaved, abandoned and despised

beings."[36]   Marx, however, did not pay any attention to
the **costs** of this action of overthrowing.   One who
believed in the liberation of people and in the vision
of a truly free and humane society, but who had experienced the alienating and oppressive structures in the
revolution itself, was the German socialist poet
Bertolt Brecht.   He wrote:

> We, who wished to prepare the soil for
> kindness
>
>> could not be kind ourselves.
>
> But you, when at last it will come to pass
> that
>
>> man is a helper to man,
>
> Remember us with forbearance.[37]

"Remember us with forbearance":   in a secular way,
Brecht has taken up what the continuous plea for the
forgiveness of sins and for reconciliation means for
the Christian faith.   This is what I would call the
necessity of the liberation and reformation by the
spirit in the revolutionary struggle.   Without the
spirit of the reformation, i.e., without forgiveness of
sins, reconciliation, and rebirth to a living hope, the
revolution can be corrupted by the revolutionaries
themselves and will lose its power to convince the
people.   This is what I would call the **reformation of
freedom**.

Therefore: there can be no reformation without
the **revolution of freedom**, and there can be no revolution without the **reformation of freedom**, until God's
justice reigns over all things.

NOTES

1. *Thomas Müntzer: Schriften und Briefe*, ed. G. Franz (Gütersloh, 1968), 544-550.

2. F. Engels, *The German Peasants' War*, tr. M. Oglin (New York, 1926).

3. E. Bloch, *Thomas Müntzer als Theologe der Revolution* (München, 1921).

4. W. Pieck, "Junkerland in Bauernhand," quoted in *Illustrierte Geschichte der Deutschen Frühbürgerlichen Revolution* (Berlin, 1974), 400-402.

5. Ibid., p. 224.

6. Quoted in the speech of W. Pieck.

7. *Martin Luther: Ahnherr der DDR?* <u>Friedrich Ebert Stiftung</u> 983, 8.

8. Quoted in "Thesen über Martin Luther zum 500. Geburtstag," *Einheit: Zeitschrift für Theorie und Praxis des wissenschaftlichen Sozialismus* (1981), 890, see also 903.

9. G. Maron, "Die Entdeckung Luthers in der DDR," *Journal für Geschichte* (1983), Heft 2, 16-19.

10. G. Zschäbitz, *Martin Luther, Grösse und Grenze* (Berlin, 1967), 202.

11. W. Elliger, *Thomas Müntzer: Leben und Werke* (Göttingen, 1975), 65.

12. WA 7, 49-73; LW 31, 333-377.

13. WA 6, 497-573; LW 36, 11-126.

14. WA 6, 404-469; LW 44, 123-217.

15. G. Franz, s.v. "Müntzer," *Die Religion in Geschichte und Gegenwart* IV, 3rd ed. (Tübingen, 1960), 1183.

16. *Schriften und Briefe*, 495-505.

17. WA 10 III, 1-64; LW 51, 70-100.

18. *Schriften und Briefe*:   "German Evangelical Mass,"
     157-206; "German Church Office," 25-155.

19. WA 19, 72-113; LW 53, 61-90.

20. *Schriften und Briefe*, 218-224.

21. WA 15, 210-221; LW 40, 49-59.

22. *Schriften und Briefe*, 242-263.

23. Ibid., 395-397.

24. Ibid., 322-343.

25. Ibid., 454.

26. WA 11, 245-281; LW 45, 81-129.

27. WA 15, 210-221; LW 40, 49-59.

28. LW 40, 57.

29. H. Böhmer, *Urkunden zur Geschichte des Bauernkrie-
     ges und die Widertäufer* (Bonn, 1910), 3-10; LW 46,
     8-16.

30. WA 18, 291-334; LW 46, 17-43.

31. LW 46, 25.

32. LW 46, 28.

33. WA 18, 357-361; LW 46, 49-55.

34. LW 46, 53-54.

35. *The Heidelberg Catechism*, in the *Constitution of
     the Presbyterian Church (U.S.A.)*, Part I, *Book of
     Confessions* (New York-Atlanta, 1983), 4.001-4.129.

36. K. Marx, *Towards a Critique of Hegel's Philosophy
     of Right: Introduction*, in: *Selected Writings*,
     ed. D. McClellan (Oxford, 1977), 69.

37. B. Brecht, "An die Nachgeborenen," in: *Gedichte*
     (Frankfurt, 1981), 725.

Marilyn J. Harran

LUTHER AND FREEDOM OF THOUGHT

At the very outset, one must acknowledge that the theme "freedom of thought," unlike such motifs as the "freedom of a Christian" or the "Christian in church and state," is not one upon which Luther directly and deliberately focused his own attention in his many writings. Our concern with the topic "freedom of thought" reflects in part our modern response to political realities - to totalitarian governments, for example, which seek to repress not only outward freedom of speech but inward freedom of thought. This topic also reflects our concern with contemporary anthropological and psychological models of human existence, particularly that of the behaviorists which has severely limited the rational, thinking dimension in human responses and decisions.[1] The use of the computer, the development of super computers able to do millions or even a billion operations per second, and progress in creating artificial intelligence systems have also added a new dimension to our concern with the topic "freedom of thought." The earlier description of the human being as a machine may soon be replaced by the question of whether a person is a superior or inferior thinking machine when compared with the computer of the future.

Such issues appear far different from those which concerned Luther and the thinkers of the 16th century.

Luther was pre-Copernican, not only pre-computer, in
his thinking, and one is hard put to know what he would
think not only of the computer, but of the enterprise
of genetic engineering, clonal reproduction, and
embryonic transfer. As we consider the issue of Luther
and freedom of thought, we must be cognizant and
respectful of the differences between Luther's world
and ours. At the same time, we must ponder whether or
not Luther's convictions on the possibilities and
limitations of reason, of thought, speak to us and our
modern concerns. Certainly, Luther esteemed highly the
human intellectual capacity and affirmed the responsibility which humankind bears for this ability *coram
Deo*, before God. Our task is to ask whether the
inter-relationship of reason, conscience, and will
asserted by Luther illuminates our query regarding
humanity and its possibilities. We must be cautious at
the outset to assume that Luther's definition of a
concept such as "reason" is the same as ours. Indeed,
we must be even more careful when we turn our attention
to that complex idea called "freedom."

In this essay I will concentrate specifically on
Luther's understanding of reason, its possibilities and
limitations, and I will examine how Luther relates
reason to will. This discussion will provide the
foundation for a consideration of Luther's statements
on education, the goals he believed it could achieve
and the responsibilities it must meet. In conclusion I
will offer some thoughts on the relevance of Luther's
ideas to our technological, diverse, and secular
society.

In the classic debate with Ernst Troeltsch,
Wilhelm Dilthey portrayed Luther as the liberator, the
hero who through the Reformation liberated people from

the domination of the medieval hierarchy, fostered
inner liberty, and freed humankind from obsession with
sin and its status before God.[2] According to this
assessment, Luther also urged his contemporaries to a
new attitude toward matters social and political.[3]
Troeltsch, in contrast, described Luther as the authoritarian, supernaturally oriented religionist who
diffused the Renaissance spirit of outward, secular
concern and led Western Europe back into a repressive,
ecclesiastical culture.[4] A similarly negative apprais-
al of Luther was offered by Friedrich Engels in his
book *The Peasant War in Germany*.[5] Engels portrayed
Luther, in contrast to Thomas Müntzer, as not merely
regressive but reactionary. More recently, Herbert
Marcuse criticized Luther for preaching an inner
freedom which permitted and sanctioned a lack of
freedom in the social and economic spheres.[6] Given
such samples of negative assessments, we must question
in what ways, if any, Luther's name can be linked with
freedom of thought.

I

The first warrant, the one most often cited, in
arguing for Luther's contribution to freedom of thought
is his speech before the emperor and the highest
authorities of the land at the Diet of Worms in 1521.
For his defense Luther called on the authority of
Scripture, conscience, and reason, by declaring:

> Since then your serene majesty and your
> lordships seek a simple answer, I will give
> it in this manner, neither horned nor tooth-
> ed: Unless I am convinced by the testimony
> of the Scriptures or by clear reason (for I

do not trust either in the pope or in councils alone, since it is well known that they
have often erred and contradicted themselves), I am bound by the Scriptures I have
quoted and my conscience is captive to the
Word of God. I cannot and I will not retract
anything, since it is neither safe nor right
to go against conscience....may God help me.
Amen.[7]

Much has been written on Luther's understanding of
reason and his reference to its authority in his
address at Worms.[8] But also his 1536 *Disputatio de
homine* has been the focus of special attention.[9] In
the first theses of the disputation Luther established
his high regard for reason, while at the same time
acknowledging its limitations. With the greatest
appreciation and esteem, he wrote:

4. And it is certainly true that reason is
the most important and highest in rank among
all things and, in comparison with other
things of this life, the best and something
divine. 5. It is the inventor and mentor of
all the arts, medicines, laws, and of whatever wisdom, power, virtue, and glory men
possesses in this life. 6. By virtue of
this fact it ought to be named the essential
difference by which man is distinguished from
the animals and other things.... 9. Nor did
God after the fall of Adam take away this
majesty of reason, but rather confirmed it.
10. In spite of the fact that it is of such
majesty, it does not know itself *a priori*,
but only *a posteriori*. 11. Therefore, if
philosophy or reason itself is compared with

theology, it will appear that we know almost
nothing about man.[10]

Obviously, Luther both praised reason and defined its
limits. Unlike theology, it cannot reveal knowledge to
human beings about themselves, but can only report to
them about themselves after the fact.

Luther defined reason in three different ways: 1.
natural reason, the high gift of God which Luther
described in the *Disputatio de homine*; 2. **arrogant
reason**, which seeks to attain salvation in its own way
and through its own efforts; and 3. **regenerate
reason**, the ability of the converted individual who is
led by grace and faith.[11] As positive as Luther could
be in describing regenerate reason and even natural
reason, so could he be unmercifully negative in his
evaluation of arrogant reason and the damage it can do.
Reason errs most gravely when it attempts to reach
knowledge of God by its own efforts, short-circuiting
revelation and faith. In this instance reason constitutes an intellectual parallel to the effort to attain
salvation by works, through merit. Arrogant reason
ignores the fact that salvation comes to humans only on
God's terms, not on their own terms.

Luther condemned these two errors of arrogant
reason and salvation by works in his 1525 *Lectures on
Jonah*. He described the human situation and ability to
comprehend God in this way:

> The only true form of God is for us to grasp
> Him by faith, namely, to learn that God is
> always a well-disposed Father and the Father
> of mercies. This understanding is given only
> by the Holy Spirit, and this is the only true
> and genuine knowledge of God. All other
> opinions are idolatrous, as when, with our

own reason as leader and teacher, we make up
certain works for ourselves, by which we
think that we will be pleasing to God and
imagine that we are going to win His rewards
or favor.[12]

Of course, natural reason may easily degenerate
into arrogant reason, the Devil's whore, *Frau Hulda*.
However, it also has the ability to restrain human
beings from evil action and to inform them, if not of
what God is, at least of what God is not. As Luther
argued in his tract *De votis monasticis*, written in
1521 (the same year as his stand at Worms):

> when it [natural reason] asserts affirmative
> statements... its judgment is wrong, but when
> it asserts negative statements its judgment
> is right. Reason does not comprehend what
> God is, but it most certainly comprehends
> what God is not. Granted, reason cannot see
> what is right and good in God's sight (faith,
> for instance), but it sees quite clearly that
> infidelity, murder and disobedience are
> wrong.[13]

Thus, natural reason - the knowledge inscribed on the
heart of every person - both offers negative insight
into the nature of God and positive knowledge of what
is ethically required from a human being. It would be
too positive an evaluation, however, to regard this
ethical knowledge as the same as Christian love or
self-sacrifice; instead, it is the ethical precept
necessary for survival.

In his 1526 *Lectures on Jonah*, Luther asserted
that natural reason is able to recognize that God is
"kind, gracious, merciful, and benevolent."[14] Natural
reason is able to attain to a certain basic and

important knowledge about God. But, natural reason is unable to apply this general perception of the deity to the specific circumstances of humankind. Consequently, this knowledge remains in the most fundamental sense meaningless. Natural reason, operating on empirical evidence, is capable of perceiving God as a terrible, wrathful judge while not also seeing God as a loving father.[15] Thus, "reason believes in God's might and is aware of it, but it is uncertain whether God is willing to employ this in our behalf, because in adversity it so often experiences the opposite to be true."[16]

This limitation in attaining specific knowledge about God and God's will toward the individual is not only the fault of reason but also of the will which cannot proceed beyond the point of recognizing that God may be gracious to others but not to oneself. In other words, the will is incapable of reaching a position of trust or faith in God as one's personal savior. For Luther, the powers and limits of the will and of reason are closely connected. Freedom of thought is limited by the bondage of the will to sin and self-love. Thus, reason is not free to come to the correct perception of God because it is absorbed in its own desires and concerns.

Natural reason is unable to identify God accurately, for

> it calls that God which is not God and fails
> to call Him God who really is God. Reason
> would do neither the one nor the other if it
> were not conscious of the existence of God or
> if it really knew who and what God is.
> Therefore it rushes in clumsily and assigns
> the name God and ascribes divine honor to its
> own idea of God. Thus reason never finds the

true God, but it finds the devil or its own
concept of God, ruled by the devil. So there
is a vast difference between knowing that
there is a God and knowing who or what God
is.[17]

It is precisely natural reason's limited ability that
leads it astray when it attempts to attain to revealed
knowledge about God and God's relation to human beings.
Its inability truly to know God makes natural reason
arrogant as it assigns its invented attributes to a god
of its own creation. The cliché that "a little knowledge is a dangerous thing" describes also Luther's
perception of the role of natural reason in attaining
knowledge about God. Even in his last sermon in
Wittenberg, on January 17, 1546, Luther preached
against the arrogance of natural reason. He linked
this abuse of reason to fanaticism and said:

the devil's bride, reason, the lovely whore
comes in and wants to be wise and what she
says, she thinks, is the Holy Spirit. Who
can be of any help then? Neither jurist,
physician, nor king, nor emperor; for she is
the foremost whore the devil has. The other
gross sins can be seen, but nobody can
control reason.[18]

Arrogant reason questions the value of baptism,
the efficacy of eating bread and wine in the eucharist,
and asserts that Mary should be called upon as the
intercessor with Christ.[19] For Luther these positions
appear on the surface to be reasonable, but they are in
reality the sure route to hell. Therefore, one must
place the catechism over against arrogant reason, and
when faith requires one to do so, one must trample upon
reason.[20] Following Paul, Luther taught:

We are to quench not only the low desires but also the high desires, reason and its high wisdom. When whoredom invades you, strike it dead but do this far more when spiritual whoredom tempts you. Nothing pleases a man as much as self-love, when he has a passion for his own wisdom. The cupidity of a greedy man is as nothing compared with a man's hearty pleasure in his own ideas.[21]

This critique does not mean that Luther was opposed to reason or thought. Indeed, in the *Disputatio de homine* he declared that as a person's power for thought, reason is the highest gift which distinguishes humankind from the rest of creation.[22] Luther did not criticize thinking or even freedom of thought, but rather, he condemned specific thoughts.[23] As his last Wittenberg sermon indicates, he condemned people's lustful pleasure in their own intellect, in their own thoughts which concentrate on human power and ability. Accordingly, sin for Luther did not consist in thinking *per se*, in utilizing the capacity God has given human beings, but in using that capacity for one's own selfish purposes and ends. This perversion or prostitution motif, i.e., the misuse of a right endowment for wrong purposes, is the reason why Luther called reason a whore.

Luther focused throughout his writings and sermons not on the issue of freedom of thought but on the necessity for **responsible** thought. He condemned those people who seek to make reason into a deity and who rejoice in the greatness of their thoughts when they should be directing their reason toward such areas as proper governance and appropriate response to the neighbor in need. This abuse of reason is another sign of the sinful *amor sui* of humankind, of the human being *incurvatus in se ipsum*. The misuse of reason is such a terrible sin and affront to God precisely because it is the abuse of the highest gift humans have received from God. Because Luther had such high regard for reason, for the power of thought, he spoke so bitterly of its misuse and corruption.

In his strongest statement on the abuse of reason, he asserted that reason must indeed be murdered lest it interfere with the act of faith, which so often appears, at least outwardly, to contradict reason. The divine demand placed upon Abraham to sacrifice Isaac is the supreme example of the disjunction between the decision of reason and the decision of faith. In this situation, Abraham acted rightly, putting the voice of reason to death. In Luther's judgment,

> Faith conquered in him, slaughtered and sacrificed that bitterest and most pestilential enemy of God. All the pious do so, going with Abraham into the darkness of faith, they kill reason saying, 'Reason, you are a fool. You do not know the things of God. So do not get in my way, but be quiet. Do not judge, but hear the Word of God and believe.'[24]

Moving beyond a simple contrast of faith and reason, Luther indicated that faith itself kills reason.[25] At other times, he described reason not as being slaughtered and annihilated by faith, but as being illuminated by it.[26]

At the Diet of Worms Luther appealed to regenerate or illuminated reason. For him, regenerate reason is not supernatural insight received through mystical visions, but it is reason taken captive by grace, so

that it realizes that its place is to serve faith, not
to challenge or displace it.[27]

This reason plays an important role in doing
theology. According to one *Table Talk* account from
early 1533:

> Reason that is under the devil's control is
> harmful and the more clever and successful it
> is, the more harm it does. We see this in
> the case of learned men who on the basis of
> their reason disagree with the Word. On the
> other hand, when illuminated by the Holy
> Spirit, reason helps to interpret the Holy
> Scriptures.[28]

Yet in this role too, the path of reason is filled with
pitfalls and snares. For example, reason must not
resort to interpreting Scripture on the basis of
philosophy but must rely on the word: "Reason that is
illuminated takes all its thoughts from the Word."[29]
It is the task of regenerate reason to expound and
interpret Scripture so that faith is guided and
encouraged:

> Prior to faith and a knowledge of God, reason
> is darkness, but in believers it is an
> excellent instrument.... Faith is now fur-
> thered by reason, speech, and eloquence,
> whereas these were only impediments prior to
> faith. Enlightened reason, taken captive by
> faith, receives life from faith, for it is
> slain and given life again.[30]

Should reason encounter Scriptural passages which
conflict with reason's own assumptions, reason must
surrender to the word. Regenerate reason, guided by
grace, knows its limits, accepts the boundaries imposed
by faith, and does not seek to change miracle and

revelation into commonplaces of everyday life.[31]
Luther's optimism regarding regenerate reason stems, of
course, not from his confidence in reason, but from his
confidence in grace. Grace at work within the Christian so guides reason that it keeps to its appointed
task, restraining it from subverting theology into
philosophy and from constructing a god of its own from
the God proclaimed in Scripture. Reason, even regenerate reason, remains subject to faith, but, paradoxically, it is only within this bondage that reason is
truly free and able to operate as the divine gift
which it is.[32] Like Christians in their entire being,
reason is only free when it serves God. Conversely,
reason is in true slavery when it is obsessed with
finding its own means to salvation and is absorbed in
self-concern, unable to believe that God so loved the
world that God would send God's Son to die in order to
redeem it.

When Luther referred to the testimony of clear
reason in his speech at the Diet of Worms, he recognized himself as a man in bondage - "I am bound by the
Scriptures I have quoted and my conscience is captive
to the Word of God."[33] In this bondage to Christ,
Luther stood free through faith to affirm both his
conscience and his reason. Through his reason, illuminated by grace, Luther could employ its God-given
abilities to recognize the errors in the accusations
hurled against him by his opponents.

For Luther, the total person, including both
reason and will, is in bondage either to God or the
devil.[34] His most famous writing on the topic of the
will was his 1525 *De servo arbitrio*, a direct response
to Erasmus' *De libero arbitrio*.[35] By this writing
Luther struck a death blow to an alliance between

humanism and the Reformation, alienating many humanists.[36] In her assessment of the historic confronta-
tion between Luther and Erasmus, Margaret Phillips has
asserted that "Erasmus is at his best as the champion
of human liberty against determinism."[37] Clearly, in
her view, Luther's position established him as a
determinist.

However, Paul Tillich has offered a persuasive
answer to the charge of determinism levelled against
Luther. Locating the bondage of the will within the
context of a person's total being, Tillich wrote:

> Man's will in bondage to demonic structures
> is meaningful only if man, in his essential
> nature, is free. Luther's (as well as Paul's
> and Augustine's and Aquinas') statement loses
> its profundity and its paradoxical character
> if it is identified with philosophical
> determinism. Only a being that has the power
> of self-determination can have a *servum
> arbitrium*, a 'will in bondage,' because a
> being without the power of self-determination
> has no *arbitrium* ('capacity for decision') at
> all.[38]

The question is not whether or not one has a will, any
more than the question is whether or not one has a
capable reason. The question is by what authority
one's will, like one's reason, is governed or directed.

Gerhard Ebeling pointed out that for Luther the
issue was not the **freedom** of the will, but the **power** of
the will.[39] Although the will, similar to reason, may
perceive itself as free and self-determining with
regard to matters of salvation, it is in reality
limited by the power of sin and not free. As Luther
described the situation in a famous passage:

> If we are under the god of this world, away
> from the work and Spirit of the true God, we
> are held captive to his will.... But if a
> Stronger One comes who overcomes him and
> takes us as His spoil, then through his
> Spirit we are again slaves and captives -
> though this is royal freedom - so that we
> readily will and do what he wills. Thus the
> human will is placed between the two like a
> beast of burden. If God rides it, it wills
> and goes where God wills... If Satan rides
> it, it wills and goes where Satan wills; nor
> can it choose to run to either of the two
> riders and seek him out, but the riders
> themselves contend for the possession and
> control of it.[40]

The will experiences genuine freedom only when it
perceives itself as led by grace and knows itself to be
totally dependent for salvation on the will of God.
Regenerate reason and the will directed by grace work
together in guiding the life of a Christian.[41] It
cannot be affirmed too often that Luther saw the
individual as a whole, *totus homo*, directed either by
sin or grace. When reason is enlightened by grace we
know our will to be in bondage to God. Yet it is that
very bondage which allows one freely and joyfully to
act, governing one's actions by conscience.

For Luther, freedom of the will is not the truly
crucial question. Far more central is the issue of
freedom of conscience. As Luther described the situation,

> Even if I lived and worked to eternity, my
> conscience would never be assured and certain
> how much it ought to do to satisfy God. For

whatever work might be accomplished, there would always remain an anxious doubt whether it pleased God or whether he required something more, as the experience of all self-justifiers proves, and as I myself learned to my bitter cost through so many years. But now, since God has taken my salvation out of my hands into his, making it depend on his choice and not mine and has promised to save me, not by my own work or exertion but by his grace and mercy, I am assured and certain both that he is faithful and will not lie to me.[42]

Luther's purpose in writing the *De servo arbitrio* was not to diminish humankind, but in the area of the spirit and of salvation to exalt God. "Luther asserts the bondage of the will for the sake of the freedom of the conscience."[43]

As Gerhard Ebeling observed, Luther had "no intention" in his *De servo arbitrio* "of denying the situation which is experienced as the psychological freedom of the will, that I can choose between different possibilities of action."[44] Luther affirmed the individual's ability to decide freely regarding all matters not related to salvation - a very large realm, indeed.[45] Especially within the secular realm of politics and government each person through the use of natural reason is active and responsible.[46] By virtue of the gift of reason, humans are in fact the creative force within culture and cooperate with God in making history. Luther extolled the role regenerate reason plays in the world by cooperating with God:

He does not work without us, because it is for this very thing that he has recreated and preserves us, that he might work in us and we might cooperate with him. Thus it is through us he preaches, shows mercy to the poor, comforts the afflicted.[47]

The activity of arrogant reason, however, stands starkly contrasted with the positive attributes which Luther assigns to both natural and regenerate reason. He directed a series of harsh questions toward arrogant reason and the self-motivated will, asking:

> What now can reason dictate that is right when it is itself blind and ignorant? What can the will choose that is good when it is itself evil and worthless? Or rather, what choice has the will when reason dictates to it only the darkness of its own blind ignorance? With reason in error, then, and the will misdirected, what can a person do or attempt that is good?[48]

The will, guided by ignorant reason and self-love, rather than by grace and faith, can do no good, no matter how intently it struggles.

Total dependence on God for salvation gives, paradoxically, true freedom to act responsibly and responsively toward one's neighbor. Bondage of the will to God in matters of salvation means freedom from self-anxiety and self-concern. It is this freedom that allows the Christian to act joyously and spontaneously in the world. As Luther wrote in his 1520 treatise *The Freedom of a Christian*: "So also our works should be done, not that we may be justified by them, since, being justified beforehand by faith, we ought to do all things freely and joyfully for the sake of others."[49] Christian freedom is the liberty to act and the liberty to use one's reason to reach individual decisions, guided by a conscience that is informed by grace and faith. In a very profound sense, this bondage to God means freedom of thought, as well.

II

In affirming the role of natural reason, Luther also recognized that reason properly instructed and educated could play a far more constructive part in the world than that reason left untrained and untaught. Along with the humanists, Luther shared the goal of reforming the university curriculum, stripping it of scholastic dialectic, and replacing it with a new emphasis on languages and history.[50] Luther and the humanists parted company, however, in their respective expectations as to what education could accomplish.

Luther never believed that education could make a person **essentially** better. Grace, not education, transforms arrogant into regenerate reason and directs the will from self-love to love of neighbor. Education cannot move a person from a state of sin to a state of grace, because of the absolute difference which exists between knowing the good and being able to accomplish it:

> They are not the best Christians who are the most learned and abound in many books. For all their books and all their learning are the 'written code' and death of the soul. But rather they are the best Christians who with a totally free will do those things which the scholars read in the books and teach others to do. But they do not act out of a totally free will unless they have love through the Holy Spirit. Therefore in our

age it is to be feared, that by the making of
many books we develop very learned men but
very unlearned Christians.[51]

Nonetheless, Luther remained cautiously optimistic
and realistic about what education could accomplish,
and therefore made a number of important contributions
to education on all levels. In this regard, too, he
was a real proponent of the advancement of "freedom of
thought."

Yet, in spite of his many statements calling for
new schools, libraries, and reformed curricula,[52]
Luther was criticized both in his own time and thereaf-
ter for being responsible, in part, for the decline of
learning, especially on the university level. For
example, in a letter of 1527 Erasmus wrote to the
Nürnberg humanist Willibald Pirckheimer, "Wherever
Lutheranism prevails, there we see the downfall of
learning."[53] The scholar of education Friedrich
Paulsen came to a similar negative evaluation of
Luther:

> Nor did he cherish any strong desire for
> learning and education; these things were far
> removed from his main interest, and those who
> pursued them as the most vital aims of life,
> like Erasmus of Rotterdam, he looked upon
> without sympathy, if not with suspicion.[54]

Let us consider each of these critiques separately.

Erasmus' statement reflects the very real situation that university enrollment did decrease dramat-
ically during the first decade of the Reformation, as a
result not only of religious controversy, but of
plagues and poor harvests, enabling fewer people to
have the funds to send their sons on to higher education.[55] Curricular reform also progressed slowly, so

that, for instance, the reform of the curriculum of the University of Wittenberg was itself only completed in 1536.[56] Nevertheless, humanistic reform of established universities and the founding of new ones, beginning in the 1530's, continued through the age of confessionalism and into the 17th century. These universities, reformed and new, relied heavily on the humanistic educational goals set forth by Philipp Melanchthon, the man who became known as the *praeceptor Germaniae*.[57] In the 1530's the universities of Tübingen, Greifswald, and Copenhagen were reformed, followed in later years by such institutions as Frankfurt-an-der-Oder and Rostock. New universities, such as Marburg, Jena, and Giessen were founded. Thus, although Erasmus' charge correctly reflects the turbulent situation in the 1520's, in the long run the Reformation led to the reorganizing, reforming, and founding of many universities, thereby leading to a vast improvement in learning, not to its downfall.

Perhaps the best response to Paulsen's charge that Luther had no genuine or central interest in education is to cite Luther's own words in his writing *To the Councilmen of All Cities in Germany That They Establish and Maintain Christian Schools* 1524:

> Now if (as we have assumed) there were no souls and there were no need at all of schools and languages for the sake of the Scriptures and of God, this one consideration alone would be sufficient to justify the establishment everywhere of the very best schools for both boys and girls, namely, that in order to maintain its temporal estate outwardly the world must have good and capable men and women.... Now such men must

come from our boys and such women from our
girls. Therefore, it is a matter of properly
educating and training our boys and girls to
that end.[58]

No better statement could be adduced to demonstrate
Luther's overriding concern for education. Paulsen's
judgment of Luther may be regarded as correct if we
understand it to mean that Luther did not look upon
education and learning as goals in and of themselves,
but rather as tools for attaining far more important
goals. These goals consisted in the study of Scripture, so that piety and the Christian life might be
guided and encouraged, and the study of languages and
history, so that civil life may be conducted in a just
and honorable manner. In Luther's view a city's wealth
does not only consist in its many fine buildings or in
a full treasury, but rather: "A city's best and
greatest welfare, safety, and strength consist...in its
having many able, learned, wise, honorable, and well-
educated citizens."[59]

Luther was convinced that the formation of such
well-educated men and women was a civic responsibility
- a responsibility, however, which began first within
the life of the family. The family figured signifi-
cantly in his division of the world into three orders,
the *status politicus*, *status ecclesiasticus* and *status
economicus*.[60] Yet these three orders do not constitute
separate compartments, but interlocking spheres.
Although no sphere is superior or inferior to the
others, Luther saw the *status economicus*, with the
family at its core, as the basis for all three.

Luther also linked the family to his reinterpreta-
tion of the meaning of *vocatio*. In contrast to a
spiritual and hierarchical conception of *vocatio* he

proposed a radical horizontalizing or levelling of the term so that all callings be regarded as of equal value since all stem from God.[61] Consequently, a person's role within the family is a *vocatio* in and of itself.[62] As a member of a family, each person has special and important responsibilities. Since education takes place first within the home, Luther affirmed that a parent bears an especially heavy responsibility for properly directing those first steps in learning which a child takes. From the parents a child should learn the willing obedience which characterizes the relationship with the heavenly father throughout a life time. The father is indeed the bishop within his own household, i.e., a *viva lex*, to be obeyed except when his law conflicts with the civil law.[63] The mother, on the other hand, is also acting within the family as God's representative, but by displaying in her works "God's protecting, preserving, and guiding activity without cessation."[64] The relationship between the parents and the child is a living model for relationships within the domestic, political, and religious spheres.

Luther frequently stressed parental responsibility before God for the proper education and upbringing of the child:

> But this at least all married people should
> know. They can do no better work and do
> nothing more valuable either for God, for
> Christendom, for all the world, for them-
> selves, and for their children than to bring
> up their children well. In comparison with
> this one work, that married people should
> bring up their children properly, there is
> nothing at all in pilgrimages to Rome,
> Jerusalem, or Compostella, nothing at all in

building   churches,   endowing   masses,   or
whatever   good   works   can   be   named.   For
bringing up their children properly is their
shortest road to heaven... By the same token,
hell is no more easily earned than with
respect to one's own children.[65]

Thus, the beginnings of education within the family
must include the teaching of the proper relation
between spiritual and worldly matters and concerns.
For example Luther asserted that it is the father's
duty to lead the family in prayer.[66] This activity
provides the foundation for all future education. Conversely, wherever the father neglects this obligation,
the home "becomes a pigsty and an institute for the
instruction of rascals."[67]

Beginning in the 1520's, Luther and his colleagues
devoted themselves to composing works which praised and
outlined the right qualities to be practiced in the
married life and in rearing and educating children.[68]
With the family and its needs in mind, Luther prepared
his *Small Catechism* which appeared in its first version
in May of 1529. He believed that the father was
obliged to check on his children's reading, memorizing,
and reciting of the catechism at least once a week, as
well as on that of the servants. "If the children
would not learn, they should not eat; if the servants
declined to study, they should be dismissed."[69] The
Christian household must be administered with love but
also with firmness. In Luther's view, the family was
the training ground, the primary place of education for
the young, and the cornerstone of society for one and
all.

While Luther emphasized the function of the
parents as a spiritual one, he also saw the educational

process within the family as part of the worldly or
civil, secular realm.[70] In its secular dimension
education within the family involves the proper governing of the children, paralleling the role of the
magistrate in society. Children must be properly
instructed in the rules and laws of society, so that
disorder does not prevail. Even within the family,
education is in large part a "worldly" matter, a
concern belonging to the sphere of natural reason. As
Luther expressed it in his address *To the Councilmen*:

> It is a sin and a shame that matters have
> come to such a pass that we have to urge and
> be urged to educate our children and young
> people and to seek their best interests, when
> nature itself should drive us to do this and
> even the heathen afford abundant examples of
> it.[71]

It is the task of the civil authorities to aid the
parents and to further the cause of education. It is
worth noting that Luther directed his pleas on the
necessity of education *To the Councilmen*, to the
secular authorities. Although in his vocation as
professor and preacher Luther did not assume responsibility for presenting a new pedagogy or assuming
control over the course of German education, he nonetheless saw it as part of his responsibility to remind
the secular authorities of their obligations:

> It therefore behooves the council and the
> authorities to devote the greatest care and
> attention to the young. Since the property,
> honor and life of the whole city have been
> committed to their faithful keeping, they
> would be remiss in their duty before God and
> man if they did not seek its welfare and

improvement day and night with all means at
their command.[72]

The participation of the civil authorities in the
educational process is necessary since parents either
deliberately fail in their responsibilities or are
unable properly to perform them. In his *Sermon on
Keeping Children in School* 1530, Luther recognized that
many parents have a lower opinion of the benefits of an
education for their children as a result of the success
of the Reformation. They assume since "monkery,
nunning and priestcraft no longer hold out the hope
they once did, there is therefore no more need for
study and for learned men, that instead we need to give
thought only to how to make a living and get rich."[73]
Therefore, both natural reason and Christian love
dictate that others must then take over the responsibility for educating children lest they grow up "to
poison and pollute the other children until at last the
whole city is ruined, as happened in Sodom and Gomor-
rah."[74]

Through his own experience Luther had become aware
of the failures of the schools. Hence, he directed the
magistrates to the need for a revised curriculum and a
new approach to education. A valid pedagogy, he
affirmed, makes use of a child's natural playfulness
and strives to make learning itself enjoyable: "Today
schools are not what they once were, a hell and purgatory in which we were tormented with *casualibus* and
temporalibus and yet learned less than nothing despite
all the flogging, trembling, anguish and misery."[75]

First and foremost, the Scripture must be the
center or core of the curriculum. Already in his 1520
treatise *To the Christian Nobility of the German
Nation*, Luther said:

> Above all, the foremost reading for every-
> body, both in the universities and in the
> schools, should be Holy Scripture - and for
> the younger boys, the Gospels. And would to
> God that every town had a girls' school as
> well, where the girls would be taught the
> gospel for an hour every day either in German
> or Latin... A spinner or seamstress teaches
> her daughter her craft in her early years.
> But today even the great, learned prelates
> and the very bishops do not know the gos-
> pel.[76]

However, after the core curriculum of Scripture the
humanities found a place, too, in the course of study.
The only limitation Luther placed on the humanities was
that they not contain materials which contradicted or
deprecated Scripture.[77] Thus, revitalized schools and
reformed curricula were seen as results of both humanism and the religious Reformation. This was a time
when the gospel could be taught freely and when Germany
was experiencing a "golden year" for the study of the
languages and the liberal arts.[78] Both the gospel and
the humanities occupy important places in the curriculum, the one pertaining to the spiritual realm, the
other primarily to the secular.

This curricular viewpoint is exemplified in
Luther's praise for the study of the languages. He
wrote *To the Councilmen*:

> And let us be sure of this: we will not long
> preserve the gospel without the languages.
> The languages are the sheath in which this
> sword of the spirit...is contained; they are
> the casket in which this jewel is enshrined;
> they are the vessel in which this wine is

held; they are the larder in which this food
is stored; and, as the gospel itself points
out..., they are the baskets in which are
kept these loaves and fishes and fragments.[79]

This statement, however, constitutes only the first
part of Luther's understanding of the importance of the
languages. Turning his attention to what we may
consider to be more secular or humanistic concerns, he
wrote:

If through our neglect we let the languages
go (which God forbid!), we shall not only
lose the gospel, but the time will come when
we shall be unable either to speak or write a
correct Latin or German. As proof and
warning of this, let us take the deplorable
and dreadful example of the universities and
monasteries, in which men have not only
unlearned the gospel, but have in addition so
corrupted the Latin and German languages that
the miserable folk have been fairly turned
into beasts, unable to speak or write a
correct German or Latin, and have well-nigh
lost their natural reason to boot.[80]

Study of the languages is not only essential in order
that the gospel may not be lost, but also that civilization and culture will not falter and decay.

In the *Instructions for the Visitors of Parish
Pastors in Electoral Saxony* 1528, Melanchthon and
Luther outlined an essential and basic curriculum for
the schools.[81] What we would term grammar and secondary schools were divided into three levels, beginning
on the first level with those children who are just
beginning to learn to read and ending on the third
level with those advanced students who have been chosen

by their parents and teachers to continue their studies.[82] In their directions to teachers on all levels
the Reformers demonstrated considerable pedagogical
sensitivity by insisting that children should not be
overburdened with memorization, but that such work
should proceed slowly and patiently. On the first
level of schooling, children proceed through a simple
primer, to Donatus and Cato, gaining expertise in
reading and gradually building up a vocabulary through
memorization. In conjunction with this study, and on
all three levels, the teaching of music is emphasized
so that the children might not only learn songs but
through singing together learn how to work together.
At the second level, composed of those students who can
read, both music and reading are continued, along with
more formal exposition of the principles of grammar and
with homework which includes the memorization of a
phrase or two from a Latin poet or writer. One day
from each week of school should be set aside for
Christian instruction, including recitation of the
Lord's Prayer, the Creed, and the Ten Commandments.
With reference to this spiritual training, too, the
teacher should not lay too heavy a burden on the
children:

> The schoolmaster should not undertake to read
> other books than these [some Psalms, Matthew,
> some of Paul's epistles, if the students are
> older, along with the first epistle of John
> and Proverbs]. For it is fruitless to burden
> the youth with hard and deep books. It is
> for their own reputation that some have
> assayed to read Isaiah, the Epistle of Paul
> to the Romans, the Gospel of St. John and the
> like.[83]

Luther again explicitly affirmed the need for both the gospel and the humanities:

> Some are taught nothing out of holy Scrip-
> ture. Some teach their children nothing but
> holy Scripture. We should yield to neither
> of these practices. It is essential that the
> children learn the beginning of a Christian
> and blessed life. But there are many reasons
> why also other books beside Scripture should
> be given the children from which they may
> learn to speak.[84]

This spiritual and humanistic training should be continued on the third level where students continue to practice music, to read the classics, including Virgil and Ovid, to learn grammar, to study dialectic and rhetoric and to practice writing, by composing letters and poems.

The *Instructions for the Visitors* certainly does not constitute a startling pedagogical breakthrough. The Reformers advocated the use of several of the books traditionally employed in monastic and cathedral schools, such as *Aesop's Fables*.[85] It is important, though, to remember that Luther did not consider himself a pedagogue but the advisor to those who are formulating the educational curriculum. Children should learn languages and history, as well as singing, music and mathematics, instead of being compelled as he was in his own education to read philosophy, "the devil's dung," rather than poetry and history, for which he had an especially high regard.[86]

Luther also recognized that education costs money beyond what an individual family could supply. He called upon the magistrates to reassess their own standards of priorities for the cities:

My dear sirs, if we have to spend such large
sums every year on guns, roads, bridges,
dams, and countless similar items to insure
the temporal peace and prosperity of a city,
why should not much more be devoted to the
poor neglected youth - at least enough to
engage one or two competent men to teach
school?[87]

The magistrates were also obliged not only to
provide schools and teachers, but, when necessary, to
compel children to attend school.[88] As a logical
consequence of his doctrine of the priesthood of all
believers, Luther believed it was absolutely essential
that children at least be able to read and understand
Scripture for themselves. In this sense, secular
education is spiritually propaedeutic. Moreover,
education is essential so that secular leaders and
authorities may be trained. Indeed, in his *Sermon on
Keeping Children in School*, Luther asserted that the
very brightest children should be directed toward
secular and civil office, not to the ministry:

There is need in this office for abler people
than are needed in the office of preaching,
so it is necessary to get the best boys for
this work; for in the preaching office Christ
does the whole thing, by his Spirit, but in
the worldly kingdom men must act on the basis
of reason - wherein the laws also have their
origin - for God has subjected temporal rule
and all of physical life to reason (Genesis 2
[:15]). He has not sent the Holy Spirit from
heaven for this purpose. This is why to
govern temporally is harder, because

conscience cannot rule; one must act, so to speak, in the dark.[89]

With typical humanist concern, Luther also stressed the necessity of education, especially in the languages, so that the Germans may not be regarded as inferior to other peoples: "I am only too well aware that we Germans must always be and remain brutes and stupid beasts as the neighboring nations call us, epithets which we richly deserve."[90] Although Germans treasure outlandish personal goods such as silks and spices, they do not give equal value to the foreign languages and arts:

> Languages and the arts, which can do us no harm, but are actually a greater ornament, profit, glory and benefit, both for the understanding of Holy Scripture and the conduct of temporal government - these we despise. But foreign wares, which are neither necessary nor useful and in addition strip us down to a mere skeleton - these we cannot do without. Are not we Germans justly dubbed fools and beasts?[91]

Luther's vocal support of compulsory education, for both boys and girls, stands as one of his major contributions to freedom of thought. Without an educational foundation in both the Scriptures and humanities, no person has an adequate ability to decide respectively matters of conscience with regard to spiritual concerns or to decide matters of reason with regard to secular concerns.

Luther made a further contribution to the development of education, and eventually to freedom of thought, by honoring those who are called to the vocation of teacher. In his *Sermon on Keeping Children in School* Luther insisted that a pious and industrious schoolteacher can never be sufficiently rewarded.[92] He even asserted that if he had to give up preaching, he would turn to teaching, "for I know that next to that of preaching, this is the best, greatest and most useful office there is."[93] A comparison of the work of a knight and a scholar shows that the work of a scholar is by far the more difficult:

> True, it would be hard for me to ride in armor; but on the other hand I would like to see the horseman who could sit still all day and look in a book - even if he had nothing else to care for, write, think about, or read. Ask a chancery clerk, preacher, or speaker whether writing and speaking is work! Ask a schoolmaster whether teaching and training boys is work![94]

In short, "it is true, as they say, that learning is easy to carry but armor is heavy. On the other hand, though, the wearing of armor is easily learned, whereas learning is not easily acquired, nor easily put to work."[95]

Neither teachers nor scholars can accomplish their work without the proper tools and facilities. Of these, perhaps the most important is a carefully chosen library. Luther himself had the greatest respect for books. He once said: "There never yet have been, nor are there now, too many good books."[96] Of course, not all books are good or useful; books may indeed be "foul and poisonous."[97] Therefore, in selecting a library one should not simply heap

> together all manner of books indiscriminately and think only of the number and size of the collection. I would make a judicious

> selection, for it is not necessary to have
> all the commentaries of the jurists, all the
> sentences of the theologians, all the *quaes-*
> *tiones* of the philosophers and all the
> sermons of the monks. Indeed, I would
> discard all such dung, and furnish my library
> with the right sort of books, consulting with
> scholars as to my choice.[98]

Luther placed high value on including the Scriptures in
Latin, Greek, Hebrew, German and other available
languages, and on the best commentaries and grammars,
as well as a judicious selection of liberal arts
volumes, and books on law and medicine. Special care
should be given to acquiring chronicles and histories,
for "they are a wonderful help in understanding and
guiding the course of events, and especially for
observing the marvelous works of God."[99]

Although Luther emphasized the necessity of a
basic education for all, it was as a reformer of
education on the highest level, at the university, that
he first wrote about curricular reform. In his 1517
Disputation on Scholastic Theology, he criticized the
intrusion of Aristotle and philosophy into the realm of
theology. Consequently, the reformation of the church
necessitated reform of the university curriculum - the
training ground for both pastors and professors. In
May of 1518 he wrote:

> I am absolutely persuaded that it is impossi-
> ble to reform the church unless from the
> ground up, the canons, decretals, scholastic
> theology, philosophy, logic, as they are now
> pursued, are rooted out and other subjects
> taught. And I go so far in this conviction
> that I daily ask the Lord to let things so

transpire that a fully purified study of the
Bible and of the holy fathers will be restored.[100]

While Luther initiated reform of the university
curriculum at the top, with the theology faculty, his
younger colleague Melanchthon, appointed to the university in 1518, began at the bottom, with the faculty of
arts.[101]   Although some of Aristotle's writings, such
as the *Logic*, *Rhetoric*, and *Poetics*, were retained, the
entire university curriculum was infused with a humanist spirit which emphasized the languages, history, and
rhetoric.   Melanchthon's   inaugural   oration   at   the
University of Wittenberg, *De corrigendis adolescentiae
studiis*, provided a pattern for the reform of higher
learning, with the *studia humanitatis* replacing scholastic dialectic as the core of the curriculum.[102]

Even more than Luther, Melanchthon stressed the
role of education in promoting the public welfare and
furthering the secular state.   In his *Oration in Praise
of a New School* 1526, delivered at the founding of the
new Nürnberg gymnasium, Melanchthon stated:

> For what else brings greater benefits to the
> whole human race than letters?   No art, no
> work, not, by Hercules, the very fruits born
> of the earth, not finally, this sun, which
> many have believed is the author of life, is
> as necessary as the knowledge of letters!....
> Therefore, above all things in a well-consti-
> tuted state, schools are necessary where
> youth, which is the seed-plot of the state,
> will be educated.   For if anyone thinks that
> genuine virtue can be acquired without teach-
> ing, he is very much deceived.   Nor is anyone
> capable of governing the state without the

knowledge of those letters with which every principle of ruling states is maintained.[103]

Thus, Melanchthon intensified Luther's stress on the necessity of education for both secular and spiritual well-being. This same emphasis was continued in the second generation of Protestantism when the citizens of Geneva pledged to support Calvin's new *Academy*, designed for promoting the welfare of both church and state. On another continent, John Knox, proposed in 1560 *The First Book of Discipline*, a plan for a national educational system, although it was not fully realized until the 1890's.[104] Already by the end of the 16th century primary education (*Volksschulwesen*) was flourishing in the German territories of Saxony, Hesse, and Württemberg.[105]

With regard to education, then, Luther's name can be linked to three specific accomplishments: 1. the establishment of compulsory education; 2. the new respect and appreciation for the vocation of teacher; and 3. the emphasis, in all levels of education, from 'first grade' through the university, on the classical curriculum, the humanities.

While Luther insisted on the teaching of Scripture as the foremost educational obligation, he did not fail to stress secular or humanistic studies. Certainly, education is intended primarily to teach the rudiments of the Christian faith. But it also serves to train the students in using their reason for worldly affairs. Luther expected each educated person to apply knowledge, to utilize reason, and to think independently. He understood education as a right for all people, not merely for the aristocracy, those who could afford it. In this respect Luther was both "modern" and "democratic" in his thinking. Luther made a significant contribution to the cause of freedom of thought by emphasizing that the secular is not inferior to the spiritual. He gave both a place in the curriculum and emphasized particularly the training of leaders for the secular sphere. Of course, Luther limited human freedom with respect to matters of salvation; a person is not saved by reason. But through his writings on education, he left a wide realm open for the exercise of human reason and decision. He regarded with great appreciation human reason and the human ability to learn.

III

In conclusion, by emphasizing individual responsibility, the wide expanse open to human reason and judgment, and by insisting on compulsory education so that each individual might know the Scriptures and make decisions on the basis of an informed conscience, Luther contributed to the cause of individual rights and freedom. The Cambridge historian Herbert Butterfield has given the following assessment of Luther: "Luther became the father of our modern individualism in religion, even though he did not mean to be - even though he had never imagined that other people should be able to decide on matters of belief in the way he had done."[106] Butterfield's judgment may in fact be too negative. Certainly, Luther had no notion at the Diet of Worms that his affirmation of the right of conscience would lead to such divergent beliefs. Within his own lifetime, however, he saw the proliferation of sects as diverse as the revolutionary spiritualists and the pacifist anabaptists. Disturbed though he was by these events, Luther never retreated from his

affirmation of the right of each individual to stand
before God and his or her fellow human beings guided by
faith and with a conscience instructed by grace.

At this point a word of caution is necessary. As
Karl Barth wrote in his famous 1933 essay, *Reformation
als Entscheidung*, the decision for faith was never for
Luther or the other reformers a decision for one of a
variety of human possibilities and options. In this
sense, Luther was most definitely **not** a proponent of
freedom of thought. Rather, Luther called the people
of his time to a "decision to surrender one's freedom
in freedom."[107]   By this decision a person binds the
self

> irrevocably without any prospect of doing
> otherwise in the future, without any remain-
> ing possibility of overhauling this decision
> in the future... This decision in contrast
> with all others is the ultimate decision.
> For in this decision man has sacrificed his
> freedom, that is, precisely the possibility
> of being able to do otherwise in the fu-
> ture... The way to other decisions in the
> future is barred to him, for he has now
> actually and ultimately surrendered his
> freedom not to believe.[108]

Thus, the decision to serve both God **and** mammon is now
forever foreclosed to the Christian.

Luther believed that it was precisely this decision for faith which gives one true freedom - freedom
from self-concern, freedom to serve one's neighbor in
love. This decision gives to the Christian freedom of
thought, freedom within the secular sphere to utilize
natural reason; freedom to learn, freedom to experi-
ment, freedom to engage in a vast variety of activities

which make human life a never ceasing source of joy and wonder. For us, secular modernists, it may seem that Luther limited freedom of thought by emphasizing that it is bounded and limited by the truths of revelation, truths not open to human probing and experimentation.

For Luther, however, it was precisely this fact revealed in Scripture that human salvation is a divine gift, not a goal which a person must attain through "correct" thought or action, which gives an individual real freedom of thought. No longer living in fear for the future, a Christian is able to utilize reason to its fullest. Within this life, the Christian has freedom of thought, not an abstract freedom, or a freedom without content, for such a freedom would be meaningless. Luther's recognition of the limits of natural reason and the dangers of arrogant reason does not sound so "medieval" to us in these days of recognizing that so many of our problems remain unsolved by reason and all of our technological developments. Reason has not succeeded in ending wars or stopping massacres or preventing the threat of a nuclear holocaust.

Luther put his faith not in the power of thought, of reason, but in the power of thought guided by grace, what he understood as regenerate reason. He perceived freedom of thought as this freedom to think responsibly and joyfully before God. He understood true freedom of thought, not as an unending possibility of choices, but as thought guided by the decision of faith, giving one the freedom to act joyfully in the world as the servant of others.

NOTES

1. Among many works addressing the situation of contemporary humankind, see J. Moltmann, *Man: Christian Anthropology in the Conflicts of the Present*, tr. J. Sturdy (Philadelphia, 1974), especially 22-45. For contrasting views see W. Pannenberg, *What is Man? Contemporary Anthropology in Theological Perspective*, tr. D. A. Priebe (Philadelphia, 1970), especially chapters 9-11, and Th. Hanna, *Bodies in Revolt: A Primer in Somatic Thinking* (New York, 1970), particularly 83-104 and 230-255. The essay by Paul Tillich, "The Protestant Message and the Man of Today," *The Protestant Era*, tr. J. L. Adams (Chicago, 1948), 192-205, remains insightful and relevant.

2. W. Dilthey, "The Interpretation and Analysis of Man in the 15th and 16th Centuries," in: *The Reformation: Basic Interpretations*, ed. L. W. Spitz, 2nd ed. (Lexington, Mass., 1972), 11-24. On Dilthey and his contemporaries see H. Bornkamm, *Luther im Spiegel der deutschen Geistesgeschichte*, 2nd rev. ed. (Göttingen, 1970), 100-107.

3. *Op. cit.*, p. 23.

4. E. Troeltsch, "Renaissance and Reformation," in: *The Reformation*, ed. L. W. Spitz, 25-43. See also H. Bornkamm, *Luther im Spiegel der deutschen Geistesgeschichte*, 107-110, and G. Ebeling, "Luther and the Beginning of the Modern Age," in: *Luther and the Dawn of the Modern Era*, ed. H. A. Oberman (Leiden, 1974), 11-39.

5. Tr. M. J. Olgin (New York, 1926).

6. H. Marcuse, *Reason and Revolution: Hegel and the Rise of Social Theory* (London, 1941), 14. Marcuse developed this argument at more length in his "Studien über Autorität und Familie," (1936), in: *Aufsätze aus der Zeitschrift für Sozialforschung 1934-1941*, Herbert Marcuse Schriften 3 (Frankfurt - Main, 1979), 85-185, esp. 85-110. See further O. Bayer, "Marcuses Kritik an Luthers Freiheitsbegriff," *Zeitschrift für Theologie und Kirche* 67 (1970), 453-478; W. Maurer, *Autorität in Freiheit: Zu Marcuses Angriff auf Luthers Freiheitslehre* (Stuttgart, 1970).

7. WA 7, 838; LW 32, 112-13. Debate continues over whether Luther spoke the words "I cannot do otherwise, here I stand" which are added in German to the Latin text. See LW 32, 113, n. 8. For differing views, see M. Brecht, *Martin Luther: Sein Weg zur Reformation 1483-1521* (Stuttgart, 1981), 438-439 and 506, n. 24, and R. Bainton, *Here I Stand: A Life of Martin Luther* (New York-Nashville, 1950), 185.

8. Cf. B. Lohse, *Ratio und Fides: Eine Untersuchung über die ratio in der Theologie Luthers* (Göttingen, 1958); B. Gerrish, *Grace and Reason: A Study of the Theology of Luther* (Oxford, 1962); G. Ebeling, *Lutherstudien*, II: *Disputatio de homine* (Tübingen, 1982), and *Evangelische Evangelienauslegung: Eine Untersuchung zu Luthers Hermeneutik* (Darmstadt, 1969), 376-382; K.-H. zur Mühlen, *Reformatorische Vernunftkritik und neuzeitliches Denken* (Tübingen, 1980), 44-158.

9. G. Ebeling, *Disputatio de homine*; K.-H. zur Mühlen, *Reformatorische Vernunftkritik*, 129-134.

10. WA 39 I, 175; LW 34, 137.

11. B. Gerrish, *Grace and Reason*, especially 26, and 71-83; B. Lohse, *Ratio und Fides*, 55-136.

12. WA 13, 246; LW 19, 11.

13. WA 8, 629; LW 44, 366.

14. WA 19, 206; LW 19, 54.

15. WA 17, 431.

16. WA 19, 207; LW 19, 55.

17. WA 19, 207; LW 19, 55.

18. WA 51, 126; LW 51, 375.

19. WA 51, 128-129; LW 51, 375-376.

20. WA 51, 129-130; LW 51, 376.

21 WA 51, 130; LW 51, 377.

22. WA 39 I, 175; LW 34, 137 (theses 4-6).

23. B. Gerrish, *Grace and Reason*, 169.

24. WA 40 I, 362.

25. WA 40 I, 362.

26. WA 42, 486; LW 2, 313; cf. B. Lohse, *Ratio und Fides*, 91.

27. See L. W. Spitz, "Luthers Bedeutung als Gelehrter und Denker für den anthropologischen Realismus," in: *Humanismus und Reformation als kulturelle Kräfte in der deutschen Geschichte*, ed. L. W. Spitz (Berlin, 1981), 5-9; B. Gerrish, *Grace and Reason*, 22-27; B. Lohse, *Ratio und Fides*, 50-54.

28. WA TR 1, 191, no. 439; LW 54, 71.

29. WA TR 1, 191; LW 54, 71; B. Lohse, *Ratio und Fides*, 114 f.

30. WA TR 3, 105, no. 2938 b; LW 54, 183.

31. WA TR 4, 613-614, no. 5015; LW 54, 377-378.

32. WA 51, 133; LW 51, 379.

33. WA 7, 838; LW 32, 112. See M. Brecht, *Martin Luther*, 439; also B. Lohse, *Ratio und Fides*, 106-119; "Luthers Antwort in Worms," in: *Luther: Mitteilungen der Luthergesellschaft* 29 (1958), 124-134; "Conscience and Authority in Luther," in: *Luther and the Dawn of the Modern Era*, 158-183; see also L. W. Spitz, "Luthers Bedeutung als Gelehrter," 9. For a view of the events leading to Luther's speech at Worms, see D. Olivier, *The Trial of Luther*, tr. J. Tonkin (St. Louis, 1971).

34. See H. A. Oberman, *Luther: Mensch zwischen Gott und Teufel* (Berlin, 1981), especially 223-234.

35. WA 18, 600-787; LW 33.

36. On Erasmus and Luther, see E. H. Harbison, *The Christian Scholar in the Age of the Reformation* (New York, 1956), 69-135, and on the relation between Luther and humanism, see L. W. Spitz, "Humanism in the Reformation," *Renaissance Studies in Honor of Hans Baron*, ed. A. Molho and J. A. Tedeschi (Dekalb, Ill., 1971), 643-662; "Headwaters of the Reformation: *Studia Humanitatis*,

Luther Senior, et Initia Reformationis," in: *Luther and the Dawn of the Modern Era*, 89-116; and H. Junghans, "Der Einfluss des Humanismus auf Luthers Entwicklung bis 1518," *Luther-Jahrbuch* 37 (1970), 37-101. See also B. Moeller-K. Stackmann, "Luder-Luther-Eleutherius: Erwägungen zu Luthers Namen," in: *Nachrichten der Akadamie der Wissenschaften in Göttingen I, Philologisch-Historische Klasse*, no. 7 (1981), 171-203.

37. M. Mann Phillips, *Erasmus and the Northern Renaissance* (London, 1949), 201.

38. P. Tillich, *The Protestant Era* (Chicago, 1948), 129.

39. G. Ebeling, *Luther: An Introduction to His Thought*, tr. R. A. Wilson (Philadelphia, 1972), 220.

40. WA 18, 635; LW 35, 65-66. See further, H. J. McSorley, *Luther: Right or Wrong? An Ecumenical-Theological Study of Luther's Major Work The Bondage of the Will* (New York-Minneapolis, 1969), 297-366, and W. Behnk, *Contra Liberum Arbitrium Pro Gratia Dei: Willenslehre und Christuszeugnis bei Luther und ihre Interpretation durch die neuere Lutherforschung* (Frankfurt, 1982).

41. On the limitations and temptations even of regenerate reason, see B. Lohse, *Ratio und Fides*, 100-106.

42. WA 18, 783; LW 33, 288-289.

43. See G. Ebeling, *Luther*, 217; see further his *Lutherstudien* I (Tübingen, 1971), 308-329, especially 320-329; also M. Baylor, *Action and Person: Conscience in Late Scholasticism and the Young Luther* (Leiden, 1977).

44. Cf., *Luther*, 218.

45. WA 18, 638; LW 33, 70.

46. See G. W. Forell, "Luther and Politics," in G. W. Forell, H. J. Grimm, Th. Hoelty-Nickel, *Luther and Culture*, <u>Martin</u> <u>Luther</u> <u>Lectures</u> 4 (Decorah, Iowa, 1957). See also WA 40, 292-293; LW 26, 173-174.

47. WA 18, 754; LW 33, 243.

48. WA 18, 762; LW 33, 255.

49. WA 7, 67; LW 31, 368. See also O. H. Pesch, *Hinführung zu Luther*, 2d rev. ed. (Mainz, 1983), 178-188.

50. K. Bauer, *Die Wittenberger Universitätstheologie und die Anfänge der deutschen Reformation* (Tübingen, 1928); M. Grossmann, *Humanism in Wittenberg* (Nieuwkoop, 1975), especially 76-85; H. J. Grimm, "Luther and Education," *Luther and Culture*, especially 73-93; S. Ozment, "Humanism, Scholasticism, and the Intellectual Origins of the Reformation," in: *Continuity and Discontinuity in Church History: Essays Presented to George Huntston Williams on the Occasion of his 65th Birthday*, ed. F. F. Church and T. George (Leiden, 1979), 133-149.

51. WA 56, 338; LW 25, 326.

52. See Luther's letter *To the Councilmen of All Cities in Germany That They Establish and Maintain Christian Schools* (1524), WA 15, 27-53; LW 45, 347-378. See also WAB I, 170, no. 74.

53. Erasmus, *Opus epistolarum*, Vol. 7, ed. P. S. Allen *et al.* (Oxford, 1928), 366 (20 March 1528).

54. F. Paulsen, *German Education Past and Present*, tr. T. Lorenz (London, 1908), 48. See also H. G. Good, *A History of Western Education* (New York, 1947), 153-158.

55. L. W. Spitz, "The Impact of the Reformation on the Universities," in: *University and Reformation: Lectures from the Copenhagen Symposium*, ed. L. Grane (Leiden, 1981), 13.

56. G. A. Benrath, "Die Universität der Reformationszeit," *Archiv für Reformationsgeschichte* 57 (1966), 40 f.

57. K. Hartfelder, *Philipp Melanchthon als Praeceptor Germaniae* (1889; Nieuwkoop, 1964); C. L. Manschreck, *Melanchthon: The Quiet Reformer* (New York, 1958), especially 131-157; and G. Müller, "Philipp Melanchthon und die Studienordnung für die hessischen Stipendiaten vom Mai 1546," *Archiv für Reformationsgeschichte* 51/2 (1960), 223-242.

58. WA 15, 44; LW 45, 368.

59. WA 15, 34; LW 45, 356.

60. Cf. thesis 52 of Luther's *Zirkulardisputation* 1539
     (WA 39 II, 42): "God ordained three hierarchies
     against the devil, that is the household, the
     polity, and the church (*oeconomiam, politiam, et
     Ecclesiam*)," p. 175. See W. H. Lazareth, *Luther
     on the Christian Home: An Application of the
     Social Ethics of the Reformation* (Philadelphia,
     1960); F. E. Cranz, *An Essay on the Development of
     Luther's Thought on Justice, Law, and Society*
     (Cambridge, Mass., 1964), 173-178.

61. WA 6, 407; LW 44, 127.

62. WA 10 I, 308.

63. W. Elert, *The Christian Ethos*, tr. C. J. Schindler
     (Philadelphia, 1957), 84. See also G. Strauss,
     *Luther's House of Learning: Indoctrination of the
     Young in the German Reformation* (Baltimore, 1978),
     especially 108-131.

64. W. Elert, *The Christian Ethos*, 83. For the
     influence of Luther's mother on his understanding
     of the mother's role, see I. Siggins, *Luther and
     His Mother* (Philadelphia, 1981), especially 71-79.

65. WA 2, 169-170; LW 44, 12-13.

66. W. J. Kooiman, "Luther's Later Years," in Th. G.
     Tappert, W. J. Kooiman, L. C. Green, *The Mature
     Luther*, <u>Martin</u> <u>Luther</u> <u>Lectures</u> 3 (Decorah, Iowa,
     1959), 73.

67. WA 38, 368.

68. G. Strauss, *Luther's House of Learning*, 111-131.

69. R. Bainton, *Here I Stand*, 337; G. Strauss,
     Luther's House of Learning, 123-127.

70. I. Asheim, *Glaube und Erziehung bei Luther: Ein
     Beitrag zur Geschichte des Verhältnisses von
     Theologie und Pädagogik* (Heidelberg, 1961), 46 f.

71. WA 15, 32; LW 45, 353.

72. WA 15, 34; LW 45, 355; see I. Asheim, *Glaube und Erziehung bei Luther*, 20-24.

73. WA 30 II, 522-523; LW 46, 217.

74. WA 15, 34; LW 45, 355.

75. WA 15, 46; LW 45, 369. See also G. M. Bruce, *Luther as an Educator* (1928; Westport, Conn., 1979); and K. Petzold, *Die Grundlagen der Erziehungslehre im Spätmittelalter und bei Luther* (Heidelberg, 1969), 69-94.

76. WA 6, 461; LW 44, 205-206. The question as to whether Luther placed schools within the sphere of the secular or the spiritual realm has been greatly debated. The most plausible interpretation, offered by Asheim, is that the schools, like parents, participate in both realms (*Glaube und Erziehung bei Luther*, 67-73). The modern debate concerning the role of religion in the schools would be entirely foreign to Luther. His goal was to achieve in Germany the establishment of *Christian* public schools.

77. I. Asheim, *Glaube und Erziehung bei Luther*, 75-83.

78. LW 45, 351, n. 10: "Luther is alluding to the papal practice of proclaiming from time to time a jubilee year, which in Germany was popularly called a '*Güldenjahr*.'"

79. WA 15, 38; LW 45, 360.

80. WA 15, 38; LW 45, 360.

81. WA 26, 195-240; LW 40, 269-320. Melanchthon wrote the *Instructions*, but in doing so, closely followed Luther's ideas. Luther himself wrote the Preface and made revisions in subsequent editions. LW 40, 266-267.

82. WA 26, 237-240; LW 40, 315-320.

83. WA 26, 239; LW 40, 319.

84. WA 26, 238; LW 40, 318.

85. WA 26, 237; LW 40, 316.

86. WA 15, 46; LW 45, 369-370.

87. WA 15, 30; LW 45, 350.

88. WA 30 II, 586; LW 46, 256.

89. WA 30 II, 562; LW 46, 242.

90. WA 15, 36; LW 45, 357-358.

91. WA 15, 36; LW 45, 358.

92. WA 30 II, 579; LW 46, 252-253.

93. WA 30 II, 580; LW 46, 253.

94. WA 30 II, 573; LW 46, 249.

95. WA 30 II, 575; LW 46, 250.

96. WA 54, 3.

97. WA 15, 51; LW 45, 375.

98. WA 15, 51-52; LW 45, 375-376.

99. WA 15, 52; LW 45, 376.

100. WAB I, 170, no. 74, 9 May 1518. Cited in L. W. Spitz, "Luther as Scholar and Thinker," in: *Renaissance Men and Ideas*, ed. R. Schwoebel (New York, 1971), 87.

101. G. A. Benrath, "Die Universität der Reformations-zeit," 39-40.

102. *Melanchthons Werke in Auswahl*, Vol. 3: *Humanistische Schriften*, ed. R. Nürnberger (Gütersloh, 1961), 29-42. See also K. Hartfelder, *Philipp Melanchthon als Praeceptor Germaniae*, especially 62-76.

103. *Humanistische Schriften*, 64, and 69. Cited in L. W. Spitz, "Humanism and the Reformation," in: *Transition and Revolution: Problems and Issues of European Renaissance and Reformation History*, ed. R. M. Kingdon (Minneapolis, 1974), 172, and 175.

104. L. W. Spitz, *The Renaissance and Reformation Movements* (Chicago, 1971), 558.

105. K. Holl, "Die Kulturbedeutung der Reformation,"
     in: *Gesammelte Aufsätze zur Kirchengeschichte*
     Vol. 1 (Tübingen, 1921), 396.

106. H. Butterfield, *Liberty in the Modern World*
     (Toronto, 1952), 11.

107. K. Barth, "Reformation as Decision," in: *The
     Reformation*, ed. L. W. Spitz, 158.

108. Ibid., 160. On Luther's concept of freedom, see
     also K. D. Schmidt, "Luthers Auffassung von
     Freiheit," *Luther: Mitteilungen der Luthergesell-
     schaft*, Heft 1 (1953), 1-11.

Hans-Christoph Rublack

REFORMATION AND SOCIETY

The Reformation of the 16th century has been
conventionally interpreted as marking the beginning of
the modern era,[1] although Luther posed a thoroughly
medieval question. The Reformation has been called a
revolt, even a revolution,[2] although its impact on
social structures was apparently less than powerful.
The Reformation has been viewed as a one-man-show, or
alternatively a two- or even three-men-show, as
Luther's, Zwingli's, and Calvin's ideas spread rapidly,
were received and accepted by the masses,[3] although it
is questionable whether many simple folk really understood what modern interpreters find so difficult to
explain to enlightened scholars.

Looking at the Reformation in its relation to
society we see changes on a less far-reaching scale
than is often suggested. If we search for common
denominators we can find certain tendencies inherent in
the process we term "Reformation." These tendencies
would be: **abstraction, contraction,** and **inclusion.**[4]
They reflect the direction of the Reformation process
on various levels: **abstraction** of **beliefs, contraction**
of **religion, inclusion** as to **social integration.** These
levels are not independent of each other; they are, of
course, closely interrelated, and for a short time they
even coincided - a fact which explains the powerful
effects of the Reformation. Moreover, these levels are

held together by communication. The **ACI** dimensions
(abstraction, contraction and inclusion) point to the
direction of the process, whereas communication provided the movement with its essential **dynamics**. Thus the
Reformation can be viewed as a process of communication
within a social system, which at once destroyed and
reconstructed the traditional beliefs by abstracting
them, the old religion by contracting it into newly
defined essentials (changing the institutional framework of what was one church into various confessional
churches), and the social context by levelling the
distinctions between clergy and laity which seemed to
be "*mieux adaptés*," as Lucien Febvre put it, to a
social system.[5]

One of the metaphors favored by 16th century
Reformers to signify the change intended was "light."[6]
This was an even more powerful symbol of change in an
age that was not able to blur the rhythms of day and
night, or winter and summer by using electric light.
"Light" meant the beginning of life and work; night
stopped everything, activity and movement. Darkness
was the time when haunting, paralyzing fears of the
uncontrollable forces outside were prevalent. Light,
on the other side, had all the beauty of capturing the
minds of the society in its concrete existence. It
was, moreover, not a new-fangled term but one of old
standing: Christ is the light. The sacred had for a
long time been depicted by sun, halos, gold. "Light"
was used by the Reformation writers to refer back to
the original message of Christ, i.e., to an older
religion that was to be restored.

Certainly, Reformation in this sense was not
identical with "enlightenment," as the age of rationalism had it, which did not see its terms of reference in

the past, but transferred them to a future to be improved by reason. While "rationalism" moved forward, "Reformation" change was interpreted as referring back to the truth once and for all established by the original message, i.e., the truth revealed in Christ. Light symbolized change as moving away from the previous age to an age of recapturing the original truth. The previous centuries were thereby cast into the shadow of darkness. Error, human depravity, human laws were seen as secular, constituting the principal sin of darkness. Light symbolized decisive and abrupt change, comprising everything and everybody. The whole world appeared in a new light. Hence, the Reformation truth claimed to re-interpret theology, religion, society, church, and state. Light overcame darkness and made an old world new. Light came from above, could not be produced, but was something granted, a gift from God. It signified the sacred, because God, the Sacred One, was the creator of light and life. All truth was centered in God's light.

Clearly, "light" was a metaphor signifying restoration as well as newness. It did not mean something totally new or unknown as for instance the "New World" discovered at that time by Columbus. Truth was rediscovered. The minds of the people at the beginning of what we call the "modern era" were not prepared to appreciate the quality of something new as something essentially better. Improvement meant restoring the old, the true meaning. So light had traditional overtones; it did not indicate a break with the old truth. The new interpretation of the gospel appeared as a restoration of a tradition lost after an age of darkness and sin. Something latent was made manifest.

It was a representation of a truth, which for a long time had been kept hidden.

In one of the many woodcuts of Reformation pamphlets, the principal media of communicating the new meaning to society, Luther is depicted as leading the Christians out of a dark cave. Luther shows them the way out of the Egyptian darkness in which the believers had been held for so long to Christ the crucified.[7] Reformation was the liberating force which made it possible for believers to gather around Christ. The inscription elucidates this: "The Exodus." Christian believers are led from the Egyptian darkness of human teaching into the light of the holy gospel, full of God's grace, teaching, and truth. Light as opposed to darkness is spelled out in terms of a process, an exodus[8] from Egypt, from the bondage of darkness to the freedom of Christ's light.

Since truth is characterized by its singularity it is unambiguous and straight-forward. Everybody can comprehend truth, for it possesses the virtue of unity and identity. In Luther's teachings this truth is expressed by his famous soleisms, *sola fide, sola gratia, sola Scriptura*, all of which refer to God **alone.** In the minds of more or less simple folk this precipitated a reduction from confusing complexity to simplicity. A city scribe at Constance, Jörg Vögeli, described the change as one from a labyrinth in which he had been entangled and encircled to walking along a royal highway, i.e., a straight path, with a clear and well defined goal. The twists and turns that had always led him to dead ends were replaced by a straight way; he moved ahead.[9] Truth brought clarity, a clear orientation for a life that led towards eternity. Frustrating complexity was turned into simplicity: a clear path to truth and true life. One could also point to inferences of the "light" metaphor in the Reformers' references to Scripture as the "pure" and "clear" "word of God."[10]

In historical terms, the self-defining images of the Reformation experience signify that Luther called Christians, and they responded by becoming Lutherans. In other words his ideas, which referred to the Christian truths, challenged lay persons, and they received the Lutheran message by converting to Luther's ideas. Thus the principal pattern of the relation between the Reformation and society seems to be one of **challenge** and **response:** an individual's ideas were transformed into action. Although those to whom the ideas were communicated responded in a more passive way, the ideas created a new religious and social reality through them. Therefore, the relation of Luther to the society of his time may be described as essentially "removed," as detached from social reality. That is to say, his relationship to society was on an ideological level. Society was altered through his ideas. Whether Luther is viewed as a hero, as a liberator, or as an instrument of divine action, social change **was** human-made, a human response to a human being - from the secular historian's point of view, at least.

It has long been debated how precisely Luther may be restored to his historical and social background. After all, he was an integral part of society. Already his biography necessitates describing his relations to the contemporary social positions and institutions. Luther was born into a society, socialized by schooling and training, teaching in a university, and addressing himself to the public at large. His father had moved from one class (peasant) to another (citizen), when he became a fairly successful manager and co-owner of a copper mine. He directed his son's career, paid for elementary and Latin schooling and financed his university education.[11] Martin was expected to improve his social status, too. Two possibilities for advancement presented themselves. A career in the church might provide the security of a well-endowed prebend, or an influential position in an ecclesiastical institution. The leading positions in the church were, however, primarily the preserve of the aristocracy. More promising seemed the possibility of attaining an influential political position, such as a lawyer in one of the recently established bureaucracies of territorial princes, or in the magistracy of major cities. The latter option was Hans Luther's plan for his son.

However, Martin chose to join the seemingly classless society of monks. Now, monastic life as such brought with it no secular reputation. Furthermore, the order which Luther entered was characterized by humility and strict seclusion from the world - a total reversal of his father's wishes, for whom life within the monastery walls had no meaning other than the religious prestige of a person nearer to God. His time, effort and money were spent in vain. Martin's conversion to monasticism meant that he had become indefinable in terms of social standing. For instance, the woodcuts in his early tracts depict him as a monk.[12] The halo around his head appears somewhat out of place in the light of his rejection of sainthood, but it was meant to indicate his otherworldliness. Although his authority was socially not definable, he could so much more be taken to be a messenger of divine truth.

And yet again he broke also with this position when he married. For the rest of his life he remained in the marital estate as a university professor. However, this switch in social position seems to be of no consequence for his theological theory, for even before he married, Luther had already advocated marriage.[13] Thus his marriage appears rather to be an action deduced from his belief.

Luther's relations to social realities, as defined in class or estate, demonstrate that it is highly questionable to consider him as a "bourgeois." Until recently those who have advocated the interpretation of the Reformation as an "early bourgeois revolution" (*frühbürgerliche Revolution*)[14] have not been able to clearly identify the principal Reformer with a bourgeois position. Therefore, they called him an "exponent" of a class position.[15] The term "exponent" carries at least two meanings. "Exponent of a bourgeois ideology" signifies that Luther interpreted a bourgeois set of ideas. But such ideas must have already been in existence. Luther, however, obviously was himself the cause for the people to reinterpret their situation. In fact, it is hard to find reformed bourgeois thought before the early bourgeois revolution. So a second meaning would apply, namely, that Luther was a "representative of his class." His dominant interests were symbolic of the bourgeois interests of his time, making explicit what was hidden in social reality.

Such an interpretation of Luther's Reformation and its relation to society, then, does not have to focus on the **person** and his ideas transforming a social context, but on the **class position** more or less defined by those interests, desires, and expectations which produce congenial ideas in individuals who are more or less limited by their conformity to this position. Consequently, there is no need to prove biographically that the ideas were produced in an individual's life. Rather, the exponent's subjective theory is considered to be a reflection of objective needs, i.e., ideas are assumed to conform with structures. To put it more succinctly, Luther did not teach anything new or unexpected: his Reformation simply reflected the interests of a social group. He thought what his class would have wished him to think.[16] The poles of activity and passivity have thus been switched: society is essentially active, while the Reformer's role is basically passive, i.e., receptive to classbred notions.

This interpretation has recently been revised. We can offer only a sketch of this new Marxist understanding of Luther, Reformation, and society. The revision has been advanced by Gerhard Brendler in his model Luther biography in the German Democratic Republic.[17]

Brendler's approach is characterized by a high degree of differentiation and flexibility. This is true of both Luther's social biography and of the analysis of the society of his time. Stressing the varying roles and positions in Luther's life, this more flexible interpretation freed itself from the previous, more static definitions of the relation between social status and exponential ideas. Luther is now essentially part of the intellectual elite and it is his professional work which defined his ideas most clearly. Surprisingly, or maybe not, Luther is accepted as a theologian. Yet theology is a function of the early modern society.

According to Brendler this social function of theology is one of **integration** and **legitimization**. Luther found an individual solution to his personal problems which forced him to oppose the church. However, there was also a corresponding, growing opposition in the society at large which, though it preceded Luther's and was widely scattered through different social groups, was less consciously felt and lacked a focal point. Therefore Luther's attack on the church as an hegemonial power of feudalism crystallized all opposition and so became the take-off for a bourgeois revolution. Various interests attached themselves to this incipient Reformation ideology. Nevertheless, Luther's concept of authority and his emphasis on the need for stability (ideas compatible with his own social standing) necessarily impeded the fusion of the early bourgeois revolution with the Reformation. Luther sided with authority, stabilized his new church, cared for the needs of ministers and schoolmasters, and opposed the peasants.

Whereas much of Brendler's functional analysis is compatible with what non-Marxist scholars find acceptable for elucidating social reality, one is in the end left with an unsatisfactory impression. It seems that Brendler rationalizes a basic Marxist attachment to class consciousness as he rediscovers Luther's professorial role because he attributes to him a split personality, with two loyalties and even two pieties, which alternately worked as opposition and appeasement to authority. All the same, Brendler's attempt is open to scholarly debate rather than being simply a net of hypotheses which make for a closed system. This is encouraging.

One can visualize the problems Brendler tried to deal with as identical with those scholars all over the world have struggled with for years. Why was Luther successful? Why was there a change ca. 1525 in Luther's attitude toward authority? Why his lack of understanding for the religious motives of the peasants' revolt? These are questions to which scholars have yet to provide an adequate answer. How was it that Luther found a solution to the main problems of society at a time when he was most detached from social experience? Which were the factors by means of which Luther's ideas were deflected according to varying interests?

Where these questions need to be tested is the empirically based analysis of **communication**, i.e., Luther's ideas moving within society and being received by various individuals and social groups, and vice versa, interests of social groups and individuals being transformed by Luther's ideas. In this respect, Brendler has gained no more ground than his non-Marxist colleagues. Nor does he completely depart from older concepts. Not only does he still use the concept "exponent," even where he found more flexible terms such as **congruence** or **correspondence**, but he also proposes a "one-way-communication," for in stressing the importance of the whole problem, Luther alone is taken as instrumental in providing a solution. A more flexible method would see society grant it to the theologians to discuss their problems independently and thus would recognize the considerable importance of theology itself. These theological discussions and solutions may or may not have appealed to different sectors of society. Even more importantly a more differentiated method would view religion as the medium by which theology was communicated to various social groups. Such an approach, as advanced by the non-Marxist scholar Rainer Wohlfeil,[18] works with a set of variables, the relations among which are contingent, i.e., conjunctive and disconjunctive as the case may be. There is no reason to exclude the possibility that personal theology and social religion may show different characteristics.

It is in this sense of a flexible connection between variables that I would stress the vital role of religion in the process of communicating Luther's ideas to the society, as much as the transforming role of the various groups within society in receiving them. It is, of course, a preconceived assumption to assign theology an **extra**-social status, since in fact it was related to society. This relation, however, cannot be articulated either by determining its contents, nor by merely reflecting on social problems. Theological thinking had a dynamic of its own, and a lot of it remained alien to social groups other than professional theologians. Society granted its theologians the right to define their themes and work out their problems independent of social needs. This very independence was criticized by humanists and reformers alike as "scholasticism." Luther, too, moved along this separate track before 1517. It was only when theological theory was translated into religious terms that social needs as defined by religion would be met. And it was Luther himself who translated his academic *95 Theses* into terms of a religious appeal.

This beginning point of Reformation history was already the result of a complex process. The development was initiated by a problem which Luther encountered in his pastoral practice, namely, his

parishioners returning from Tetzel's sale with their
pockets filled with letters of indulgence to disburden
them from guilt feelings. Luther transposed this
experience onto a doctrinal level, his Latin theses
published for academic discussion. After the theses
had been attacked by defenders of the church, Luther
turned in a larger Latin book to theologians and in a
smaller pamphlet to the literate German lay people.[19]

We cannot follow Luther's and the Reformation's
progress closely step by step. The dynamics of public
opinion are known in general, but not in detail. If
only our knowledge of Reformation communication equal-
led that of our understanding of political events, we
would be better equipped to describe the Reformation in
its approximation to social reality. But it is clear
from Luther's early German pamphlets that he appealed
to literate lay persons whose religion he wanted to
change. His object was to reform piety.

This is most accurately reflected by a citizen at
Freiburg who, when asked to purge his library of
Luther's books, stated that he had read devotional
books by the Strasbourg preacher Geiler von Kaisers-
berg, by the mystic Tauler, and by the famous Gerson
and "other teachers of Holy Scripture. I have read
them for myself and to my household, knowing of no
better leisure." And in the same way he had also read
Luther who taught him how to pray, to fast, to venerate
the saints and the virgin, and to obey the authorities
and the precepts of God and the church. "I do not ask
for controversy," he added, "but for the teaching of
doctrine, as Paul wrote, 'we are to read everything and
keep good things and leave bad things behind.'"[20] If
we check this testimony against Luther's early German
works from 1518 to 1519, this is what a pious layperson

could actually learn from Luther's writings: Luther was at first read in German as a devotional author, though we cannot quite ascertain whether it was his sincerity and integrity that made him a spiritual authority, or his recent fame for attacking the church that attracted the readers. Probably both notions contributed to his reputation as it was by no means an unusual thing in a church as diversified as the late medieval church was, for a monk to initiate a movement of pious devotion.

What we have to get rid of is the notion of a monolithic church. The lives of simple folk were determined by local conditions. Alternative forms of religious devotion were rarely offered to peasants. Citizens usually had the option of worship in the parish church or monastery. There was the high mass, a Latin liturgy consisting of ritual actions. There were private masses, asking God, Christ, and the saints for intercession for souls of deceased relatives. There was the ritual which accompanied the main stages of life: birth, marriage, death, the "rites of passage." Once a year there was confession, for which laypeople were asked to prepare a list of sins committed.

On the communal level processions and benedictions marked the course of the year giving rhythm and religious meaning to life, day and night, summer, spring, fall, and (the season of darkness) winter. Life brought expansion with sun and heat during the harvest, despair when the harvest failed, collapse into fears. But with favorable harvest one might survive winter and spring. All this was basic life on short term cycles, not reaching much beyond the locality in which one was born. The higher nobility was never or rarely seen:

the local gentry was the authority common folk were accustomed to.

This was admittedly a simple life, but for most people, the simple folk, there was work, food and drink, warmth and chill, summer and winter, marriage and childbirth, and the sorrows of life and death, and that was that. It was a life dependent on religion that pervaded everyday life and seasons, making life tolerable and adding some meaning, some light, to the darkness. What our books tell us - the splendid Emperor Maximilian, the brilliant Erasmus pouring his ideas into the printing press, a council debating at Rome, the Pope and his luxurious court - all this was removed, if not unknown, and in no way touched the lives of the simple folk.

It is true, though, that their lives were touched by religion, and religion was centered around the activity of the priest. His action in the church was a social action: it addressed the layfolk, integrated their lives, gave comfort in death, provided God's blessing and kindled hope for this world and the next. "Priest," however, is a simplifying term for a whole variety of ecclesiastical positions: parish priests, curates, mendicant friars, bishops of aristocratic descent, the chapters, cardinals, the pope - they all functioned in diversified precincts of social action. Likewise the term "lay person" must be spelled out. How many could read? Approximately up to 5 percent, maximally 10 percent, mostly in the cities. How many were pious, diligent, negligent? How many could afford to spend more than a penny for endowments, or could commission an artist to paint an altar? Citizens and country folk, rich and poor, had unequal chances of religious achievement.

It is in this social context that we have to
evaluate statements like: 'the German people hailed
Luther;' 'almost every German was provided with a copy
of Luther's pamphlets;' 'the peasants misunderstood
Luther's message;' 'the Reformation was an urban
event.'

What did Luther teach his lay readers? His
religion devalued good works. Religious achievement
had run high; people were asked to spend more and more
of their money to obtain grace. Those who could afford
it invested heavily in achieving salvation for themselves and for their relatives. They contributed to
relieving the suffering in purgatory, hell, and damnation. Luther, however, taught that good works are of
no avail. Only through faith does God come to the
human being. No human efforts and means can bring
security or hope: it is God alone who freely gives
salvation by grace. The human heart, a person's
innermost being, must be directed toward Christ's
redemptive act and God's saving grace. So, Luther
abstracted God from human means: he interiorized
religion in recommending that the hearts turn away from
good works and solely be directed toward God.[21]

Knowing God's grace, learning about faith in
Scripture is essential and so living by faith means not
to rely on any active accomplishment but to turn one's
heart to God. This **abstraction**, this concentration on
faith, this orientation toward God and Scripture
constituted the core of Luther's religion. Later, when
a new church had to be established in an institutional
setting, this tendency toward abstraction would turn
into cognitive training: the Scripture read as a text,
children memorizing short statements on doctrine, and
sermons preached expanding the evangelical teaching.

The major change was one from ritual action to knowing
and knowledge. Luther moved the emphasis from the
visual to that of the abstract, the interiorized, the
invisible.

The consequence of this abstraction of religion
was a redefinition of what the church was and of how
its ministers were to act. Luther addressed himself to
Christians, without reference to human institutions.
As long as the word of God is preached, God's presence
is insured. This is to be done by local ministers,
because preaching, needless to say, can be effected
only through verbal communication. However, everything
above that local level is mere organization, necessary,
of course, for institutionalizing the new church (such
as visitations and superintendents to make sure that
sound and regular preaching is available), but essentially, i.e., spiritually, indifferent to the proclamation of God's word.

Luther's indifference to church organization is
well known, as long as bishops preached they were
allowed to stay in office. Luther saw the greatest
danger in the pope, who in his position of power had
perverted God's religion into human statutes, into a
legal code, upon which the privilege and the hegemony
of the church were founded and which denied the poverty
and humility of Christ and his word. From the 1520's
on the pope was defined as the Antichrist.[22]   So
Luther's, and for similar reasons, Zwingli's and
Calvin's church was contracted into preaching by
reducing the number of sacraments, curbing the luxury
of church pageantry, and limiting the variety of
worship services. Communal life was purged from
processions and benedictions. This was a contraction
which allowed concentration on the essentials. The

purity of the light asked for purification of the church. In the end the universal church was contracted into territorial, national, and local churches.

A new limitation of the secular and the sacred (God, Christ, and his word alone are sacred, while previously pious actions, such as good works, and previously sacred places or holy times are secularized) deprived the clergy of their status of holiness. They could no longer grant salvation, but proclaimed God's grace and law. Baptized Christians were expected to do likewise. Only reasons of order and of the need for training made an orderly procedure at first advisable and then mandatory to select and ordain clerical staff to administer the word and the sacraments. Ministers were called "servants of the word." Although they were soon distanced from the congregation, as symbolized in the location of the pulpit, they shared with their parishioners a bourgeois life style. They were first allowed then expected to marry. Their life became as socially controlled as that of any other citizen. The cities subjected them to taxes by making them citizens. They lost their privilege of special courts and their separate privileged status. This **inclusion** marks a major change in social structure: there was no escape from secular power: clerical privileges and immunities were abandoned.

On the whole, then, **abstraction**, **contraction**, and **inclusion** mark the essentials of the relationship between the Reformation and society.

How was the Reformation received by the laity? Obviously we have to move into a mode of differentiation again. Certainly, the Reformation did not remain within the inner circles of an intellectual elite; rather, it developed into a lay movement. This

suggests that it had an inner **unity**, which was provided
by Luther's teachings. But the closer we move to
social reality, the more diversified are their real
appeal and the motives for their adoption. After all,
the Reformation was a movement within society and
Luther himself took advantage of the diversified effect
of his appeal. Nonetheless, Luther's power of attraction consisted in the fact that his religion promised
identity. Luther himself repeatedly described works
righteousness as a mere "running to and fro."[23]
Everything possible was being done to escape the threat
of eternal damnation by achieving salvation through an
endless variety of good works. In providing abstraction, contraction, and inclusion Luther was promising
identity and unity: by faith alone. In fact this
development had been in the making for some time, for
devotion and education of the inner self, a higher
degree of reflexivity was already practiced in monasteries and lay circles of the elite spiritual groups.[24]
Such pre-Reformation practices found with Luther a
theoretical, theological confirmation.

Contraction appealed to those who could experience
religion only in a local context. It was also favored
by the city magistrates who had long fought for an
identity of their local churches with the urban community. Likewise, princes found it attractive in order
to avoid constant interference with their rule from
outside their territories. Furthermore, they tended to
welcome the reduction of the complex organizational
structures of ecclesiastical institutions, such as
chapters, episcopal curiae and courts, and monastic
orders. The Reformation pattern of church organization
simplified them and attached them to local churches.
Last but not least, contraction appealed to the

peasants, as evidenced in the *12 Articles of the Peasants* 1525: they wished to elect their own parish pastor.[25]

Inclusion fulfilled the aspirations of all who for various reasons had objected to the separation and arrogance of the clergy, and the moral and financial burdens imposed by them. Anticlericalism disappeared as soon as the special status of the priests was abolished. Ministers in Protestant territories were not allowed to claim special social privileges. The laity reacted unfavorably when ministers assumed positions which interfered in what it claimed as its preserve. The Lutheran confirmation of secular authority enabled the laity firmly to tell its ministers to stay within the spiritual realm. Lay authorities expected domesticated ministers. They resented doctrinal controversies disturbing the peace, for conscientious ministers did not always live up to their role expectations.

All of this means that both the religious attraction of and the reaction to the Reformation were predisposed by the aspiration and the discontent in pre-Reformation times. What Luther did was to provide a fundamental religious solution to a variety of problems. Religion was founded on a new theological theory as soon as it found it compatible. However, since the new theological theory was used as a solution to a variety of problems, further deductions were made to meet specific problems. With a variety of predispositions, ranging from discontent with, and enmity to the clergy, to power struggles, religion reacted to Luther's theology, by not only integrating it into itself as a theological rationale for its opposition to existing conditions, but also by altering it according to the motives of various groups within society, and according to times and places.

We can already outline the degree of participation in the Reformation movement of the estates: nobility, higher and lower; citizens, upper and middle class; peasants. Clearly, social interests prevented the **nobility** from too strongly advocating the Reformation message. As a class they were not overly responsive to Luther's appeal in 1520 to promote ecclesiastical reform.[26] They soon sensed that in fact the Wittenberg Reformer had the princes and magistrates in mind. This increased their apprehension that the Reformation church enhanced the power of both the territorial princes and their bourgeois advisers who were educated enough to govern the church with a university trained staff. The nobility was as much aroused by Zwingli's anti-aristocratic attitude, as they later resented the presbyters in Calvin's Geneva where ecclesiastical functions traditionally performed by the nobility were transferred to the common people.[27]

Moreover, the nobility, whether high or low, had vested interests in chapters and better endowed convents and monasteries, the prebends of which provided not only for a more than adequate living but also insured influence. In addition the nobility and gentry feared that their rights of patronage over their local churches would be eliminated, thus depriving them of an instrument of social dominance and control.[28] When the social pressure from below subsided after the Peasants' War there was no real need to press ahead with reform or to adapt to progress to appease religious opposition. Individually some nobles became convinced adherents of the Reformation movement, mostly of the Lutheran type. But as a group they give strong evidence to the assumption that personal and social forms of religion could indeed move along separate lines. Depending on the constellation and situation, regional nobility resisted the centralizing effect of the new gospel which undergirded the opposition against a Catholic prince and provided an element of coherence. But this movement for a larger degree of political autonomy dwindled and the nobility regained their old advantages.

There was a strong disposition in the cities to advance the Reformation. They were ideal centers culturally equipped to spread a literate religion. They were centers of printing, of communication, with geographical mobility being surprisingly high. As a rule citizens were not forced to rely on prebends, since they were sufficiently mobile to move into other branches of the economy. Upper class citizens did not really have to depend on church positions other than to enhance their prestige and influence. There was a growing search for identity of city and parish church. Freed from outside interference the parish churches contracted into local congregations. The cities were generally the first to assimilate their priests as citizens, though they tended to keep the clergy from full political participation. By adopting the Reformation the cities were able to solve quite a few problems: provisions for the poor now were financed from former ecclesiastical holdings; the social control exerted by the church courts in marriage matters was eliminated and transferred to the magistrates; and a long series of saints' days was abolished so that more work could be done and more profit could be made.

Financing the new church was relatively easy because of the appropriation of ecclesiastical income.

However, political changes in the imperial cities gave
rise to the possibility of conflicting interests which
joined the interests of the upper classes in the
church. But the potentiality of conflict diminished
since the emperor, source of legitimate government and
privileges, was prevented from taking a strict stand
against the Reformation because of the Smalcaldic
League,[29] a political and military alliance which
promised an empire-wide protection for Protestant
territories and cities. Oligarchies in the cities
found it easier to heal the rifts and tensions within
their communities by yielding their reluctance to
reform their churches. This again did not mean that
among the urban elite there were not convinced Protestant individuals. But as a socio-political group they
exhibited more or less non-devotional motives to
embrace the Reformation of the church, which made them
hesitate.

All the same, motives to accept reform were on the
whole stronger. There was pressure from the **middle
classes** who were not only less connected to interests
outside the city but also prepared by experience and
education to find the new gospel commensurate with
their spiritual needs, or with their discontent with,
and protest against the church. Moreover, they soon
realized that condemning good works meant that they
could very well keep their profit to be reinvested in
shops and firms. All this would sooner or later move
the citizens more readily into the Protestant reform.
Luther's, and even more Zwingli's and Calvin's reform
was found readily adaptable to social aspirations. As
Luther himself experienced at Wittenberg,[30] the middle
class citizens showed an unwillingness to sacrifice
money to assist the ministers and the poor, which

demonstrated that although the citizens were converted to the new faith they lacked in love to the neighbor which was to follow from it. A little known fact is that Luther's wrath over the avarice, as he termed the civic economic prudence[31] of his Wittenbergers, reached such proportions that for a few weeks, in 1530, he refused to preach his sermons.[32]

Luther similarly realized that the **peasants'** way of converting his gospel into their lives perverted his intentions: he blamed them for contaminating the word with their worldly concerns.[33] As Gerald Strauss' extensive research has shown, this is no surprising fact: The Reformation message was spread in an intellectual and a literate form alien to the peasants' needs.[34] Such a world of inner spirituality to be reaffirmed by Scripture reading and reflection rather than action and movement, was totally foreign to their necessities. Even in the process of acculturation to the now officially adopted doctrine, the peasants hardly found words meaningful enough to express their life which was pervaded by the activity to produce food and to avert imminent threats to their only means of survival. The pastors' complaints about their ignorance and indifference point to a limitation which could only be gradually removed by the impact of training in literacy. Consequently, the peasants' way of viewing the Reformation had to be selective according to their social conditions. They evidently felt the ecclesiastical burdens and they sensed the promised expansion of control in communal life. But this was more a concern of the village elite (again one would have to distinguish groups within village societies). It is here that historians discover the limits of their research since cultures that did not produce written

documents are barely accessible, thus defying historical analysis. Still, more research is in progress,[35]
but easy generalizations might in the long run be more
misleading than helpful.

There are no general parameters with which the
social movement of the Reformation can readily be
measured. Estates, the dichotomy of rich and poor,
literate and illiterate, distance and proximity to
cultural centers, ecclesiastical dominance and effective rule of princes and nobles, political risks and
need of protection, all these criteria get hold of the
Reformation in particular terms. It is important to
realize that theology in its religious forms had to
take on social forms in order to be launched into the
channels of **communication**. This transformation is what
happened within social groups. So, what an input of a
religious appeal of reliance on God alone meant when it
was filtered through to the lower social ranks, is
probably typified by the experience of the Upper Rhine
count, whom an evangelical peasant addressed in 1525
with the claim: "Brother George, your body, my body,
my body, your body, my goods, your goods, your goods,
my goods, we all are brethren in Christ."[36] We have to
take such a statement as a genuine part of the Reformation religion, just as much as we can see a religious
quality in citizens' eating meat during Lent.[37]

The means of communication were not all conducive
to delivering unambiguous spiritual messages. Since
research on Reformation communication is but in its
early stages,[38] it would be precarious to give more
than a preliminary outline. Rainer Wohlfeil has
summarized the hitherto known facts and pointed out the
problem that 16th century public opinion was in its
structure widely different from what we have inherited

from the 19th century.[39] Miriam U. Chrisman's pioneer
work has clearly documented that the Reformation
pamphlets were in great demand for a brief period in
the 1520's.[40] Bob Scribner's work gives us a comprehensive view of the uses of images and illustrations
which Reformation agitators employed.[41]

We have, therefore, to analyze an upsurge in the
production of texts, differentiated as to various
levels, like scholarly commentaries and Latin doctrinal
expositions, popular pamphlets, and the Bible published
in German, which the Reformers claimed to contain the
fundamentals of true religion, a text accessible to
scholars both as a source for solving theological
problems and for instruction for life, and to literate
laity as an aid in devotional needs and religious
judgment - a book to be used in prayer and as a weapon
in conflict. It is here that the multi-functional use
of books in print is most evident.

The Reformation Bibles in German were illustrated.
Hence the Bible could serve as a model for the various
forms in which a message could be communicated: it
could be read privately, illustrations would reinforce
the content. The Bible was of course regularly read
aloud in church, and so acquired an authority relative
to public opinion. It was used for teaching purposes,
served as a text for sermons and was a source from
which psalms could be sung, as the Calvinists did. The
Bible comprised the whole range of media characteristic
of Reformation public opinion.

The communication process of the Reformation
period bears the mark of expansion, not only in quanti-
ty, but also in the development of specific media uses
to open up specific ways to achieve specific aims. In
contrast to the preference given to the sacred and

learned book in pre-Reformation times, there occurred an extension of the range of media, at least as far as production is concerned, a proliferation of media uses and aims which can be analyzed in its effects and coherence as a "media profile."

Yet such an approach only narrowly defines the means used, as most of the communication was non-textual, i.e., oral. This is true, of course, of sermons, the medium that gained predominance in Protestant churches during the Reformation. Its role can hardly be underestimated. As the word of God preached Sundays and weekdays the sermon obtained the monopoly position of communicating meaning and behavioral patterns to life. Nevertheless, sermons must not be overrated since they were oral in delivery and thus limited to the congregation present and restricted in time, and their sheer regularity did not automatically increase their effect. But sermons set the style for religious communication, however locally restricted their effect.

Oral communication in fact was the basic form for the simple, illiterate folk: news of any kind, conflict or consent, was communicated in houses, streets, and taverns. Being the only available general means of information, oral communication was not limited to topics agreed on by convention, so that other topics would have been excluded and reserved to different media. Rather, religion in times of conflict was discussed in inns; political events were reported by songs; rumors and discussions had, as the authorities very well knew, political undertones and could develop into a revolt.[42]

It is only above this level of oral communication that textual communications arose. Communication by written word had the advantage of a wider range beyond regional impact, as Luther's writings did. Moreover, printed texts could be combined with media of a different kind, such as title woodcuts, and could be used in new communication contexts. But even these texts used to be orally communicated by reading them aloud, as much as conversely, real dialogues may have served as blueprint for the texts.[43] Texts were performed as plays in public, songs sung in various places were circulated as texts not only for use as hymns in churches but also as rallying songs in demonstrations.

Non-verbal forms of communication were equally common: gestures, such as by the two students in Nördlingen, who raised their hands to their ears to signify that the preacher was a fool.[44] This must have been a conventional sign, for people from Augsburg did the same when Cardinal Campeggio moved into town.[45] Bob Scribner has written a useful article on carnival rites which were used to signify religious perversion and change.[46]

All this can be considered part of the social means of communication, and my point is, that the interpretation communicated was not necessarily in line with the intention of the authors. Even now historians find it difficult to prove whether something like the destruction of a saint's image was a religious act or an act of social revolt against the ostentatious luxury the rich displayed in sacred places - or possibly both.[47] There was a butcher's son in Augsburg who spilt blood on carved gravestones in the cathedral cemetery, where prominent people were buried. His landlord explained that a scribe was living in his house who daily read the Bible and from whom the boy had learned that images were to be destroyed.[48] Yet it was not always the poor people who were prone to

destroy images. Thomas Kleinbrötli of Zürich contended
that the donors of images were more pious than those
who destroyed them. He distrusted the written word,
for it might tell also lies indicating thereby that the
illiterate had no way of viewing things spiritual if
images were destroyed.[49]

All spoken communication moved words and texts
along the avenues of various sectors of society. Words
and texts were imbued with the communicators' spirit
and interests. These were deformed or genuinely
assimilated according to various interests, highlight-
ing or distorting the meaning the original authors
wished to express. Consequently, the general tendencies of the Reformation were subject to a process of
transformation. However, while continued analysis of
the Reformation pamphlets will indeed amount to a huge
step forward in understanding the Reformation as a
social process, it will give us but a glimpse into a
non-textual, a verbal reality.

The short-term effects of the Reformation are not
the only dimension social historians have to consider.
Ever since the debate on "social mentalities" began,[50]
it was understood that fundamental behavioral patterns
are established by a coordination of consciousness and
social norms - a synthesis in the process of socialization and affirmed by enduring social conditions. Did
the Reformation contribute to forming 'mentalities',
and in this way produce long-term effects?

This historical dimension is the time scale of
Weber's **extension** or Braudel's "*longue durée*." Though
Luther's and Calvin's influence was not limited to
early modern times, it was at that time that they were
accepted as undisputed authorities among the members of
their churches. Not until recently has the Roman

Catholic teaching of that age come to prominence as competing with Protestantism for being a contributing factor to modernization. Delumeau and Muchembled contended that the Reformation and Counter-Reformation had similar effects; namely literate, learned and written culture was superimposed on popular culture, thereby destroying it.[51] Gerald Strauss maintained that this was not an easy achievement.[52]

On a **long term** scale, then, we again have to work our way through details of instruction of the elite groups, such as ministers and priests, to identify the influence they, judges, and officials exerted on people high and low, to analyze the virtues they recommended and the vices they forbade, and to assess the resistance offered by town and country.

Again, we are only at the beginning of research in this field. Significant is the fact that recent scholarship attributed a rather modest role to the influence of the Reformers. For instance, Luther did not essentially change the lowly role which **work** played - in fact Max Weber was correct not to place Luther into the catalytic role of having spawned the spirit of capitalism.[53] Luther opened the door, as one recent interpreter said, but he did not know what precisely the consequences would be.[54] Luther conceived of work as the medieval authors did, i.e., it was a troublesome, laborious drudgery. This view was realistic and corresponded to most people's experience. Just the same, Luther changed the frame of reference: it was God's command to work: there was to be no longer any pious escape into monastic leisure: work and its profits had to be used to help the neighbor.[55]

Luther could not go any further in attaching positive significance to work. He did not herald a

future when work is taken to be the essential means of
changing the world by improving it. Anything that
would make use of profits to make new profit was alien
to him. Even the simple accumulation of money and
goods to provide for the exigencies of an unknown
future was judged as a vice, since it withheld aid from
suffering neighbors. "Avarice," said Luther, in
repetition of a Biblical tradition, "is the root of all
evil."[56]   Nonetheless, the extent to which Luther
stressed the love of the neighbor is surprising,
perhaps even paradoxical in view of his devaluation of
good works. Yet since the early 1520's he more and
more stressed this second dimension of his theology of
faith, namely works of love, the consequence of faith.
His sermons addressed to his Wittenberg congregation
strongly emphasize this aspect.[57]

The Reformation certainly gave a fresh impetus to
the issuance of ordinances for the relief of the **poor**.
This impact was, as a modern researcher has shown,
widespread.[58]   However, it would be more important for
social history to take a look at the social aims in the
care for the poor. Such an approach would show that
even though with regard to spiritual **motives** early
Protestant ordinances for the relief of the poor relied
heavily on Luther's new teaching on grace alone to be
followed by mercy to the poor, Protestant social **aims**
do **not** appear to have differed widely from Humanist or
Roman Catholic aims. The poor were not to be advanced
to rise in social status, but rather they were assisted
to be able to stay where they were, in their station in
life - just above a minimum standard of living. As
there was no achievement by works in religious matters,
so Luther did not advocate any achievement, advancement
or improvement in social status or wealth. Another aim

seems to have been that the poor were to serve as a potential pool from which cheap labor could be recruited. This was certainly a matter of social control, as evidenced for instance by the fact that vagrancy was disprivileged, the local poor were to be preferred (another indicator of growing localism) and the poor to be marked by special signs. Social control was to insure decent and pious behavior.

More recent research has shown that less change than hitherto assumed is to be attributed to Luther's notion of **married life**.[59] Of course, the Reformation eliminated the distinction of celibate life as preferred by God. But for Luther the principal aim for marriage remained the containment of sexual desires. Luther viewed marriage as essentially remedial. Now, the begetting and educating of children could be elevated to a superior aim, if conflict with the aim of the containment of lust could not be resolved. Mutual aid, traditional as this secondary purpose was, was indeed mentioned, but the social nature of marriage as partnership in life and mind was in no way upgraded to be the **principal** aim. Still, by evaluating marriage as a divine ordinance Luther at least paved the way to an unequivocally positive evaluation of married life. Once again, he appears to represent an intermediate position, but leaning more to the medieval past. It was rather the relaxation of eccelesiastical control that made the shift toward a positive understanding of marriage possible, together with socio-economic changes which prefigured the major change to romantic love around 1800.[60]

More of a change can be noticed in the documents indicating new attitudes toward **death**. Here Protestantism devalued the peremptory character of the battle

on the deathbed, deciding between salvation and condem-
nation. Instead the grave was a place to rest and wait
for the resurrection. Grace abounding disburdened this
last effort to achieve salvation. This seems to have
been accepted widely among Protestants, as epitaphs
show.[61] On the other hand, there is some doubt whether
the attitude toward the **procreation of life** changed as
a consequence of the Reformation. Even in the Geneva
society with its high quality of self-control and
rationality of life, there was obviously no move toward
the idea of family planning as ranking superior to the
conditions of social life. Rather, it was the urban
context that changed demographic habits.[62] Although in
homogeneous circumstances between two confessional
groups, one finds the birth rate of Protestants lower
than that of Catholics,[63] it is not clear as to what
degree this was caused by superior social status and
improved standards of hygiene.

A more decisive influence toward modernization may
be seen on the socio-cultural level. Protestantism
required a high degree of intellectual training and it
promoted **schools.**[64] Again, the exact ways and modes
have not been researched in detail for Germany. But
there is reasonable ground for the assumption that the
Protestant cognitive culture favored not only a decline
in magic but also a higher degree of consciousness of
individuals by elementary and Latin schooling.

On the whole, then, the Protestant culture does
not appear to have been the matrix which anticipated
the modern culture. Early progressive moves were
followed by contraction when the Reformation began to
be transformed into institutions. This transformation
necessarily adapted to patterns set by socio-economic
conditions as well as by the demands of a state

centralizing its power, controlling as it did life in
order to domesticate and mobilize its resources. It
still seems to be true that the modern age was advanced
by a revolt against these established forms of Protestantism.[65] The Reformation did indeed pave the way as
abstraction of faith induced a higher degree of religious reflection, as **contraction** made religion adaptable to social reality, and as **inclusion** moved along
its functional trend. But it is equally true that the
light of the Reformation was in no way secular "enlightenment," for it was seen as shining forth from the
inflexible, eternal truth which had been revealed in
the past.

It was rather in the modes of communication that
mental tools were implemented which later on could be
used to change the traditional environment for the
take-off into the modern age. Even though local social
systems could be changed by the Reformation (the
clearest cases being Zwingli's Zürich and Calvin's
Geneva), a more comprehensive change of the national
and rural societies was required to usher in the modern
period. It was where the social progress initiated by
the Reformation came to a standstill that additional
energies were necessary to move on. The Reformation
certainly did not leave the world untouched, but a new
light was required to change social and economic
conditions. It was in this second turn of the revolutionary era around 1800 that the Protestant Reformation
was used as a model for possible revolt. 19th century
Protestants liked to view their Reformation as an
"early bourgeois revolution" and to think of Luther as
the hero of bourgeois liberty.[66] However, this uti-
lization of the Reformation again reduced the complexity of the dynamics of early modern culture.

Nevertheless, the Reformation served as a prime example
that successful revolt against oppressive laws and the
power of tradition was possible.

NOTES

1. H. A. Oberman, "Reformation: Epoche oder Epi-
    sode," *Archiv für Reformationsgeschichte* 68
    (1977), 56-109.

2. Cf. M. L. Bauemer, "Sozialkritische und revolutio-
    näre Literatur der Reformationszeit," *Interna-
    tionales Archiv für Sozialgeschichte der Literatur*
    5 (1980), 169-233, especially 212 ff.; W. Becker,
    Reformation und Revolution, Katholisches Leben und
    Kirchenreform im Zeitalter der Glaubenspaltung 34
    (2nd ed. München, 1983); Th. A. Brady, Jr.,
    "Social History," in: *Reformation Europe*, ed. S.
    Ozment (St. Louis, 1983), 172 ff.

3. W. Rochler, *Martin Luther und die Reformation als
    Laienbewegung*, Institut für Europäische
    Geschichte Mainz, Vorträge 75 (Wiesbaden, 1981);
    R. W. Scribner, "The Reformation as a Social
    Movement," in: *The Urban Classes, the Nobility
    and the Reformation in England and Germany*, ed. R.
    W. Scribner, Publications of the German Historical
    Institute London 5 (Stuttgart, 1979), 49-79.

4. These terms are borrowed from N. Luhman, *Funktion
    der Religion*, Suhrkamp taschenbuch Wissenschaft
    407 (Frankfurt/M., 1982), 234 f.

5. L. Febvre: *Au coeur religieux du XVIe siècle*
    (Paris, 1957), 26.

6. There is no general study on this topic. Useful
    articles are: J. Ratzinger, "Licht," *Handbuch
    Theologischer Grundbegriffe* (München, 1963), II,
    44-54; D. Mathieu, P.-Th. Camelot, and M. Schmidt,
    "Lumière," *Dictionnaire de Spiritualité* (1976),
    IX, 1142-1174; *Lexikon der christlichen Ikono-
    graphie* (1971), III, 95-99. H.-Chr. Rublack, *Die
    Einführung der Reformation in Konstanz von den
    Anfängen bis zum Abschluss 1531*, Quellen und
    Forschungen zur Reformationsgeschichte 40 (Güters-
    loh, 1971), 271, expanded by B. Hamm: "Laientheo-
    logie zwischen Luther und Zwingli. Das reformato-
    rische Anliegen des Konstanzer Stadtschreibers
    Jörg Vögeli aufgrund seiner Schriften von
    1523/24," in: *Kontinuität und Umbruch*, ed. J.
    Nolte, et. al., Spätmittelalter und Frühe Neuzeit
    2 (Stuttgart, 1978), 222-295. As to Luther see WA
    10 III, 236: "*Dann allain das Euangelium ist das*

liecht," and 238: "*Also ist die schrifft jr selbs
aigen liecht.*" Th. Stör, *Von der Priester Ee
disputation* (1524), f. Aiijr: "*heyter liecht
sines heyligen Euangelion.*"

7. Reproduced in: *Martin Luther und die Reformation
    in Deutschland*, Katalog der Ausstellung Nürnberg
    1983 (Frankfurt, 1983), 223.

8. References in H.-Chr. Rublack, *Eine bürgerliche
    Reformation: Nördlingen*, Quellen und Forschungen
    zur Reformationsgeschichte 51 (Gütersloh, 1982),
    107, n. 7, to which Zwingli in Z1, 170 f.; 2, 311
    could be added. Further evidence in B. Hamm,
    "Laientheologie," 237 f.

9. A. Vögeli, ed., *Jörg Vögeli. Schriften zur
    Reformation in Konstanz 1519-1538* (Tübingen –
    Basel, 1972), I/1, 472; H.-Chr. Rublack, *Einführ-
    ung der Reformation in Konstanz*, 27; B. Hamm,
    "Laientheologie," 222-295.

10. Cf. for instance WA 10 I/1, 728; LW 52, 286; D.
    Demandt – H.-Chr. Rublack, *Stadt und Kirche in
    Kitzingen*, Spätmittelalter und Frühe Neuzeiti 10
    (Stuttgart, 1978), 205, 222; H. Krabbe, H.-Chr.
    Rublack, eds., *Akten zur Esslinger Reformationsge-
    schichte*, Esslinger Studien – Schriftenreihe 5
    (Esslingen, 1981), 141.

11. M. Brecht, *Martin Luther. Sein Weg zur Reforma-
    tion 1483-1521* (Stuttgart, 1981), esp. 19; see
    also G. Brendler, *Martin Luther. Theologie und
    Revolution* (Berlin, 1983), 19.

12. R. W. Scribner, *For the Sake of Simple Folk.
    Popular Propaganda for the German Reformation*
    (London, 1981), 14 ff.; reproductions in J. Rogge,
    *Martin Luther. Sein Leben, seine Zeit, seine
    Wirkungen* (Gütersloh, 1982), 160, 167, 171; W.
    Hofmann, *Köpfe der Lutherzeit* (München, 1983),
    Nos. 14, 40, and 41.

13. A. Stein: "Luther über Eherecht und Juristen,"
    in: *Leben und Werk Martin Luthers von 1524 bis
    1546*, ed. H. Junghans (Berlin, 1983), I, 171-185;
    II, 781 ff.; A pointed interpretation: H. A.
    Oberman, *Luther. Mensch zwischen Gott und Teufel*
    (Berlin, 1982), 286 ff.; narrative: H. Bornkamm,
    Luther in Mid Career (Philadelphia, 1983).

14. R. Wohlfeil, *Einführung in die Geschichte der deutschen Reformation* (München, 1982), 174 ff.; id., *Das wissenschaftliche Lutherbild der Gegenwart in der Bundesrepublik und in der Deutschen Demokratischen Republik* (Hannover, 1982); G. Zschäbitz, *Martin Luther. Grösse und Grenze* (Berlin, 1967), 219.

15. G. Brendler, "Revolutionäre Potenzen und Wirkungen der Theologie Martin Luthers," in: *Luther und die Folgen*, ed. H. Löwe and C. J. Roepke (München, 1982), 160-180. See also Brendler's recent biography, *Martin Luther. Theologie und Revolution*, and "Thesen über Martin Luther," *Einheit* 9 (1981), 893.

16. G. Zschäbitz, *Martin Luther. Grösse und Grenze*, 218; "Thesen über Martin Luther," 893.

17. G. Brendler, *Martin Luther. Theologie und Revolution*.

18. R. Wohlfeil, *Einführung in die Geschichte*.

19. *Explanations of the Ninety-Five Theses*, WA I, 522-628; LW 31, 83-252; *Eynn Sermon von dem Ablasz unnd Gnade ...*, WA I, 239-246. Cf. M. Brecht, *Martin Luther. Sein Weg zur Reformation*, 173 ff.

20. H.-Chr. Rublack, "Die Reformation in Vorderösterreich und Konstanz," in: *Luther und die Reformation am Oberrhein.* Katalog der Ausstellung der Badischen Landesbibliothek (Karlsruhe, 1983), 103-127.

21. Cf. my article: "Martin Luther and the Social Urban Experience" (forthcoming, Trinity College Dublin).

22. G. Seebass, s.v. "Antichrist IV." *Theologische Realenzyklopädie* 3, 28 ff., here 29.

23. See for instance WA 2, 140; LW 42, 12-13; WA 10 III, 137 and 326.

24. Such as the *Devotio moderna*, see R. Mokrosch, "Devotia moderna," *Theologische Realenzyklopädie* 8, 605-616; H. A. Oberman, *Werden und Wertung der Reformation. Vom Wegestreit zum Glaubenskampf* (Tübingen, 1977), 56-71.

25. P. Blickle, *The Revolution of 1525. The German Peasants' War from a New Perspective* (Baltimore - London, 1981).

26. *To the Christian Nobility of the German Nation*, WA 6, 404-469; LW 44, 123-217.

27. V. Press, "Adel, Reich und Reformation," in: Mommsen, ed., *The Urban Classes*, 330-383; id., "Soziale Folgen der Reformation in Deutschland," Vierteljahresschrift für Sozial - und Wirtschafts- geschichte Beiheft 74, 196-243.

28. J. Sieglerschmidt, *Territorialstaat und Kirchenre- giment: Studien zur Rechtsdogmatik des Kirchenpa- tronatsrechts im 15. und 16. Jahrhundert.* (Diss., Universität Konstanz, 1982).

29. Th. A. Brady, Jr., "Phases and Strategies of the Schmalkaldic League. A Perspective after 450 Years, *Archiv für Reformationsgeschichte* 74 (1983), 162-181.

30. WA 27, 403-411 (Sermon, November 8, 1528), here: 409 ff.: "you ungrateful folk, you are avaricious because of money and do not contribute (to the common chest)... I am shocked and do not know whether I am to preach any longer, you base creatures." Later in this sermon he named the Wittenbergers "ungrateful beasts."

31. N. Luhman, "Knappheit, Geld und die bürgerliche Gesellschaft," *Jahrbuch für Sozialwissenschaft* 3 (1972), 182-210.

32. H. Junghans, "Luther in Wittenberg," in: *Leben und Werk Martin Luthers*, 11-37, here 21.

33. WA 18, 291-334; LW 46, 17-43; e.g. WA 18, 314; LW 46, 31-32; S. Bräuer: "Luthers Beziehungen zu den Bauern," in: *Leben und Werk Martin Luthers*, 457-472.

34. G. Strauss, *Luther's House of Learning* (Baltimore, 1978). Contradictory evidence in J. Kittelson, "Successes and Failures in the German Reformation: the Report from Strasbourg," *Archiv für Reforma- tionsgeschichte* 73 (1982), 153-175.

35. F. Conrad, "Die bäuerliche Reformation. Die Rezeption der Reformationstheologie auf dem Land,"

paper delivered at the congress "Zwingli und Europa" (Bern, 1984), based on her dissertation: "Die Rezeption der Reformationstheologie in der ländlichen Gesellschaft" (Saarbrücken, 1982). For a summary analysis see P. Blickle, *Die Reformation im Reich*, Uni-taschenbücher 1181 (Stuttgart, 1982), 97-103.

36. H.-Chr. Rublack, "Die Reformation in Vorderösterreich," 112.

37. The famous incident at Froschauer's, the printer's house in spring 1522: G. W. Locher, *Die zwinglische Reformation im Rahmen der europäischen Kirchengeschichte* (Göttingen, 1979), 95-98.

38. H.-J. Köhler, ed., *Flugschriften als Massenmedium der Reformationszeit*, Spätmittelalter und Frühe Neuzeit 13 (Stuttgart, 1981). B. Moeller, "Flugschriften der Reformationszeit," *Theologische Realenzyklopädie* 11, 240-246; S. Ozment, "Pamphlet Literature of the German Reformation," in: *Reformation Europe*, 85-105.

39. R. Wohlfeil, *Einführung in die Geschichte*, 123-133.

40. M. U. Chrisman, *Lay Culture, Learned Culture. Books and Social Change in Strasbourg, 1480-1599* (New Haven - London, 1982).

41. R. W. Scribner, *For the Sake of Simple Folk*.

42. Cf. H.-Chr. Rublack, "Das 'Lied' des Nördlinger Contz Anahans, April 1525," in: *Speculum Sueviae. Festschrift für Hansmartin Decker-Hauff zum 65. Geburtstag*, ed. H.-M. Mauer and F. Quarthal (Stuttgart, 1982), II, 58-74. For a general study, see: E. Kleinschmidt, *Stadt und Literatur in der frühen Neuzeit. Voraussetzungen und Entfaltungen im südwestdeutschen, elsässischen und schweizerischen Städteraum*, Literatur und Leben, Neue Serie 22 (Köln - Wien, 1982).

43. "Ein gesprech auff das kurtzt swischen eynem Christen vnd Juden / auch eynem Wyrthe sampt // seynem Haussknecht / den Eckstein Christum // betreffendt / so noch Gotlicher schrifft // abkunterfeyt ist / wie alhie bey // gedruckt figur auss // weysset." O. Clemen, ed., *Flugschriften*

aus den ersten Jahren der Reformation (1907, Nieuwkoop, 1967), I, 373 ff.

44. H.-Chr. Rublack, *Eine bürgerliche Reformation*, 91 f.

45. F. Roth, *Reformationsgeschichte Augsburgs* (2nd. ed. München, 1900), I, 156.

46. R. W. Scribner: "Reformation, Carnival and the World Turned Upside-Down," in: *Städtische Gesellschaft und Reformation*, ed. I. Batori, Spätmittelalter und Frühe Neuzeit 12 (Stuttgart, 1980), 234-264.

47. Th. A. Brady, Jr., *Ruling Class, Regime and Reformation at Strasbourg, 1520-1555*, Studies in Medieval and Reformation Thought 22 (Leiden, 1978), 218 f.; B. Moeller, "Luther und die Städte," in: *Aus der Lutherfordschung. Drei Vortrdge*, Gerda Henkel Vorlesung (Opladen, 1983), 21 ff.; C. Christensen: "Reformation and Art," in: Ozment, *Reformation Europe*, 251 f.

48. Augsburg Stadtarchiv Urgichten 1524, no. 29 - 8.5.1524; F. Roth, *Reformationsgeschichte*, I, 156.

49. E. Egli, *Actensammlung zur Geschichte der Zürcher Reformation* (Zürich, 1879), Nos. 416, 161.

50. R. Reichardt, "Histoire des mentalités," *Internationales Archiv für Sozialgeschichte der Literatur* 3 (1978), 130-166.

51. J. Delumeau, *Catholicism Between Luther and Voltaire* (London - Philadelphia, 1977). R. Muchembled, *Culture populaire et culture des élites* (Paris, 1978).

52. G. Strauss, *Luther's House of Learning*.

53. M. Weber, *Die protestantische Ethik und der Geist des Kapitalismus: Gesammelte Aufsätze zur Religionssoziologie* (5th ed. Tübingen, 1963), I, 17 ff., esp. 72 ff.

54. C. Frey, "Die Reformation Luthers in ihrer Bedeutung für die moderne Arbeits- und Berufswelt," in: *Luther und die Folgen*, 110-134, here: 114; K. Wiedemann, *Arbeit und Bürgertum. Die Entwicklung des Arbeitsbegriffs in der Literatur Deutschlands*

an der Wende zur Neuzeit, Beiträge zur neueren Literaturgeschichte 3, Folge 46 (Heidelberg, 1979). Cf. W. Conze: "Arbeit," in: Brunner, Conze, and Koselleck, *Geschichtliche Grundbegriffe* (Stuttgart, 1972), I, 163-167.

55. WA 10 III, 236 and 227.

56. WA 10 III, 228 quoting I Timothy 6, 10. WA 10 III, 274.

57. See my article, "Martin Luther and the Social Urban Experience."

58. J. P. Gutton: *La société et les pauvres en Europe (XVIe-XVIIIe siècles)* (Paris, 1974); Th. Fischer: *Städtische Armut und Armenfürsorge im 15. und 16. Jahrhundert. Sozialgeschichtliche Untersuchungen am Beispiel der Städte Basel, Freiburg i.Br. und Strassburg,* Göttinger Beiträge zur Wirtschafts- und Sozialgeschichte 4 (Göttingen, 1979); H.-Chr. Rublack, *Gescheiterte Reformation,* Spätmittelalter und Frühe Neuzeit 4 (Stuttgart, 1978), Exkurs I, 128 ff.

59. See my article "Gesellschaft und Christentum (Reformationszeit)," in: *Theologische Realenzyklopädie,* (forthcoming 1984).

60. A recent summary of the Shorter debate in: M. Mitterauer, *Ledige Mütter. Zur Geschichte illegitimer Geburten in Europa* (München, 1983), 86-89; cf. R. I. Rotberg, Th. K. Rabb, eds., *Marriage and Fertility. Studies in Interdisciplinary History* (Princeton, 1980).

61. Ph. Ariès, *Geschichte des Todes* (München, 1980); B. Vogler, "Attitudes devant la mort et cérémonies funèbres dans les églises protestantes Rhénanes vers 1600," *Archives des sciences sociales des religions* 20 (1975), 139-146; P. Zahn, ed., *Die Inschriften der Friedhöfe St. Johannis, St. Rochus und Wöhrd zu Nürnberg,* Die Deutschen Inschriften 13, Münchener Reihe 3 (München, 1972), and other volumes of the same series.

62. A. Perrenoud: *La population de Genève du XVIe au debut du XIXe siècle. Étude démographique* (Genève - Paris, 1979); id., "Malthusianisme et protestantisme: un modèle démographique weberien,"

Annales: Economies, Societes, Civilisations 29 (1974), 975-988.

63. See my short discussion in: "Konfession als demographischer Faktor?" in: *Festgabe für E. W. Zeeden zum 60. Geburtstag*, ed. H. Rabe, et. al., Reformationsgeschichtliche Studien und Texte, supplement vol. 2 (Münster, 1976), 62-96.

64. WA 15, 27-53; LW 45, 347-378. I. Asheim, *Glaube und Erziehung bei Luther* (Heidelberg, 1961); id., "Bildung V, Reformationszeit," *Theologische Realenzyklopädie* 6, 611-623. B. Moeller, K. Stackmann, eds., *Studien zum städtischen Bildungswesen des späten Mittelalters und der frühen Neuzeit* (Göttingen, 1983).

65. See my discussion of Troeltsch in: "Gesellschaft und Christentum;" E. Troeltsch: "Luther, der Protestantismus und die moderne Welt," *Aufsätze zur Geistesgeschichte und Religionssoziologie, Gesammelte Schriften* IV (Tübingen, 1925), 202-254. C. Seyfarth, "Protestantismus und gesellschaftliche Entwicklung: Zur Reformulierung eines Problems" in: *Seminar: Religion und gesellschaftliche Entwicklung. Studien zur Protestantismus-Kapitalismus-These Max Webers*, ed. C. Seyfarth and W. M. Sprondel, Suhrkamp taschenbuch Wissenschaft 38 (Frankfurt/M., 1973), 338 ff., esp. 346.

66. M. L. Baeumer, "Sozialgeschichte und revolutionäre Literatur," 212 f.; G. Ebeling, "Der kontroverse Grund der Freiheit. Zum Gegensatz von Luther-Enthusiasmus und Luther-Fremdheit in der Neuzeit," in: *Luther und die Neuzeit*, ed. B. Moeller, Schriften des Vereins für Reformationsgeschichte 192 (Gütersloh, 1983), 9-33.

ABBREVIATIONS

BC   *The Book of Concord.* Translated and edited by Theodore G. Tappert. Philadelphia, 1959.

BSLK   *Die Bekenntnisschriften der evangelisch-lutherischen Kirche.* 3rd ed., rev. Göttingen, 1930.

DS   *Enchiridion Symbolorum Definitionum et Declarationum de Rebus Fidei et Morum.* Edited by H. Denziger and A. Schönmetzer. 33rd ed. Freiburg, 1965.

LW   *Luther's Works.* American Edition. Edited by Jaroslav Pelikan and Helmut Lehmann. Philadelphia and St. Louis, 1955- .

PE   *Works of Martin Luther.* Philadelphia Edition. Philadelphia, 1943.

WA   *Luthers Werke.* Kritische Gesamtausgabe. (Schriften) Weimar, 1883- .

WAB   *Luthers Werke.* Kritische Gesamtausgabe. Briefwechsel. Weimar, 1930- .

WATR   *Luthers Werke.* Tischreden. Weimar, 1912-1921.

CONTRIBUTORS

Martin Brecht   -   Professor of Church History, University of Münster, West Germany

Marilyn J. Harran   -   Assistant Professor of Religion, Barnard College, Columbia University, New York City

Manfred Hoffmann   -   Professor of Historical Theology, Emory University, Atlanta, Georgia

George A. Lindbeck   -   Pitkin Professor of Historical Theology, Yale University, New Haven, Connecticut

Jürgen Moltmann   -   Professor of Systematic Theology, University of Tübingen, West Germany

Otto Hermann Pesch   -   Professor of Systematic Theology, University of Hamburg, West Germany

Hans-Christoph Rublack   -   Professor of Modern History, University of Tübingen, West Germany

Lewis W. Spitz   -   William R. Kenan, Jr., Professor of History, Stanford University, Stanford, California

TORONTO STUDIES IN THEOLOGY